MARK KERMODE'S SURROUND SOUND

Also by Mark Kermode
It's Only a Movie
The Good, the Bad and the Multiplex
Hatchet Job
How Does It Feel?

Also by Jenny Nelson (as Jennifer Nelson)
Saturday Night at the Movies

MARK KERMODE'S SURROUND SOUND

THE STORIES OF MOVIE MUSIC

**Mark Kermode
and Jenny Nelson**

PICADOR

First published 2025 by Picador
an imprint of Pan Macmillan
The Smithson, 6 Briset Street, London EC1M 5NR
EU representative: Macmillan Publishers Ireland Ltd, 1st Floor,
The Liffey Trust Centre, 117–126 Sheriff Street Upper,
Dublin 1 D01 YC43
Associated companies throughout the world

ISBN 978-1-4472-3056-4 HB
ISBN 978-1-0350-7236-1 TPB

1 3 5 7 9 8 6 4 2

A CIP catalogue record for this book is available from the British Library.

Typeset in Minion by Six Red Marbles UK, Thetford, Norfolk
Printed and bound in the UK using 100% Renewable Electricity by CPI Group (UK) Ltd

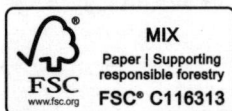

MIX
Paper | Supporting
responsible forestry
FSC
www.fsc.org FSC® C116313

Visit **www.picador.com** to read more about all our books
and to buy them.

This book is dedicated to:
Ezra
Georgia and Gabriel
And the next generation of film music lovers.
Onward!

CONTENTS

'Do you want it good or do you want it Wednesday?'

ELISABETH LUTYENS

OPENING TITLES

'Just the Music'

Sometime back in the early seventies, when I was at primary school in Finchley, North London, my mother took me to a cinema in Muswell Hill to see *Dougal and the Blue Cat* – the feature-length animation based on the popular TV series *The Magic Roundabout*. The film was an Anglo-French stop-motion production which, like the TV show, had been directed in France by Serge Danot, and then later dubbed into English by Eric Thompson (father of Emma), who largely made up his own dialogue.

It was a bizarre and occasionally nightmarish adventure about a cat named Buxton who plans to take over the Magic Garden and eliminate all colours except his own – blue. Part of the action took place in a deserted treacle factory that looked like something out of Robert Wiene's 1920 horror classic *The Cabinet of Dr Caligari* – all angular expressionistic shapes and strangely theatrical forced perspectives. Here, Buxton had to prove his worth to the disembodied 'Blue Voice' (played in fantastically fruity tones by the great Fenella Fielding) by facing his worst nightmares in the 'Room of Dreams' – a hallucinatory collage of screaming faces and whispered threats accompanied by demonic howls of laughter.

The film was completely bonkers.

I absolutely loved it.

A few days later, Mum and I found ourselves in the local Woolworths store, which was selling a Music for Pleasure album of the soundtrack of *Dougal and the Blue Cat* for 99p. I pleaded with Mum to buy it for me and eventually she caved in and forked out the necessary pence. Back at home, I was too young to be allowed to operate my dad's treasured gramophone set, but he agreed to let me listen to the record on the massive 'electrostatic' headphones that were his pride and joy.

What an experience it was! Almost the *entire* film was there in long-playing record form (although, admittedly, it wasn't a very *long* film), with Eric Thompson's narration leading the proceedings, interspersed with haunting musical numbers, composed by Joss Baselli and sung by Thompson himself. As soon as it was finished, I got my dad to start again from the beginning of Side One, and I sat there in rapt attention, mesmerized by the idea of being able to *hear* a movie – to effectively rewatch it with my ears! Because, in those days before the arrival of video, the chance of being able to relive a movie at will seemed little short of astonishing.

What I didn't realize at the time was that *Dougal and the Blue Cat* was *not* a typical soundtrack album, and that generally the music from a film was the only thing you'd get on such a disc. Yes, *some* soundtracks contained fragments of dialogue – something that would be popularized decades later, in the nineties, when Quentin Tarantino started to litter CDs of *Reservoir Dogs* (1992) and *Pulp Fiction* (1994) with quotable exchanges that sat in between the jukebox pop hits. But for the most part, soundtrack albums consisted of orchestral scores or pop song compilations, themes from which could be heard in the movie, often playing *underneath* the action and words.

My first inkling that soundtracks weren't literally 'soundtracks' came when my local record store put a copy of the LP of the 1973 film *The Sting* in their shop window. I was ten years old when the film came out; I'd been to see the movie (which won the Oscar for Best Picture) at the Classic in Hendon with my sister Annie. We both loved it, and after the viewing Annie bought a book of sheet music with many of the Scott Joplin piano rags that Marvin Hamlisch had arranged and adapted for the movie. Annie was a really good pianist, and within a matter of days she'd learned to play 'The Entertainer' (which was effectively the film's main theme) in pretty convincing fashion. Now she'd moved on to 'Pine Apple Rag', which was also in the movie, although I couldn't for the life of me remember which scene it accompanied, or introduced – something I found oddly frustrating.

The next time I was in the record shop (I'd pop in there on my way home from school, to stare at garish album covers like Supertramp's *Indelibly Stamped* or BeBop Deluxe's *Axe Victim*) I saw that soundtrack LP of *The Sting* hanging in the window and noticed that it had all the tunes from the movie listed on the back cover. I went up to the counter and asked a guy in an obviously much-loved Yes T-shirt to play 'Pine Apple Rag', which he did (again, this was a different age, when asking to hear a particular track from a record didn't get you thrown out of the store – at least not immediately). He put the track on the record player behind him, and I stood there at the counter, listening to it intently.

When it finished, the Yes-T-shirt man went to pick the needle off the disc, at which point I blurted out, 'No, no, leave it, let it play on. I want to hear where it comes in the film.' He looked at me as if I were a fool. Which of course I was. I was expecting the dialogue to pick up at the end of the song, just like it did on the soundtrack LP of *Dougal and the Blue Cat*, when the tunes finished and the narration returned. Yet all that happened was that the next music track started to play, with no identifying speech or sound effects to indicate its placement in the film.

I looked baffled.

'Where's the rest of it?' I asked, confused.

'The rest of *what*?' he replied blankly.

'The rest of the *film*,' I said. 'You know, the rest of the "soundtrack".'

'You mean you want to hear *another* track?' he asked.

'Yes. Well, no. I mean . . . the record sleeve says it's the "original motion-picture soundtrack", right?'

'Right.'

'So . . . where's the *rest* of the "soundtrack"?'

The Yes-T-shirt guy looked at me with an expression suggesting that he couldn't quite decide whether I was having him on or I was really that stupid.

'What are you talking about?' he said, his voice measured, but with a hint of exasperation.

'You know, the *words*,' I said. 'Where are they?'

Long pause.

'It's an instrumental,' he said, quietly but sternly. 'There are no words.' At which point he picked the disc off the turntable and started to slide it back into its dust-sleeve.

'No, I mean the words of the *movie*,' I said, my voice becoming squeaky with agitation. 'Not the words of the *music*. I know the *music* is instrumental. But where are the words of the *movie*?'

4

Yes-T-Shirt guy looked me squarely in the eye, took a deep breath, and said: 'There are *no* words. It's just the music. That's what "soundtracks" are. They're just the music.'

And with that he and his T-shirt turned their backs on me, indicating (in case I hadn't already figured it out) that this conversation was over.

Not the whole movie.

Just the music.

Huh?

At first, I was genuinely disappointed. I'd been saving up to buy a new long-playing record for a few months now, and I thought that being able to listen to *all* of *The Sting* over and over again would be well worth £2.50, since I had really enjoyed the movie in the cinema. Yet, as I walked out of the store, shoulders dropped in shame at my ignorance, that phrase started to rattle around in my head: 'Just the music'.

Just the music.

And it was then that it first occurred to me that maybe that was all you really needed. Maybe the *music* of a film could tell its own story. Maybe you didn't *need* the words or sound effects after all.

Many decades later, I found myself talking to the British film-maker Edgar Wright about his favourite soundtrack albums. I was making a programme for BBC Radio 2 called *The Soundtrack of My Life*, for which I'd been interviewing directors and musicians about the film soundtrack albums that had proved formative for them. I mentioned to Edgar that, in the age before videos, I had owned and learned by heart the spoken-word-and-song LP for *Dougal and the Blue Cat*, which had mistakenly convinced me that 'soundtrack' albums contained the entire soundtrack of the film – a ridiculous notion! And then Edgar reminded me that in the early eighties there had been a tie-in 'storybook' album for Steven Spielberg's *E.T. the Extra-Terrestrial* (1982), with Michael Jackson narrating the film and breaking down in tears when E.T. appears to die. That record, which was on the MCA label, became the subject of a lawsuit by Jackson's record label Epic, since its release pre-empted the imminent arrival of his new LP *Thriller* and they were worried that, in the weeks before Christmas, it would effectively be competing with their product. The lawsuit caused distribution problems for the *E.T.* storybook, although it went on to earn a Grammy Award for Best Children's Recording, with Jackson declaring: 'Of all the awards that I've got tonight [he bagged seven others for *Thriller*] I'm most proud of *this* one.'

'You should probably give it a listen,' Wright told me. 'But I never owned – or *heard* – the storybook album. I had the *E.T.* album with the John Williams score only. And to be honest with you, you really don't need a narrator. That music told the story better than any narrator ever could.'

Wright went on to muse upon the subject of whether Williams would prove to be the last great writer of memorably hummable movie themes – earworm tunes that would pass the proverbial 'whistle test'. But what struck me most about our conversation was his observation that the music for *E.T.* 'told the story' of the film without the need for words. That was something I had first started to understand after that bruising encounter in my local record shop, all those years ago, and now it seemed to make perfect sense.

The first movie music LP I owned (apart from that *Dougal and the Blue Cat* album) was the music from Stanley Kubrick's *2001: A Space Odyssey* (1968). Or rather, it *wasn't* the music from *2001*, which had been issued on the MGM label in the year of the film's release. Instead, it was a Decca recording of Richard Strauss's *Also Sprach Zarathustra*, performed by the Los Angeles Philharmonic under the baton of Zubin Mehta. Kubrick's movie famously begins with the opening movement of *Also Sprach Zarathustra*, performed by the Vienna Philharmonic Orchestra under Herbert von Karajan (although for complicated reasons the original MGM disc apparently featured a *different* version of the same piece, with Karl Böhm conducting the Berlin Philharmonic – don't ask). But after those opening few moments, with their ascending horns and booming timpani, Strauss and Kubrick go their separate ways, with the director cherry-picking tracks by György Ligeti and Aram Khachaturian (alongside Johann Strauss II's 'The Blue Danube'), giving a wide berth to the music that filled up the remaining two sides of the LP of which I was now the proud owner.

The reason I had the 'wrong' LP was simple. I had asked my parents if they could get me the music from *2001* after I had been to see a rerelease screening of the film with my friend Mark Fürst. Mark's father was the celebrated Hungarian conductor János Fürst, who had taken us both to see the sentimental 1972 science fiction charmer *Silent Running* at the Casino Cinema on Old Compton Street, the London home of Cinerama. At that screening, Mark and I had seen a trailer for *2001*, which was coming back to the Casino immediately after *Silent Running* ended its tenure there. The two movies were connected because Doug Trumbull, who had worked visual effects miracles for Kubrick on his space odyssey, had gone on to make *Silent Running* (one of only two feature films he directed) partly in response to the cold inhumanity of Kubrick's movie.

Neither Mark nor I knew anything about this connection, nor did we realize that *2001* was now several years old (this was the early seventies) and was getting a theatrical *revival* rather than a first release. We just thought it was an exciting-looking new science fiction film, and we couldn't wait for it to open. When we finally got to see it some time later, at the Phoenix (then the Rex), East Finchley, it left us completely baffled. Mark's mother had warned us that the movie was very 'symbolic', but we had no idea what that meant, nor what was going on with the old man and the space baby at the end of the movie. Yet still it made an indelible impression on me, and I became determined to figure out what it all meant. So I went to a bookshop and bought co-writer Arthur C. Clarke's novelization of his movie script, and then asked my mum and dad to buy me the music from the film so that I could listen to it while reading the book. Simple!

The problem was that my dad, who was something of a music buff (he loved everything from choral hymns to jug-band jazz), knew what the music from *2001* was actually called (most people just thought of it as 'the theme from *2001*'). So when he went to the record store to purchase the disc, he didn't say, 'I'd like an LP of the music from *2001*, please,' but rather, 'I'd like an LP of Richard Strauss's *Also Sprach Zarathustra*, please.' Which is exactly what he got.

Strangely, I didn't initially realize that only a couple of minutes of the music on that LP actually featured in the film I had watched. Indeed, as I sat there reading the book of *2001* with Dad's gigantic electrostatic headphones threatening to break my neck with their weight, I convinced myself that *Also Sprach Zarathustra* in its entirety was featured in Kubrick's film, which I had seen just the once. To this day, I can't hear any movement of that whomping great tone poem without being transported into outer space, so inexorably were the words of Clarke's book, the images from Kubrick's film (which featured on the book's jacket) and the music of Richard Strauss welded together in my confused young head. Indeed, when I finally came across a copy of the *real* MGM *2001* soundtrack album, complete with sleeve notes explaining where all the different pieces of music came from, I read them and thought, 'Well, *that's* not right . . .'

If two minutes of music from *2001* had given me the movie soundtrack bug (albeit misguidedly), then my next acquisition sealed the deal: the MCA LP of the music from *Silent Running*. When I first saw the movie with Mark Fürst, I had found it a genuinely heartbreaking experience – a tale of lonely space travel with an unforgettably tear-jerking finale that didn't so much pluck at the heartstrings as snap them in two. The score was by Peter Schickele, who had achieved fame as the musical satirist 'P.D.Q. Bach', a fictional figure who was claimed to be the 'youngest and oddest' of Johann Sebastian Bach's children.

Trumbull had first come across Schickele's name on the back cover of a Joan Baez album, on which Schickele was an orchestrator and arranger. When I was writing my BFI Modern Classics volume on *Silent Running* decades later, Trumbull confessed to me that he had asked Schickele to compose the music for his film largely because he figured it might be a way of getting Baez to agree to record a song for the movie. Which she did – two songs, in fact: the folksy 'Silent Running' and the sublimely mournful 'Rejoice in the Sun', the latter of which remains my favourite movie soundtrack song of all time.

Both of these songs featured on the soundtrack album, along with Schickele's brilliantly evocative score. I played that album to death, listening to it over and over again, gazing at the poster image on the front cover of the LP and the black-and-white stills on the back, reliving the movie in my head as the record worked its musical magic. From the majestic pomp of 'The

Space Fleet' to the haunting strains of 'The Dying Forest' and the low-key melancholia of 'Tending to Huey', every note conjured a picture – a *moving* picture. Here was the key to being able to rewatch a film whenever you wanted – a musical gateway into a world of movies that stirred the visual imagination as it surrounded you with sound.

It was heaven.

It was also strangely instructional. Once I'd discovered that it was possible to own and listen to the music from a movie, I started to watch films in a different way. For the first time I began to take note of how music cues – as in, short pieces composed for specific scenes – were used in cinema. Of course, theme tunes from hit films had long been a popular attraction (compilations of 'Big Bond Themes' and 'Best of the Westerns' were a regular part of most record collections). But the idea of listening to an entire score from a single film was something different – something a bit more . . . *obsessive*? And that sense of obsessiveness bled back into the cinema, making me take note of the music I was hearing as I watched a film, understanding just how much of the storytelling was being done by the soundtrack.

Shortly after buying the *Silent Running* LP, I snapped up a copy of the soundtrack to Norman Jewison's dystopian sci-fi thriller *Rollerball* (1975), which featured a series of pieces performed by the London Symphony Orchestra, conducted by André Previn (who I knew from *The Morecambe & Wise Show* as 'Andrew Preview'). The most famous of these pieces was Bach's Toccata and Fugue in D Minor, with organ soloist Simon Preston hammering out an arresting curtain-raiser for this future fantasy about deadly gladiatorial games ('In the not too distant future, wars will no longer exist. But there will be . . . ROLLERBALL'). The track that really caught my attention, however, was Albinoni's Adagio in G Minor, a maudlin tune that became an overused movie favourite, to which we will return later in this book. I pretty much bought that soundtrack album on the strength of that single piece, but I'd sit and listen to the entire LP while reading William Harrison's source short story 'Roller Ball Murder' and looking at the front-cover poster image of a studded fist raised in front of a helmeted head, or the back-cover montage of pictures of James Caan in action on his rollerskates.

From there I progressed to Jerry Goldsmith's angular score for *Planet of the Apes* (1968, still a firm favourite), John Williams' music for *Jaws* (1975, so much more than just the iconic opening theme!), the synthy sounds of Wendy Carlos's work on *A Clockwork Orange* (a film I wouldn't see for decades because Kubrick effectively banned his own movie from UK exhibition after its initial run in 1972) and Alain Goraguer's prog-jazz stylings for the animated oddity *La Planète Sauvage* (1973) on what I presume was a French import disc, although I bought it in a decidedly non-specialist record shop in Golders Green for £1.50 (the reduced price sticker never came off).

In the wake of the blockbuster success of George Lucas's sci-fi epic *Star Wars* (1977), John Williams' double-LP soundtrack became a record-breaking hit, although that same year I was more interested in German prog-rockers Tangerine Dream's score for William Friedkin's *Sorcerer* (1977), partly because the film had tanked in cinemas, becoming something of a lost classic (it has since been re-evaluated and is now regarded as one of the director's finest works). The next year I bought Giorgio Moroder's broodingly pulsey score for Alan Parker's *Midnight Express* (1978) and got a friend to record me a cassette tape of

Goblin's witchy accompaniment to Dario Argento's *Suspiria* (1977), all of which cemented a long-standing interest in soundtrack electronica, which is the subject of a chapter of this book.

In the eighties, I was introduced to the work of minimalist pioneer Philip Glass through his music for Godfrey Reggio's head-spinning documentary *Koyaanisqatsi* (1982), and Paul Schrader's *Mishima: A Life in Four Chapters* (1985), an introduction that would lead me to Glass's operatic works *Akhnaten* (1983) and *The Making of the Representative for Planet 8* (1988), both of which I loved despite knowing *nothing* about opera. Glass's music also featured prominently in Jim McBride's *Breathless*, a 1983 remake of *À Bout de Souffle* which I have always found infinitely preferable to Godard's revered 1960 original.

Meanwhile, Peter Greenaway's *The Draughtsman's Contract* (1982) put British composer Michael Nyman on the movie map (his previous credits had included the altogether less auspicious 1976 soft-core romp *Keep It Up Downstairs*), and American guitarist Ry Cooder scored a cult-favourite soundtrack hit with Wim Wenders's *Paris, Texas* (1984) – which became a staple of every student household, along with an obligatory poster for *Betty Blue* (1986).

Other essential hip soundtrack albums of the eighties included Trevor Jones's haunting score for Alan Parker's devilish chiller *Angel Heart* (1987), on which Courtney Pine's saxophone weaves in and out of some very well-chosen dialogue clips; and Bill Lee's score for his son Spike's controversial hit *Do the Right Thing* (1989), featuring fellow sax-legend Branford Marsalis. Both of these were must-have items for any self-respecting music *or* film fan, effortlessly bridging the gap between popular music and orchestral film scores. (We'll hear more about *Do the Right Thing* in Chapter 8, 'Pop Goes the Movies'.)

As a diehard devotee of David Bowie, I'd been to see Nagisa Oshima's *Merry Christmas, Mr Lawrence* (1983), and although I didn't care much for the film (I preferred Nic Roeg's 1976 sci-fi drama *The Man Who Fell to Earth*), I did buy the soundtrack album by Bowie's onscreen co-star, Ryuichi Sakamoto. The Japanese musician/actor (and leading light of the Yellow Magic Orchestra) would go on to share Oscar victory with Talking Heads frontman David Byrne and Chinese composer Cong Su for their joint work on Bernardo Bertolucci's *The Last Emperor* (1987), beating off stiff competition from Italian legend Ennio Morricone for his soaring score for Brian De Palma's *The Untouchables* (1987), alongside two further nominations for John Williams (*The Witches of Eastwick* and *Empire of the Sun*, 1987), who was well on his way to becoming the most celebrated and successful film composer of his generation.

In the nineties, I co-presented the BBC Radio 1 film show *ClingFilm* (a *terrible* name for which I take no credit), an hour-long programme which was divided fifty-fifty between speech and music, with pop tracks from the movies making up half of the running time. During these years I amassed a large collection of jukebox soundtrack CDs, with favourites ranging from the retro sounds of Philip Kaufman's *The Wanderers* (1979) to Iain Softley's 1995 computer romp *Hackers* and of course Danny Boyle's era-defining *Trainspotting* (1996), alongside those Tarantino CDs with their eminently clippable dialogue soundbites.

Fast-forward twenty years to 2019, and I found myself presenting a weekly two-hour film soundtracks show on the newly launched – and now sadly defunct – Scala Radio ('classical music for modern life'). I'd landed the gig because my former Radio 1 colleague (who had gone on to become my Radio 5 Live colleague) Simon Mayo had recommended me to the station's bosses when he became Scala's morning-show host. Simon and I had been working together since the nineties, and I had shackled my wagon to his star and hung on for dear life, with very effective outcomes. As a result of his patronage, I'd effectively remained employed on the radio for over two decades, and to this day we still co-present a movie podcast (*Kermode and Mayo's Take* – available *wherever* you get your podcasts, since you ask) which has become a mainstay of my working life.

Thank you, Mr Mayo.

Much had happened in film music in the years between my time at Radio 1 and my five-year tenure at Scala Radio. As you may have noticed (or perhaps not), most of the sound-track albums I've cited so far in this chapter have been by male composers, who were widely considered to have the monopoly on film scores since the earliest days of recorded sound. But in 1997, Rachel Portman made history by becoming the first woman to win an Oscar for scoring a motion picture (Douglas McGrath's 1996 Jane Austen adaptation, *Emma*), and it had started to occur to me that perhaps there was a world of film music out there that I'd been missing out on for all these years. And indeed there was, from Indian soundtrack pioneer Usha Khanna, through British composers like Doreen Carwithen and Elisabeth Lutyens, to American innovator Shirley Walker, all of whom helped to lay the groundwork for such latter-day titans as Anne Dudley (who won an Oscar for 1997's *The Full Monty*), Turkish-born Pinar Toprak (the first woman to score a blockbuster superhero movie, with 2019's *Captain Marvel*) and Icelandic composer Hildur Guðnadóttir (who provided the Academy Award-winning score for the 2019 DC smash hit *Joker*).

When my Scala producer (and co-author of this book) Jenny

Nelson and I first met in 2019, we made a pact that we would never make a show which did not feature a range of music by women, transgender and non-binary composers, and that was a rule we kept to throughout our five-year run at Scala. Our very first show, which went out on 9 March 2019, consisted entirely of two hours of tracks by Doreen Carwithen, Anne Nikitin, Nainita Desai, Kathryn Bostic, Anne Dudley, Mica Levi, Rachel Portman, Wendy Carlos, Angela Morley, Laura Karpman, Amelia Warner, Hildur Guðnadóttir, Debbie Wiseman, Anna Meredith, Pinar Toprak, Kira Fontana, Usha Khanna and Lesley Barber.

Over the next five years, Jenny and I would seek out and showcase new film music by Audrey Ismaël, Anne-Kathrin Dern, Gazelle Twin, Ariel Marx, Kate Simko, Anna Drubich, Die Hexen, Dascha Dauenhauer, Zeltia Montes, Carla Patullo, Tara Creme, Anne-Sophie Versnaeyen, Chloé Thévenin, Nadah El Shazly, Morgan Kibby, Tamar-kali, Bryony Marks, Theodosia Roussos, Fatima Al Qadiri, Anne Chmelewsky, Lucrecia Dalt and Stephanie Economou, the last of whom won a Grammy in 2023 for a videogame score.

Sarah Angliss's music for the British horror movie *Amulet* (2020) provided some wonderfully eerie broadcasting moments, while Amy Nostbakken's vocal accompaniments to the Canadian psychodrama *Mouthpiece* (2018) proved utterly mesmerizing. Jenny and I also discovered (and fell in love with) Japanese composer Aska Matsumiya through her work on the 2019 short film *Clavadista*. Aska would go on to compose extraordinary feature scores for *37 Seconds* (2020), *I'm Your Woman* (2020), *After Yang* (2022, to which Ryuichi Sakamoto also contributed) and more recently Kôsai Sekine's *Kakushigoto/Stay Mum* (2024).

French-born composer Emilie Levienaise-Farrouch (who is now based in London) and British-Indian composer Nainita Desai became mainstays of the show, which regularly featured tracks from films like *Only You* (2018), *Censor* (2021) and *Living* (2022) from the former, and *For Sama* (2019), *The Reason I Jump* (2020) and *The Deepest Breath* (2023) by the latter. You'll hear from both of those composers later in the book, along with many of the others mentioned here. I also became obsessed with Japanese singer/songwriter/musician Eiko Ishibashi's score for Ryûsuke Hamaguchi's Oscar-feted *Drive My Car* (2021) – my favourite soundtrack of that year, and for my money one of the finest film scores of the twenty-first century. We'll take a deep dive into that score later on.

If all of this reads like a seemingly endless list of composers, many of whom you may never have heard of, then that's exactly what it's meant to be, because Jenny and I became somewhat evangelical about expanding the landscape of 'celebrated film composers' beyond the established 'boys' club' with which we had both grown up. Which is not to say that the canonized greats (Erich Wolfgang Korngold, Bernard Herrmann, John Williams, Jerry Goldsmith, Hans Zimmer et al.) are not 'great' – merely that they are not *exclusively* great. Their story is not the *whole* story. There are *other* stories to be told.

The problem, of course, is that (as you've probably gleaned from this introduction) my own personal experience of film music is both scattershot and shambolic. Growing up in the age before the internet, I had stumbled upon film soundtracks as and when they appeared in my local record shops. It wasn't until I moved back from Manchester to London in the late eighties that I discovered 58 Dean Street Records, the legendary soundtrack store in Soho owned by the famously irascible

Derek Braeger, and run (at least when I was a customer) by the Masheter brothers, Martin and Philip. Browsing through the racks of vinyl at 58 Dean Street was an education, largely because it showed me just how *little* I knew about the great history of film soundtracks.

'I think the golden years were the eighties,' Philip tells me. He started work at the store in 1981 and rapidly became the manager. 'Back then, 58 Dean Street was the *only* place in London which specialized fully in film music. And because we were one street parallel to Wardour Street, a lot of film people would come in. At that time, before the internet, directors would often come in to find music to temp-track the films they were working on, when they were editing them in Soho. They'd pick out some music and ask you to suggest things. One of the people I was most pleased to meet was Terence Young, who came in a few times. Lewis Gilbert was in once too. But the store was always packed. I remember that on a Saturday I'd arrive at work at 10 a.m., and you'd usually have five or ten people waiting to go in.'

I would have been one of those people, loitering outside London's only soundtrack emporium, hoping there'd be some bargain that would catch my eye inside. I had a ton of soundtrack LPs that I loved and cherished, but I also had very little idea of where they all fitted into the wider picture of film music composition and recording. It wasn't really until I started working with Jenny on the Scala show that she began to lend some form of context to my unruly (and largely uneducated) film music passions, not least because, as the *producer* of that show, it was her job to make some sense of the random hotchpotch of tracks and titles that I absolutely insisted we should play in full.

Jenny had previously been an executive producer at Classic

17

FM, where she had produced the extremely popular film music show *Saturday Night at the Movies*, working first with composer and presenter Howard Goodall, and then with my film critic colleague Andrew Collins. Jenny had also written an excellent book with the same title as that Classic FM show, which focused on twelve key collaborative relationships between film composers and directors. When we first met, she gave me a copy of her book, and I gave her a list of unbroadcastable atonal squonkfests that I wanted to play on our show. Somehow, we met in the middle, with Jenny making sure that my own zealous enthusiasm for 'challenging' obscurities ('Yes, Jenny, I *do* think the listeners need to hear four minutes of industrial noise from the soundtrack of David Lynch's *Eraserhead*') was matched by an altogether more disciplined overview of the kind of film music that Scala audiences might actually *like* to hear.

More importantly, Jenny broadened my horizons beyond the scope of 'music from films that mean a lot to Mark' by insisting that I put those pieces in the wider context of a history of popular film scores (that mean a lot to *everybody else*), upon which she had been drawing throughout her years at Classic FM. And, as with all the best partnerships, that creative tension produced something unique – five years of shows that genuinely tried to do something different in the field of film music broadcasting, without either scaring off the listeners with horribly unfamiliar ambient noise, or simply boring and/or pacifying them with tracks they already knew.

By the time we broadcast our final Scala show on 24 February 2024, Jenny and I had started to work together on this book, keeping pretty much the same working relationship in print that we had on the radio: I would be the presenter, she would be the producer, and the end result would navigate a course between our shared interests. This book may be called *Mark Kermode's Surround Sound*, but (as with the radio show) it has been written jointly by Jenny and me – in my voice, but with her guidance, and with both of us rewriting and rearranging each other's work.

*

So, what can you expect? Well, there's a fair amount about electronica, pop music and horror films, which should come as no surprise to anyone who's ever listened to me talking about movies. But there's also an attempt to investigate how modern movie scores are made – from composition to recording; from demo tapes to orchestration. We'll take you inside the practical process of scoring films, whether that be at home with a computer screen, or in one of the hallowed recording rooms at Abbey Road Studios in London where vast orchestras have gathered to provide music for films as diverse as Terry Gilliam's brilliantly troubling *Brazil* (1984) and Mel Gibson's Oscar-winning breast-beater *Braveheart* (1995).

We'll try to get to the bottom of how a composer can reflect and amplify the vision of a film director, and what happens when those partnerships find themselves at loggerheads. And, in the two-part chapter 'How Did We Get Here?', we'll attempt to sketch out a broad-strokes guide to the milestones of film music history, from the early twentieth century heyday of Max Steiner and Erich Korngold to the twenty-first-century era of Hildur Guðnadóttir, Mica Levi, Jonny Greenwood and Anna Meredith.

We've conducted a series of interviews for this book, for which we'd like to thank composers Michael Abels, David Arnold, Lorne Balfe, Neil Brand, Suzanne Ciani, Nainita Desai, Anne

Dudley, Warren Ellis, Germaine Franco, Jonny Greenwood, Hildur Guðnadóttir, Natalie Holt, James Newton Howard, Laura Karpman, Emilie Levienaise-Farrouch, Anna Meredith, Clint Mansell, Rachel Portman, Benjamin John Power (aka Blanck Mass) and Howard Shore, along with Abbey Road Studio engineer John Barrett, soundtrack album producer and film historian/preservationist Mike Matessino, soundtrack collector and curator Philip Masheter, and one of the first violins at the London Symphony Orchestra, Maxine Kwok.

We've also drawn on interviews that Jenny and I have conducted over the years, with Ludwig Göransson (for the *Kermode on Film* podcast), Amelia Warner and Isobel Waller-Bridge (for 'Scala Radio x Abbey Road Presents: Music for Film' at Abbey Road Amplify 2022), Yorgos Lanthimos (for *The Observer*), Nic Roeg (for *The Culture Show*), Pino Donaggio (for the 23rd Trieste Science+Fiction Festival), David Lynch (for *Q* magazine and *The Guardian*), Angelo Badalamenti (for the 2001 Edinburgh International Film Festival), Jocelyn Pook and Natalie Holt (for 'Scoring for Film & TV' at Abbey Road Equalise 2023), Prano Bailey-Bond (for *Sight and Sound* magazine), Edgar Wright and Alan Parker (for BBC Radio 2), Walter Murch, Don Letts, Ernest Dickerson, Ed Bailie, Dionne Edwards and A. R. Rahman (for BBC Radio 4's *Screenshot*), and Daniel Pemberton, Hans Zimmer, Max Richter, Eiko Ishibashi and Abbey Road's head of audio products Mirek Stiles, all for Scala Radio.

Oh, and William Friedkin, to whom I had the great pleasure of speaking on countless occasions between 1990 and 2023, and whom I miss greatly.

All of these interviews have proved invaluable in the writing of this book, and they allow the reader to hear first-hand what it's like to work at the coalface of modern film music. Unless otherwise stated, all the quotations used in this book come from those interviews. Thanks again to everyone who gave up their valuable time to speak to us.

One final note: the world of music can sometimes seem alienatingly obscure from the outside – filled with names and terminologies that are essential to the craftspeople making the music but baffling to everybody else. This is doubly true of film music, in which the process of composing for the screen has its own strange set of histories and complications, exacerbated by the fact that both film *and* music critics (and I speak as both) can have a tendency to want to let you know just how much more *they* know about their subject than *you* do.

That is not the case here.

As far as the music jargon is concerned, although I may technically be 'a musician' on some level (I was actually the 'Musical Director' for the BBC One chat show *Danny Baker After All* in the nineties), I have never had any formal music training beyond Grade 4 French horn (which I failed) and – most significantly – I cannot read music. My chosen instrument, the double bass, came to me after I had broken so many guitars that my fellow band members begged me to try something *less* breakable and forced me to play what is effectively a wardrobe with strings. Also, my favoured brand of music is skiffle, which is essentially people hitting kitchen utensils and household appliances (washboards, tea chests, wine bottles, etc.) with sticks and broom handles. So, although there are occasions in this book in which I have tried to describe in words a particular sequence of notes that occurs in a significant film score, those moments are few and far between and, when they do come up, I hope they're described in a way which *anyone* will be able to understand, regardless of their musical training, or lack of it.

You can basically skiffle your way through it.

Equally important is the fact that this book has been co-written by someone who *literally* used to think that soundtrack albums had the entire soundtrack of a movie on them, and had to have it explained to them that it was 'just the music'. I hope it's already abundantly clear that, despite being an enthusiastic collector of film soundtracks for several decades, I really didn't know *anything* about the history of film scores for most of those years, and I'm not expecting readers of this book to be any more up-to-speed than I was. Jenny and I have tried to sketch out the briefest history of film score evolution, picking out some of the biggest names from the silent age to the modern block-buster. We've also interspersed the main chapters with a series of brief dives into individual soundtrack selections that have played a major part in our own appreciation of film music, most of which are from the past fifty years, and many of which you may recognize. For those that you don't, please do check them out – we think they're all worth a listen.

So, if that all sounds acceptable, join us on a journey into sight and sound – with the occasional squonk en route.

Enjoy!

CHAPTER 1

Never Silent

It was getting on for midnight in Sodankylä, up in the top quarter of Finland, yet it was still as bright as midday. The sun showed no signs of dropping down behind the horizon. The mosquitoes, which had been rightly described as having the bodies of locusts and the attitude of Scottish midges, were still feasting on every inch of exposed human flesh, desperate to make the most of the short period in which they must eat, mate and die, impervious to the napalm-style 'protections' of all manner of insect repellent. I hadn't slept for a couple of days, since up here the days and nights blurred into one another, and my body clock was so discombobulated that I felt perpetually drunk, even though I hadn't been drinking. At least, not yet.

For all my disorientation, however, I was also elated. Earlier that evening, I had played double bass and harmonica with my skiffle band The Dodge Brothers, who had joined silent-movie maestro Neil Brand to provide an improvised soundtrack for a screening of F. W. Murnau's 1930 gem, *City Girl*. We were performing as part of the Midnight Sun Film Festival – an annual shindig established by Finnish film-making legend Aki Kaurismäki and his brother Mika. Against all expectations, we had performed a live accompaniment to a nearly century-old silent movie which was attended by just shy of a thousand punters, all of whom had reacted as if they were watching a screening of the latest *Mission: Impossible* film.

It was wonderful.

And a little bit baffling.

The Midnight Sun festival has become something of a cultural phenomenon, with guests that year including former French *enfant terrible* Leos Carax, Mexican film-maker Alfonso Cuarón and Italian auteur Alice Rohrwacher. But Neil was the real star – a regular visitor who was treated like royalty by the festival crowd. Neil had wowed them before and they were ready for more. If anyone was going to prove that silent cinema was alive and kicking in the twenty-first century, then Neil was the man to do it.

You probably know Neil from his brilliantly accessible 2013 BBC Four series *Sound of Cinema: The Music that Made the Movies* and its 2015 follow-up *Sound of Song*. He has composed gorgeous new orchestral scores for films like Alfred Hitchcock's *The Lodger* (1927) and Anthony Asquith's *Underground* (1928) and become internationally renowned for his peerless ability to perform improvised piano accompaniment for silent cinema of all genres – from comedy to horror, documentary to melodrama. To watch Neil accompany a feature-length film (which he would often be watching *for the first time*) is an astonishing experience; his eyes are on the screen, his hands are on the piano, and somehow music just flows out of him, accentuating and enhancing every nuance of the movie.

The day before we played *City Girl*, I had sat in the main Midnight Sun arena – a huge circus-style tent crammed to bursting with punters searching for seats and legroom – and watched

Neil perform live improvised piano accompaniment to three silent comedy shorts. The first was a 1928 romp entitled *From Soup to Nuts* in which Stan Laurel and Oliver Hardy find themselves employed as waiters at an upmarket dinner function – a job for which they are sorely unprepared. The crowd roared as our anti-heroes covered their guests and themselves with cake and slipped over into huge bowls of soup, with Neil accentuating every slapstick mishap without ever losing sight of the pathos at the heart of the pair's onscreen relationship.

Next came the 1922 Buster Keaton short *Cops*, a film now best known for a fleeting scene in which Keaton grabs the rear of a passing car and is literally yanked off his feet in a manner that is both hilarious and horrifying. The fact that Keaton famously did all his own stunts adds to the audience engagement, as we find ourselves wondering how the star's arm wasn't pulled right out of its socket when the vehicle hoiks him into the air and out of the frame. Then we finished off with Harold Lloyd's last short film, *Never Weaken*, a 1921 three-reeler in which Lloyd plays an office worker who spends most of the movie dangling from girders at vertiginous heights – a classic of his 'thrill comedy' oeuvre.

Never Weaken presented a number of challenges for Neil, not least because its narrative hinges upon a heartbroken Lloyd attempting to end his life by shooting himself, and then being hoisted blindfolded out of a high window in a manner that makes him believe he is ascending into heaven, accompanied by choirs of angels. Hearing Neil negotiate the tragicomic twists and turns of this thirty-minute oddity was a masterclass in making movie music. No matter how sharp the changes between laughs, gasps and groans, Neil's music hit every note bang on key, all the more remarkable since he was literally making it up as he went along. The audience, which ranged from pre-school youngsters to Zimmer-frame-wielding pensioners (and all ages in between), went wild, with Neil getting a standing ovation at the end of the performance, and everyone leaving the tent with beaming faces and a spring in their step.

This, of course, was the magic of the accomplished silent-movie pianist – the predecessor of the modern composers and musicians who are such an integral part of today's filmgoing experience, and whose work forms the substance of most of this book. Yet in this age of digitally recorded soundtracks and huge orchestral film scores, there remains something almost mystical about watching one man and his piano doing all that work, all by himself, right *there*, right before your very eyes.

The Dodge Brothers had started working with Neil in the late noughties, when his research into early cinema exhibition revealed that many movie houses would rope in local bands to accompany their film programmes, rather than just relying on a lone piano player. Neil had become fascinated by the idea of a whole band improvising simultaneously, and between us we figured out a way of everyone playing along together, without the need for sheet music. Instead, we would choose a number of key themes and motifs that seemed to fit the tone of the movie, and then we'd just watch Neil for the changes and try to keep up.

Our silent-movie repertoire began with a performance of the 1921 William S. Hart Western *White Oak* (directed by Lambert Hillyer) which we played at the Barbican in London in 2009. We flew by the seat of our pants, but as long as I kept an eye on Neil's left hand I could tell what key we were in and somehow everything else fell into place. Next, we took a swing at William Wellman's *Beggars of Life*, a 1928 drama starring Louise Brooks, Richard Arlen and Wallace Beery, for which a theme song had been written by J. Keirn Brennan and Karl Hajos, giving us a reference point for the rest of the music. Made on the cusp of the 'talking pictures' revolution, *Beggars of Life* had originally been released with a couple of sound sequences which were sent out on discs to be played in sync with the picture. Although all copies of those sound recordings are now believed to be lost, they included a sequence in which Wallace Beery (as the gruff 'Oklahoma Red') arrives with a barrel of booze, singing the boisterous drinking song 'Hark Those Bells'.

Beggars of Life came together beautifully and it became our signature film. With Neil, we'd go on to accompany a growing selection of silent classics, from Abram Room's revolutionary 1930 Soviet weirdie *The Ghost That Never Returns* (on which I started experimenting with a vaguely historically accurate theremin) to *Hell's Hinges* (1916), a tale of fire and brimstone featuring a climactic sequence in a blazing church which (like the train-wreck in *Beggars of Life*) was shot for real. But it was Louise Brooks and Richard Arlen falling in love in a succession of boxcars and haystacks to which we would return time and again.

We played *Beggars* everywhere – from the historic hall of the Bo'ness Hippodrome in Scotland to the Verdensteatret in Tromsø way up in the Arctic Circle. And, in July 2014, The Dodge Brothers made history (sort of) by becoming the first band to score a silent film live at the Glastonbury Festival, where we played *Beggars* to a tentful of people up to their ears in mud. An official brochure listing '44 Things to Do in Glastonbury' placed us at Number 38, under the headline 'See a Weird Band Play Along to a Silent Movie'. I couldn't quite figure out if that was a compliment or an insult.

Like *Beggars of Life*, Murnau's *City Girl* was another film of many moods, ranging from tentative romance to seething violence, culminating in a stormy sequence involving cantering

horses, misjudged gunfire, and plenty of breast-beating dam-
nation and redemption. We'd played the film several times
before taking it to Sodankylä, but there was something about
the almost unearthly setting of that festival, with its twenty-
four-hour daylight, that lent a weird magic to the Midnight
Sun performance. We had been somewhat nervous in advance
of the screening, since the film is fairly lengthy and the crowd
included several punters who *really* knew their cinema (Alfonso
Cuarón engaged me in a fervent discussion about Murnau being
forced to change the ending of the movie against his wishes, and
how much better the film *would* have been if his original darker
ending had been allowed to prevail). But the entire experience
became utterly thrilling as the audience reacted to both the
movie and the music in profoundly vocal fashion, and by the
time it finished I was in a state of dreamy reverie.

As we all repaired to the bar, I cornered Neil, bought him a
pint, and started to pump him for information about music in
the earliest days of cinema. What was it *really* like? What would
the audience have *heard*? Would it have been anything like what
we performed that evening? And how much do we know *for certain* about exactly how the sound and vision of modern cinema
evolved? Neil pointed out that we needed to get on a minibus
and go to some strange gathering in the middle of the woods
where an evil mixture of vodka and brandy would be served to
the festival glitterati in surroundings which seemed uncomfort-
ably like a live-action remake of *Midsommar*. But he did promise
me that he'd tell me everything he knew when the time was right,
and that was a promise to which I intended to hold him . . .

*

When it comes to the earliest days of cinema, it turns out that hard facts are even harder to come by. Because the medium of motion pictures had its roots in the somewhat disreputable arena of fairground attractions and phantasmagorical projections, a lot of it simply went unrecorded, with anecdotal evidence outweighing factual documentation by a scale of ten to one. Yet what we *can* say, with some certainty, is that the very first presentations of moving images were accompanied by music. For example, accounts of the Lumière brothers' minute-long film *L'Arrivée d'un train en gare de La Ciotat*, which was first screened in January 1896, suggest that it was seen with a musical element as part of the programme – a programme that would usually have comprised a selection of short films, presented as a sensational medley of movement.

'It was probably only a very small group of musicians,' according to Neil, 'and they were almost certainly playing music that already existed. But the assumption, from the very earliest days of cinema, was that the kind of group experience of watching a film *couldn't* happen in silence. There *had* to be sound there, which if not actually directly linked to what people were watching, was at least complementary enough not to actively clash with it. I doubt that if you went from watching *L'Arrivée d'un train en gare de La Ciotat* and then straight into *Repas de bébé* [1895, in which we watch a proud father feeding a baby while mother makes tea] that there'd be much of a change from the dramatic music of the former to the more domestic sounds of the latter. It was probably just music that would be of general interest to the audience; music that would make people relax, and would make them feel that they were in a sacred space that had already got *something* about it.'

I love Neil's use of the term 'sacred space' to define that

strange aura of a room filled with music, in which we are not just listening to the air around us, but to something that adds an element of creation, choreography and artistry. For Neil, this is always a key ingredient of the communal watching of moving pictures – the early precursors of what we now think of as the 'cinema experience', in which the atmosphere of the room itself tells us that 'what we're watching has some significance beyond the ordinary'.

That sense of seeing something 'beyond the ordinary' expanded in the early twentieth century, as moving pictures shifted from the Parisian cafes in which the Lumières first exhibited their wares into the darkened tents of fairground sideshows, where they would rub shoulders with the other oddities, curiosities and monstrosities that made up so much contemporary popular entertainment. Here, in what film historian and academic Tom Gunning would call the 'cinema of attractions', short reels of ship launches, fires, waterfalls and sometimes even natural disasters would be played with ramshackle musical accompaniment, usually to a noisy crowd for whom the music was merely a signal that *something worth watching was going to happen!* None of this music was synchronized to the picture – that wouldn't start until several years later, when the relationship between moving pictures and music began to be locked down by film companies eager to ensure that their product was getting the best possible exhibition. Instead, these musicians were simply playing along to the projected performance, providing a sense of occasion, rather than one of 'accompaniment'.

In these early incarnations, the performance of short films came with the expectation that a small group of musicians, rather than just a single pianist, would provide the aural back-drop. People had pianos in their own houses; it would take

something more than mere ivory tinkling to get potential punters to part with their hard-earned cash. How about a string
quartet, or maybe a makeshift chamber orchestra? Perhaps the
accompanists could comprise a pianist, a cellist and a violinist,
or even a trumpet player, or clarinettist? Occasionally, percussion could be introduced to add an element of pace and tension,
or to accentuate something specific, such as a bass drum being
struck while an explosion happened on screen. But such syn-
chronous accompaniment was a rarity – for the most part, the
music was simply providing that 'sense of occasion'. (There are
anecdotal accounts of early cinema reels being played to the
sound of a harpist and tuba player, although one struggles to
imagine what scenes could be comfortably augmented by that
strange collision of sounds.)

'What you need to remember', Neil tells me, 'is that we're
talking about a time when music was *everywhere*. You'd go out
on a Sunday, there'd be a brass band playing in the bandstand,
or a local choir singing. People were generally making music
vastly more than they are now. So the performance of live music
was completely normal – it came with the society you lived in.'
This surplus of sound – choirs, music guilds, orchestras, local
bands – existed as standard into the early twentieth century, so
it was simply a matter of course for music to feature heavily in
early cinema exhibition.

Feeding into this marriage between music and movies was
the legacy of the theatrical Music Hall tradition – particularly
in the UK, where the twentieth-century concept of 'the cinema'
(as in, a bespoke environment in which to show and watch
films) effectively emerged from the nineteenth-century cocoon
of musical theatre. Musical underscoring had long been a
part of the theatrical experience, with the word 'melodrama'

(an anglicized modification of the French word *mélodrame*, meaning literally 'song and drama') acknowledging the innate relationship between verbal, visual and musical performance in a manner that had none of the negative connotations of its modern usage. From the bedrock of established theatre emerged the crowd-pleasing medium of Music Hall, a populist form of live entertainment involving music, dance, spoken word, comedy and magical spectacle, creating the cradle from which cinematic pioneers like Charles Chaplin would emerge.

Just as this creative lineage saw a progression from musical theatre to sound cinema, so venues in which theatre once ruled gave way to the emerging art form of the movies, with Music Hall providing the missing link between the two. When films first started to attract public attention in the early twentieth century, music halls provided the perfect setting in which to exhibit them, not least because many music halls had resident bands on hand to provide the necessary accompaniment to the projected attractions. 'From about 1905 onwards,' Neil explains, 'you begin to get this idea of films turning up in spaces in which the audience are already used to having a small band, and even an interlocutor in the form of a Music Hall MC who could very easily become the showman-like explainer of early cinema. When it became harder to draw audiences for end-of-the-pier acts, films became the new attraction, but the venues remained the same. So music halls became a sort of halfway house between theatre and what we now call cinema. And if films could help keep the music halls' turnovers up during the summer, and pay to keep the roof over their heads, then why not capitalize upon that potential?'

When it came to pulling in the crowds, the 1905 British silent film *Rescued by Rover* proved to be a particularly reliable draw.

Produced and directed by Cecil Hepworth and Lewin Fitz-hamon, and featuring the Hepworth family (father, mother, baby, dog) who would go on to become early cinema superstars, the seven-minute one-reeler is packed with incident. The action is set in motion when a baby is dramatically kidnapped from its pram while the child's nursemaid is distracted by a handsome soldier during a visit to the park. Back at home, the grief-stricken nurse explains to the child's mother what has happened – an explanation that is heard *and understood* by the family collie dog, Rover. Leaping into action, Rover jumps out of an open window and rushes down the street, round a corner, down to a river across which he swims, arriving at the nearby neighbourhood slums. Here, the dog goes in and out of every house, boldly knocking open front doors until he arrives at the dwelling where the baby is being mercilessly stripped of its fancy clothing. The baby is distraught and its captor swigs theatrically from a bottle of booze, cruelly shooing Rover away when he comes to the rescue.

But Rover is not done! Rushing home (back across the river, back around the corner, back up the streets, back in through the open window), he wordlessly entreats his master to follow him (back down the streets, back across the river) to the slums where he finds and retrieves the stolen child. In the final shot the family is reunited, leaving the errant kidnapper with her bottle and her stolen baby clothes – a lesson to us all!

Rescued by Rover, which was made for the princely sum of seven pounds, thirteen shillings and ninepence, became so successful that it had to be reshot *twice* after the first two negatives wore out meeting the demand for prints, which sold at the rate of £8 per print. If you've never seen the film, you can find it on the British Film Institute's *Early Cinema: Primitives and*

Pioneers DVD collection (or you can hop over to YouTube, where it's been uploaded umpteen times). It's well worth seven minutes of your time, not least because it turned Blair the collie into cinema's first-ever canine star. And, as writer Michael Brooke observes in an article on the BFI's Screenonline ('the definitive guide to Britain's film and TV industry'): 'its style and canine subject matter were both highly influential', with Hepworth going on to produce *Dumb Sagacity* (1907) and *The Dog Outwits the Kidnapper* (1908), while James Williamson jumped on the bandwagon with titles like *£100 Reward* (1908). More importantly, Brooke continues, *Rescued by Rover* 'appears to have influenced the great American film pioneer D. W. Griffith, who would build on its innovations over the next few years, notably by introducing parallel cutting to present multiple plot strands in the same time frame.'

Brooke hails *Rescued by Rover* as being 'amongst the most important films ever made', marking a turning point in the art form's development from amusing novelty to the 'seventh art', 'able to hold its own alongside literature, theatre, painting, music and other more traditional forms'. It is undoubtedly a major step forward in the evolution of film grammar, using editing and camera movement to tell a fairly complex story rather than just presenting divertingly isolated scenarios. But try watching it in silence, with no music playing. Seriously – just *try* it. Although the artistry of the film-making is evident, the tone of the piece (Suspense! Tragedy! Danger!) is utterly ill-served by being viewed in an aural vacuum. Indeed, it's almost impossible to watch *Rescued by Rover* without at least *imagining* a piano cranking up the tension, or a violin adding to the scenes of wailing pathos. This isn't simply because we have become used to the cliché of a rinky-dink accompaniment being *obligatory* for any 'old movie' viewing. On the contrary, *Rescued by Rover* positively cries out for a musical backdrop, if only to dispel the eerie silence into which its rabble-rousing images (Wicked vagrants! Endangered babies! Heroic dogs!) would otherwise have to be projected.

Rescued by Rover was one of the short films that helped the music halls through some of their leaner periods, being brought back time and time again whenever crowds were flagging. And since the film became fairly well known, the musicians who played along to it got to know the rhythms of the piece – its highs and lows, its moments of grief and ecstasy. Imagine a packed music hall watching that doggy drama unfold, buoyed up by enthusiastic musicians giving it their all. This is the beginning of the modern cinema experience – a collision of sight and sound that predates the full-scale arrival of 'synchronized sound' by decades. Because, as any fan of early cinema will tell you, silent cinema was *never* silent.

'In terms of noise, early cinema was comparable to the experience of being in a football stadium,' Neil tells me. 'It was a noisy, *noisy* place. You'd have people shouting at the screen, and in some of the lower-rent venues the musicians would just be doing their best to keep up with the sound of the crowd and get through the film as best as possible. So maybe you'd have two players struggling to be heard. But then you also had the higher-end cinemas – great big picture houses in the major cities which became flagship venues with reasonably large bands who could provide the kind of music you would hear in a concert hall. But even then they'd be competing against the crowd – or more accurately, they'd be playing *with* the crowd, following their lead, reacting to their reactions.'

The importance of the audience's reaction as part of the early twentieth-century cinema experience was vibrantly illustrated in the twenty-first century when the Lincoln Center Orchestra played Oscar Micheaux's 1925 film *Body and Soul* with a score specially composed for the movie by trombonist Wycliffe Gordon. The film, which features the motion-picture debut of Paul Robeson, was part of the so-called 'race film' genre: American films produced by Black film-makers specifically for Black audiences, featuring African American casts who were often excluded from more widely celebrated US studio pictures. In *Body and Soul*, Robeson plays an escaped prisoner posing as a preacher in Tatesville, Georgia. He also plays the escapee's identical twin brother – a clever device that allows Micheaux to tell a twisty story of love and deception that involves a scheme to swindle the local church congregation, a theft, a flight from justice, a death . . . and a thoroughly unexpected dreamy revelation. It's hot-blooded fare, and when Micheaux applied to the Motion Picture Commission of the State of New York for an exhibition licence for the picture, he was flatly denied. According to the commission, *Body and Soul* was an 'immoral' and 'sacrilegious' work that would 'tend to incite crime', a verdict that forced the director to make significant edits and alterations before the film was deemed fit for public consumption.

Much of Micheaux's work in the silent era has since been lost, with only three of his twenty-something silent films still surviving: the groundbreaking 1920 masterpiece *Within Our Gates*; *The Symbol of the Unconquered* from the same year, which exists only in an incomplete form; and *Body and Soul*. But having been overlooked by (predominantly white) cultural historians for decades, Micheaux's work began to enjoy a reappraisal in the late twentieth century. In 1992, *Within Our Gates* was selected for preservation by the US National Film Registry as being 'culturally, historically and aesthetically significant', an honour which was subsequently bestowed upon *Body and Soul* in 2019.

Described by BFI silent-film curator Bryony Dixon as 'a key work' of the pioneering Micheaux in which 'the unusual structure explores the use of memory and dreams in dealing with violence and immorality', *Body and Soul* is a strange film indeed, particularly when viewed in the somewhat sterile environment of one's own home, away from the company of others. I've never seen the film projected in an auditorium, and that's something I regret, largely because Neil's account of watching it with a packed house and a live musical accompaniment makes for electrifying reading. In a guest column for *Silent London* written in 2021 under the subtitle 'An Audience for Body and Soul', Neil describes seeing the film at the Barbican, with Wycliffe Gordon's live score, and finally understanding the power of the audience and the role viewers can play in a performance. Musician Wynton Marsalis, who introduced the film, instructed the audience to be loud, and the band followed suit when they weren't playing, 'letting loose their feelings about what they were watching. Slowly, slowly . . . we all began to join in.'

Neil's description of the call and response nature of that screening paints a vivid picture of a performance in which the musicians provided an essential bridge between the film and its viewers. Here is a first-hand account of the way that live music can transform the experience of watching a projected movie, written by someone who knows silent movies inside out, but who is still discovering the excitement of those early screenings as if for the first time, over a century after the birth of cinema.

*

If audience reaction played a key role in the early cinema experience, then so too did the differing nature of the musical accompaniments available at different venues. As the appetite for cinema grew, and the number of performances increased exponentially, so the costs of staging those performances also went up. Musicians were one of the most expensive elements of any early cinema screening, and the easiest way to reduce costs would be to cut down on the number of players, giving rise to the now-familiar image of a lone pianist playing a matinee show to a half-empty auditorium in a one-horse town, with the midweek turnout too small to justify further orchestral outlay. But at the other end of the market, top-tier cinemas had started to employ musical directors (MDs), enabling them to boast that *their* screenings were of the highest possible quality, thanks to the virtuosity of the musical accompaniment. By around 1915, these MDs had become part of the upmarket cinema landscape, leading bands of players that – in the very best venues – could comprise as many as twenty-four musicians, all working in harmony, if not exact synchronization, with the movie.

The MD's role would be to source suitable music for each new movie, and then to lead the players through the significant shifts in the drama, showing them when and where to make a change. These changes wouldn't be the kind of second-by-second shifts that would come with synchronized sound and bespoke movie music, but they were broadly timed to the action of the movie and laid the groundwork for the specially recorded film scores that would follow.

A visit to Neil Brand's treasure-trove website (www.neilbrand. com) reveals a wealth of archive material that offers invaluable insight into the role of the musical director in the days of silent cinema. Among its gems is a set of instructions dated 25 August 1921, published in a supplement to *Stoll's Editorial News*, regarding the performance of Maurice Elvey's 1921 mystery thriller *The Hound of the Baskervilles*. Billed as 'Musical Suggestions by Samuel Mey, Musical Director of the Stoll Picture Theatre, Kingsway', the piece is presented in three vertical columns: the first headlined 'Title or Action'; the second, 'Character'; and the third, 'Music Suggested'. The 'Title' of that first column relates to the 'intertitles' of silent movies – interpolated frames in which dialogue or dramatic exposition would appear on screen, explaining the otherwise 'silent' action to the audience. Meanwhile, the 'character' of the second column means the mood of the scene, rather than the names of those who appear on screen. So, if we read across the first horizontal row of the vertical columns, we learn that the first intertitle will begin with the words 'Midst the desolate silence of . . .'; the character of the scene will be 'slow pastoral to mysterious'; and the music suggested by MD Samuel Mey should be 'Intro Overture "Merry Wives of Windsor" (*Nicolai*)'. Further down we find the dialogue intertitle 'Sir Henry, you are in terrible danger', introducing a scene whose character is 'restless, flowing', and for which the 'Jupiter Symphony, Part 1 (*Mozart*)' is suggested as the perfect musical counterpoint.

My favourite feature of this document is the middle column, in which Mey attempts to describe in as few words as possible the tenor of each particular scene. His descriptions are at once precise and preposterous, running the gamut from 'creepy mysterious' and 'flowing, semi-mysterious' to 'restless unmelodious', 'slightly exciting to weird' and (most convolutedly) 'restless, to mysterious, to ordinary'. The composers whose work Mey draws upon are all fairly well known, but his choice of particular pieces is wide ranging and astute, and one imagines that his musical suggestions would have been a great help to the musicians accompanying the movies.

Cue sheets sent out with the film reels added to the sense of preparation that became an increasingly common part of live cinema music at the higher end of the exhibition chain. Armed with these, the MDs could collate the music they needed, and either buy or hire it, in time for a run-through on, for example, a Friday afternoon. This would be the players' only chance to familiarize themselves with the music and scene changes, in readiness for a weekend in which they would most probably play the movie three times a day on both Saturday and Sunday. By the time Monday came, they could probably play the film with their eyes closed . . . and then Friday would roll around and they'd have to start from scratch all over again.

As for the MDs, they could either be employed by a specific venue, or they could travel from theatre to theatre, often bringing their own music with them. These peripatetic MDs soon became a favourite of the film companies, since the best of them could be relied upon to ensure that their product was presented in its finest form across a range of venues. For the film companies, the primary appeal of these MDs was not creativity but *uniformity*. In the days before the advent of recorded synchronized sound, the struggle to control the manner of a film's presentation was fraught with difficulty. Once the film reels had been sent out, it was pretty much up to the individual exhibitor to define *how* a movie would be seen – whether it would be projected correctly, at the right speed; whether the auditorium would be sufficiently darkened to ensure picture clarity; and what kind of clientele would be present for each screening. All of these elements clearly had a major impact on the way a film would be received, and in an age when word-of-mouth was the key to popular success (newspaper reviews were still in their infancy), the film companies found themselves somewhat at the mercy of the exhibitors. Having a trusted MD overseeing the musical accompaniment to a particular film in a number of locations offered a solution to this thorny problem. Although bespoke film scores had existed since the turn of the century, the landscape of musical accompaniment in general had been fairly chaotic in the early days of cinema. Here was a way of regulating that chaos – of bringing order to cinema exhibition in a manner that would maximize profits, and with any luck optimize audience enthusiasm for films.

The cinemas understood this too, and would make much show of offering the 'best musical experience' for movies that they believed had the potential to pull in large audiences. In his excellent book, *The Phoenix Cinema: A Century of Film in East Finchley*, author Gerry Turvey details the history of the cinema in which I effectively grew up – a beautiful venue that I frequented as a child, when it was called the Rex, and which showed double-bill reruns of Ealing comedies during the school holidays. Turvey's account includes fascinating details of how the Phoenix (then named the Coliseum) became engaged in a 'battle of the orchestras' with the neighbouring New Bohemia picturehouse. '[T]he two cinemas vied with each other to announce the quality of their musical provision', believing they could 'distinguish themselves competitively . . . by making much of their in-house music [and] featured performers'.

Such rivalries were commonplace, particularly when an event movie like Fred Niblo's 1925 *Ben-Hur: A Tale of the Christ* was playing. Based on a novel by General Lew Wallace that had already been adapted into a riotously popular play featuring onstage chariot races, the film rights commanded a hefty price tag for theatrical producer Abraham Erlanger, who earned both production approval and a profit participation deal, so certain was the film's success. Marketed with taglines like 'The Picture Every Christian Ought to See!' and 'The Supreme Motion Picture Masterpiece of All Time', *Ben-Hur* had audiences queuing around the block in the US, turning it into MGM's highest-grossing picture, taking over $9 million in rentals worldwide with foreign earnings in the region of $5 million, a figure that remained a record-breaker for the next quarter-century. (Ironically, due to the vast cost of production, and the overly generous deal signed with Erlanger, MGM reportedly *lost* money on *Ben-Hur* during its initial run, although several commentators have pointed to MGM's 'loss' as an early example of the kind of creative accounting that kept later smash hits like 1987's *Fatal Attraction* out of the black for decades.)

As for the cinemas that played *Ben-Hur*, their main aim would have been to ensure that this copper-bottomed blockbuster got the best possible treatment in their auditorium, thus giving potential viewers a special reason to see the film at *that* particular venue. At times, ticket prices might have to be increased to cover the expense of hiring extra musicians, but this was seen as a cost worth paying by audiences who were becoming increasingly savvy about the role of well-performed musical accompaniment.

*

One defining element of most of the movie music discussed so far is that little of it was written specifically *for* the movies. Instead, the challenge was to source existing pieces that could work in tandem with the movies, with *selection* being the key authorial element – curation, rather than composition. Yet bespoke film music *did* exist in the earliest part of the twentieth century. The 1908 French film *L'Assassinat du duc de Guise* (*The Assassination of the Duke of Guise*), for example, came with an original score composed by Camille Saint-Saëns, who also wrote music for a number of theatrical productions (and a section of whose most famous work, *The Carnival of the Animals*, has long been used to introduce films at the Cannes Festival). Saint-Saëns's score for *L'Assassinat du duc de Guise* (also known as *La Mort du duc de Guise*) is often cited as the first bespoke film score, although it is preceded by such earlier compositions as Herman Finck's music for the 1904 production *Marie Antoinette*, written for performances at the Palace Theatre in London. Such scores, however, were the exception rather than the norm, an adjunct to only a handful of film productions in a period when existing mood music was the order of the day.

According to Neil Brand, who has researched the plethora of extant source music used to accompany silent films in the first quarter of the twentieth century, the field is 'vastly bigger than anybody expected' – meaning that there is still plenty more to be uncovered about this crucial stage in film music history. Pieces such as Albert Ketèlbey's 'In a Monastery Garden' or 'In a Persian Market' may have become concert standards, but they were originally popularized as generic music for use in the silent-cinema market, which was expanding profitably in the teens and early twenties. Other generic pieces such as Maurice Baron's 'Desert Monotony' proved particularly popular as an accompaniment to the Westerns which flourished in the mid- to late twenties, many of which featured scenes in which charac-ters found themselves lost in the wilderness, under a baking sun, with no direction home. 'It's like the library music of today that could be sold on its title alone,' Neil enthuses to me. 'And its purpose was to earn money, and to be used by bands who were playing along to the movies, and who wanted new sounds that had a freshness to them.' Audiences weren't instantly familiar with the music, but it fitted with the onscreen action.

All of which, in its own way, prepared the ground for the modern synchronized movie score, which would arrive with a vengeance following the 1927 opening of *The Jazz Singer*, the first full-length feature to include synchronized recorded music, singing and speech, heralding the beginning of the end of the silent era. Of course, silent cinema didn't simply disappear in the wake of *The Jazz Singer* – there was a lengthy period of transition in which cinemas adjusted to the performance of recorded sound, and several films were issued in both sound *and* silent versions throughout the late twenties and into the mid-thirties. But the number of musicians employed to accompany silent films dropped dramatically in the years following the arrival of synchronized sound, and slowly but surely the silent era drew to a close, taking many of its secrets with it.

Except that it didn't . . .

Thanks to the work of film musicians like Neil Brand, the magic of silent cinema still thrives to this day, and there is plenty of evidence that the market for live film scores is on the increase. Today, modern audiences will pay top dollar to watch their favourite talking pictures performed with a live orchestral score. Meanwhile, silent movies are enjoying a renaissance at festivals like Midnight Sun in Sodankylä, where close to a thousand people will happily cram themselves into a circus tent to watch a skiffle band play along to a film that is the best part of a century old. What a time to be alive!

Working with Neil has been an education, and I can't stress enough that if you have *any* interest in film music (and if you're reading this book, then I presume that you do), you should try and see Neil accompanying a silent movie live. I guarantee that it will be a life-changing (or, more accurately, a life-*affirming*) experience – joyous, adventurous, informative. And yet, as is his manner, Neil retains an impressively humble sobriety on the subject of the role of the silent-movie musician, and their importance in the evolution of film music.

I'll leave the last words of this chapter to Neil, as he tells me about a novel he loves by Anthony Burgess, *The Pianoplayers* (1986). In it, a young woman replaces her drunk father as the pianist in a silent-movie cinema. She can barely play the piano, and the film she has the challenge of accompanying is . . . Fritz Lang's *Metropolis* (1927). 'She only plays these *three* chords – and *no one notices!*' laughs Neil. 'Now I think that's kind of beautiful, in a way. Because I'm afraid that at heart I think too much about getting the music for a movie *right*. But in a strange way, that novel touches something that's right at the centre of the silent-movie experience. You're deep in the middle of *Metropolis*, and as long as something – *anything* – is going on in that pit, then you probably didn't care too much what it is. Ha!'

Soundtrack Selection:
It's a Wonderful Life (1946)

About ten years ago, when I was a writer for the *Waitrose Weekend* magazine (one of the best gigs I ever had), my editors hit on the grand plan of getting their contributors to dress up as their favourite Christmas characters for their festive special edition. Stuck for ideas, I suggested that I should I dress up as George Bailey, the hero of my favourite Christmas movie, *It's a Wonderful Life* (1946). I *love* that movie – I love everything about it, from James Stewart's winning central performance to Dimitri Tiomkin's score, a few notes from which can send me into a darkly festive reverie.

Appropriate clothes (suit, waistcoat, hat, etc.) were duly sourced and provided for the Waitrose shoot, and photographs carefully taken. But, being no oil painting, I ended up looking more like the Fat Controller from *Thomas the Tank Engine* than handsome Jimmy Stewart at the height of his magical powers. I suppose that's what happens when you try to emulate your heroes; better just to watch them from afar, and revel in the majesty of their work.

Based on a short story by Philip Van Doren Stern, *It's a*

Wonderful Life may now be considered a stone-cold classic, but it got a rather lukewarm reception when first released in cinemas in December 1946. Financially, it was a dud, making an initial reported loss of $525,000. Some critics responded warmly (*Variety* praised its 'April-air wholesomeness and humanism'); many more were divided or dismissive. Writing in *The New York Times*, influential reviewer Bosley Crowther captured the general critical mood, calling the picture 'quaint and engaging' while complaining about the 'slew of cozy small-town characters' who habitually 'act juvenile and coy'. 'The weakness of the picture', he concluded, 'is the sentimentality of it all.'

The idea that *It's a Wonderful Life* is just sentimental schmaltz remains a popular cliché to this day, bolstered by a theatrical trailer, which promised 'Wonderful News . . . about Wonderful People! . . . In A Wonderful Picture!' After clips of the cast, all appearing sunny and amiable, we're treated to yet more exclamation marks with 'It's A Wonderful Love!' and 'It's A Wonderful Laugh!' Yet when one considers just how dark and disturbing key sections of the film manage to be, it's remarkable that anyone ever thought to label it mere heart-warming fluff. To borrow a phrase coined by Simon Mayo, 'There's a lot of Shawshank before you get to the Redemption, and a lot of Slumdog before the Millionaire.' And in this case, there's a *lot* of Life before you get to the Wonderful.

Consider the film's plot. Stewart's George Bailey is a beleaguered soul who has endured more than his fair share of setbacks and disappointments. As a child, he lost the hearing in one ear after saving his younger brother Harry from drowning. Later, George is savagely beaten in the drugstore where he works by an elderly chemist who is overcome with grief about the death of his own son. As a young man, George plans to go to college and travel the world. But just when George is about to escape Bedford Falls, his father dies, leaving him to take over the family business while Harry fulfils his dreams. When the Second World War arrives, George's bad ear prevents him from enlisting, but Harry signs up and becomes a decorated war hero. Finally, after his foolish Uncle Billy loses $8,000 of the business's money, George becomes so desperate that he goes to a bar, gets drunk, and decides to kill himself . . .

Despite such sombre subject matter, *It's a Wonderful Life* manages to turn tragedy to tears of joy as Henry Travers's apprentice angel, Clarence, shows George how much *worse* the world would be without him. Taking a lead from Dickens's *A Christmas Carol*, Clarence takes George on a supernatural tour of his old haunting grounds, confronting him with the spectre of 'Pottersville' – a grimly transformed vision of the small-town world he once knew, in which the lust for money has ridden roughshod over community spirit. The lesson here is simple – without decent people like George, the world would fall to rack and ruin. It all leads up to one of the most tear-jerking finales ever filmed – a ringing endorsement of the triumph of simple human kindness over venality and greed. And in a telling pre-echo of today's troubled times, America's rulers responded to this good Christian message by making the film the subject of vicious anti-communist witch-hunts, with the House Un-American Activities Committee investigating the movie, and concluding that it was guilty of 'demonizing bankers' and 'instigating class warfare'.

Capra famously never considered *It's a Wonderful Life* to be a Christmas film ('I just liked the idea,' he said), and its reputation as such was only cemented by popular TV reruns which turned it into a seasonal institution. Originally intended as a Cary

Grant vehicle, the film was shot on a tight ninety-day schedule, commencing on 15 April 1946, the same day the *Hollywood Reporter* announced that composer Dimitri Tiomkin was scoring the supernatural film *Angel on My Shoulder* (1946). *Variety* reported that Tiomkin was attached to *It's a Wonderful Life* on 3 July 1946, although he'd started composing a few months earlier, when filming began. His final recording session for the film, with an eighty-piece orchestra and forty-voice choir, was on 5 December.

Tiomkin had been busy that year, working on at least five other films in addition to *It's a Wonderful Life*. Yet despite being so in demand, he was the natural choice, having already enjoyed fruitful collaborations with Capra on several previous pictures. The director had given him his first big break by selecting him to score the adventure fantasy *Lost Horizon* in 1937. They worked together the following year on the romantic comedy *You Can't Take It with You* (1938), which also starred James Stewart alongside Lionel Barrymore, who would go on to play Mr Potter, the Trumpian founder of Pottersville in *It's a Wonderful Life*. Capra and Tiomkin collaborated again on *Mr Smith Goes to Washington* (1939) – starring James Stewart once more – and the 1941 comedy drama *Meet John Doe*, as well as the 1942 US government-funded war documentary series *Why We Fight*.

Born in Kremenchug in the Russian Empire, today part of Ukraine, Tiomkin was taught the piano at a young age by his mother, who was a musician. He studied at the St Petersburg Conservatoire, where one of his teachers was Alexander Glazunov, a renowned composer and mentor to other greats, including Prokofiev and Shostakovich. Fast-forward several decades to the 1950s, when Tiomkin was the highest-paid film composer in Hollywood, and it was his European classical forefathers like Brahms, Bach and Beethoven whom Tiomkin praised in his Academy Award acceptance speeches, rather than his American film music contemporaries.

In total, the self-taught film composer received twenty-two Oscar nominations – twenty-three if we include *Lost Horizon* (1937), which we *should*, because it was Tiomkin, rather than named nominee Morris Stoloff (the Head of the Columbia Studio Music Department), who created the score. Of those nominations, four were wins: three for scoring, for the Western *High Noon* (1952), aviation disaster *The High and the Mighty* (1954) and the 1958 Ernest Hemingway adaptation *The Old Man and the Sea*, and one for Best Original Song for 'The Ballad of High Noon', also known as 'Do Not Forsake Me (Oh My Darlin')'.

An extremely versatile composer, Tiomkin may be best remembered for his contribution to the Western film canon. His first score in this genre, *Duel in the Sun* (1946), was released the same year as *It's a Wonderful Life*, and he would go on to receive acclaim for many others including *Red River* (1948) and *Rio Bravo* (1959) on the big screen, along with the instantly hummable *Rawhide* (1959) main theme on TV. He also collaborated with Alfred Hitchcock on four of his pictures – a particularly impressive feat considering Hitch's form in picking up and dropping composers throughout his career. Tiomkin had provided the music for *Shadow of a Doubt* (1943) before Capra came calling for *It's a Wonderful Life* and, in the 1950s, he collaborated again with Hitchcock on *Strangers on a Train* (1951), *I Confess* (1953) and *Dial M for Murder* (1954).

Having originally wanted to be a concert pianist, Tiomkin only became a film composer after breaking his arm in 1937, an injury that caused a life-changing career rethink. Despite his Russian upbringing, he demonstrated an uncanny ability to create quintessentially *American*-sounding scores, not least his work depicting the vast prairies in his Western scores, or in the small-town evocations of *It's a Wonderful Life*. There's a comforting 'mom's apple pie' feel to the 'Main Title' of *It's a Wonderful Life*, although the wider score is far more nuanced, deftly skipping across a gamut of moods, from romance to despair and back again. Cues like 'Haunted House' and 'Pottersville Cemetery' are remarkably sophisticated and evocative, and the swirling, eerie choir in 'George is Unborn' makes it a standout listen.

Tiomkin proves himself to be more than adept at responding to the tonal shifts within the film. He also incorporated existing music within his original score, using familiar motifs from Mendelssohn's 'Wedding March' and Beethoven's Symphony No. 9, along with several traditional American songs like 'Buffalo Gals', which George and Mary sing on their first date.

In 2021, the great La-La Land Records (the leading purveyors of bespoke soundtrack CDs) released a limited edition, remastered seventy-fifth anniversary CD of Tiomkin's score, boasting exceptionally detailed sleeve notes by film music historian Frank K. DeWald. One of the most memorable bonus tracks on the album is a vocal version of the cue 'It's a Wonderful Life' with lyrics by Frederick Herbert. Oddly, despite Tiomkin's later popular successes with 'Do Not Forsake Me (Oh My Darlin')' from *High Noon* or 'Thee I Love' from *Friendly Persuasion* (1956), this vocal version doesn't seem to have been released as part of the film's promo. Not only might this have helped the box-office appeal when the film was released, but it's a great tune, a real earworm that could have easily nestled alongside Bing Crosby singing 'White Christmas' on future festive

51

compilations. In fact, it was overlooked to such a degree that today we don't even know who the singer is, despite DeWald's valiant efforts to investigate.

Perhaps it was a simple matter of timing. Things became rushed after the decision was made to release the film before Christmas, partly so that it would be eligible for the 1946 Academy Awards. As a result, various changes were made to enhance the seasonal elements of the film, and parts of Tiomkin's score were removed. Somewhat gallingly for the composer, several of his cues were replaced by existing music, including 'It's a Wonderful Life', which was removed to make way for 'Alleluia' from Alfred Newman's score for *The Hunchback of Notre Dame* (1939).

This can't have been easy for Tiomkin. In his 1959 memoir, *Please Don't Hate Me!*, the composer describes his collaborations with Capra up until this point as genial affairs, where the director 'had left it to me to be the judge of the music', but here he was faced with 'an all-round scissors job'. The two didn't come to blows, but their friendship suffered. Perhaps it was additionally tough for the composer who once described his approach to film scoring as: 'In general, I say "yes" to everybody, and then I go and write what I want.' Tiomkin and Capra didn't see each other for well over a year afterwards. Although they were able to patch things up, they never collaborated again.

In 1974, due most likely to a clerical error, the copyright for *It's a Wonderful Life* expired and it entered the public domain, becoming a beloved must-watch Christmas favourite, cropping up regularly on seasonal TV for a couple of decades, before Republic Pictures regained control of the copyright in the early nineties. As Capra told *The Wall Street Journal* in 1984, 'The film has a life of its own now, and I can look at it like I had nothing to do with it. I'm like a parent whose kid grows up to be president.'

CHAPTER 2

How Did We Get Here?

Part 1 – From Korngold to Williams

A long time ago in a galaxy far, far away, I turned forty.

I remember my fortieth birthday for a number of reasons, one of which was that Ken Russell, the film-maker behind such musically themed hits as *The Music Lovers* (1971), *The Boyfriend* (1971), *Mahler* (1974), *Tommy* (1975) and *Lisztomania* (1975), came to my party.

Ken lived nearby in the New Forest, and we had become friends. I had interviewed him for *Sight and Sound* magazine back in the nineties, and I had made a Channel 4 documentary about his extraordinary 1971 masterpiece *The Devils*. Somehow our professional relationship had morphed into something altogether more familiar, and we ended up spending quite a lot of time together, talking about movies and music, usually at his favourite New Forest pub in East Boldre, just round the corner from the cottage he shared with his wife, the vivaciously enchanting Lisi Tribble.

On the day of my birthday party, Ken had arrived clutching a small package to his bosom. 'It's a present,' he announced, before adding, 'but you've probably already got it.'

I opened the roughly wrapped parcel to discover inside a

CD of Erich Wolfgang Korngold's original score for the 1940 Michael Curtiz film *The Sea Hawk*.

'It's wonderful,' Ken said, 'but you've already got it, haven't you?'

I looked up at Ken's face, which had a look of genuine concern, and smiled reassuringly. 'No, Ken, I haven't got it. Thanks so much.'

Ken looked relieved, but then asked, 'But do you *like* it?'

I looked at the CD and said, 'Well, I haven't heard it yet, but I'm sure it's great.'

Ken looked puzzled. 'But you do *know* it?' he insisted.

I shook my head. He looked shocked. 'It's Korngold's score for *The Sea Hawk*,' he said. 'You know, *The Sea Hawk*. Korngold. The music from it.' I looked a little shamefaced and admitted that I wasn't familiar with either the film or its music.

'But you do *know* Korngold,' Ken said, with the slightest hint of exasperation in his voice.

'Well, I know *of* him,' I said, 'but I don't have any recordings of his . . .'

'But you're a film critic!' Ken exclaimed. 'It's your *job* to know about films. So you *must* know Korngold!'

'Well, as I said, I know *of* him . . .'

'Oh for heaven's sake!' said Ken. 'Where's your CD player?'

And with that, he put the CD on and made me sit and listen to it, and (moreover) promise to find out more about Korngold. Which I did.

The fact that I didn't really know much about Korngold's work may seem as terrible to you as it did to Ken, all those years ago. Korngold is, after all, considered by many to be one of the titans of film composition (despite the sneery 'more corn than gold' epithet cruelly coined by critic Irving Kolodin). And, as

Ken so eloquently pointed out, it was my job to know that sort of thing. Yet despite having been a fan of movies and movie music for most of my life, I had never sat down and attempted to familiarize myself with the established canon of great composers – partly because the composers who interested me most tended to be those who had worked on films that I personally loved, few of which were made before the 1960s.

I was, if nothing else, a child of my time.

Having been duly chastised by Ken, however (and pleasantly impressed by the CD of *The Sea Hawk*), I started to try to fill some of the huge gaps in my knowledge by looking back over the careers of some of the established 'greats' and trying to understand how they fitted together – how they influenced each other from decade to decade.

*

Erich Wolfgang Korngold died in 1957, six years before I was born, and about a decade before I started being taken to the movies. (The first film I remember seeing at the cinema was the 1968 adventure *Krakatoa, East of Java*.) While many consider Korngold's fellow Austrian composer Max Steiner to be the true king of the Golden Age (so much so that he's often referred to as 'the father of film music' for his significant role in creating a space and a place for film scores within the film-making process – we'll return to him later, in Chapter 7, 'Play Through the Action'), Korngold pushed things further in terms of epic action and adventure with his scores for films like *Captain Blood* (1935), *The Adventures of Robin Hood* (1938), *The Sea Wolf* (1941) and – as Ken was so keen for me to learn – *The Sea Hawk*.

A genuine child prodigy, often compared to Mozart for his

early musical talents, Korngold is credited by many film schol-
ars with the creation of the symphonic film score. He was a
well-known composer long before he arrived in Hollywood and
he would approach film in a similar way to opera, utilizing the
script as he would a libretto.

Korngold came to America in 1934, at the invitation of theatre
director and movie-maker Max Reinhardt, whose production
of *A Midsummer Night's Dream* was being filmed. Reinhardt
needed a composer to adapt the incidental music that Mendelssohn had written for the play, and Korngold proved adept
at fitting his compositions to match the dramatic timing of an
unfolding scene. His approach was practical; when he saw a
reel of film footage, he reportedly asked one of the technicians
how long one foot of film was, only to be told, 'twelve inches'.
When he asked the question again, stating that he was asking in
terms of *duration* as opposed to physical length, the technician
couldn't answer. On finding out that it came to two-thirds of a
second, Korngold was pleased, remarking that that was *exactly*
the same amount of time as the opening two measures of Mendelssohn's Scherzo for *A Midsummer Night's Dream*.

As his film career progressed, Korngold was said to have
'conducted' actors, performing their lines so that the dialogue
would work in time with the music. Soon he was working
between Vienna and Los Angeles, but his career as an opera and
concert music composer in Europe was put on hold during the
Second World War, and he became a naturalized US citizen in
1943, living and working in Hollywood.

Not only was Korngold adept at matching music to action, he
also had a reputation for turning his scores around *fast* – a real
boon in Hollywood. For his 1935 feature debut *Captain Blood*,
he composed and recorded the score in just three weeks. An

immediate hit, the film earned five Oscar nominations, including an unofficial write-in nomination (a technique used for circumventing Academy selection) for Best Score, albeit under the name of 'head of department' Leo F. Forbstein. The next year, Korngold's score for *Anthony Adverse* (1936) would win the Oscar for Best Music, Score, but again Forbstein was the named nominee. It wasn't until 1939 that Korngold won the statuette under his own name, for his work on *The Adventures of Robin Hood*.

Along with the output of other Eastern European composers who had moved to the States due to war and political upheaval in their homelands, such as Franz Waxman, Miklós Rózsa, Bronisław Kaper, Max Steiner and Dimitri Tiomkin, Korngold's big sweeping scores became the sound of Hollywood during the thirties and forties. He composed music that precisely reflected the onscreen action and, perhaps more significantly, created signature tunes – or 'leitmotifs' – to represent characters.

Popularized by the late-Romantic-era German composer Richard Wagner, creator of such bum-numbingly long operatic works as the *Ring* cycle, leitmotifs remain a hugely significant aspect of modern film scoring. As an example, look no further than the fifty-odd themes composed by Howard Shore for Peter Jackson's *The Lord of The Rings* movies in the early twenty-first century, each one associated with a distinct character, location, idea, object or event, guiding the audience through the potentially confusing landscape of Tolkien's grand creation.

As Korngold's reputation as a film composer grew, so his standing within the classical music establishment wobbled a little, an early example of the snobbery sometimes directed at film composition. Why, his classical contemporaries asked, was a composer of his stature sullying himself with an art form as vulgar and populist as cinema? Today, the rise of live film score performances has been widely credited with drawing new audiences into the classical concert halls and introducing them to orchestral music – a gateway drug to the heady world of classical composition and performance. As for Korngold, who often drew upon elements of his concert works in his film scores, he saw no distinction between the artistic merits of the diverse mediums in which he worked. 'Music is music,' he believed, 'whether it is for the stage, rostrum or cinema.'

*

While Korngold was at the height of his cinematic powers in the thirties and forties, British composer Doreen Carwithen, whose scores were comparably lush and full-bodied in terms of orchestration and musical drama, really came into her own in the fifties. One of the first women to work full time as a film composer, Carwithen demonstrated a sharp musical ability from an early age. The examiner at her Grade 8 piano exam was the Royal Academy teacher Frederick Moore, who was so impressed with her talents that he offered to give her private lessons. She went on to study at the Royal Academy and later worked there as Sub Professor of Composition.

Having become the first recipient of a J. Arthur Rank film scholarship in 1946, Carwithen went on to compose over thirty film scores in addition to works for the concert hall. There's a depth and complexity to her music as well as a spirited tunefulness. One of her best-known scores is for Val Guest's 1954 swashbuckler *Men of Sherwood Forest*, and its delightful romping orchestral 'Overture' makes a neat companion piece to Korngold's work on *The Adventures of Robin Hood*.

As with so many female film composers from the first half of the twentieth century, available recordings of Carwithen's music are patchy, but the suites from *Boys in Brown* (1950), *Mantrap/A Man in Hiding* (1953) and *Three Cases of Murder* (1955) are worth seeking out for their rich sound and visual vibrancy. In 2022, on the centenary of her birth, the inaugural Carwithen Festival took place in her birthplace of Haddenham, Buckinghamshire, helping to keep her works alive and introducing them to wider audiences.

Often uncredited for her work on film scores alongside male composers, Carwithen was aware enough of her talent to lobby for equal pay. She received her first feature film credit in 1947 and went on to gain a reputation in the industry for her professionalism and ability to work to tight deadlines; she completed her work (with Sir Adrian Boult) on Pathé's 1953 coronation film *Elizabeth is Queen* with such speed that it beat Gaumont's rival production, *A Queen Is Crowned*, into cinemas by several days.

In 1961 Carwithen's own career was put on hold when she became secretary and amanuensis to composer William Alwyn, whom she married in 1975. Following his death in 1985, Carwithen dedicated her life to launching and maintaining the William Alwyn Foundation. When asked why she had given up her career to look after Alwyn, she replied, 'Well, someone had to!' – although it's hard not to wonder what might have happened had she continued to forge her own path in the film industry.

While Carwithen stepped away from her career in 1961, over in India at around the same time, Usha Khanna was following in the footsteps of female pioneers Jaddanbai Hussain and Saraswati Devi by making a name for herself in the burgeoning Hindi film industry. A mainstay of so-called 'Bollywood' film music throughout the sixties, seventies and eighties, Khanna earned her first credit as music director/composer on the 1959 hit *Dil Deke Dekho/Try Giving Your Heart*, working with lyricist Majrooh Sultanpuri on a string of songs, several of which featured the voice of legendary playback artists Mohammed Rafi and Asha Bhosle (regulars of our Scala Radio show).

Impressed by her work on *Dil Deke Dekho*, producer Sashadhar Mukherjee enlisted Khanna to compose for *Hum Hindustani* (1960), which once again featured rising star (and screen-legend-in-the-making) Asha Parekh and helped to establish Khanna within the male-dominated Hindi film world. A talented playback singer herself, Khanna would go on to collaborate with lyricist and film-maker Saawan Kumar Tak (whom she married), and to conjure a string of hits that became film standards in India, occasionally breaking through in the global market. In 1980, vocalist K. J. Yesudas won a Filmfare Best Male Playback Singer award for his performance of Khanna's co-written song 'Dil Ke Tukde Tukde Karke Muskurake Chal Diye' ('Having Broken My Heart into Pieces You Walked Away with a Smile') from the movie *Dada* (1979). Four years later, Khanna became the first woman to earn a Filmfare nomination for Best Music Director for her work on Saawan Kumar Tak's 1983 three-way-love story *Souten*.

Khanna's place in Indian film is significant because she proved to be a pioneering woman in an industry in which artists and composers like Sneha Khanwalkar, Payal Dev and Jasleen Royal have since flourished. Her influence is immense, yet her name appears on far too few lists of 'great film composers' – lists which have all too often prioritized the work of (mainly white) men working within Hollywood, or perhaps Europe, to the exclusion of the wider world of film music. Ken Russell may have been shocked that I didn't own any Erich Korngold recordings, but by the time I turned forty I *did* have a couple of Usha Khanna soundtracks in my collection – although I confess that these had been gifted to me by a friend who insisted that 'too few British critics know *anything* about popular Indian cinema', and who had attempted to prove the point by asking if I'd even heard of Asha Bhosle *before* Cornershop's nineties hit 'Brimful of Asha' made her a household name in the UK.

I said I had.

He didn't believe me.

Among Khanna's other celebrated film credits are Sudin Menon's Indian-Malayalam drama *Moodalmanju* (1970), on which she collaborated with lyricist Puloottupadathu Bhaskaran, creating a number of infectiously catchy songs that are today regarded as stone-cold classics. Nor were her triumphs confined to the twentieth century; in 2003, for example, she provided the music for Sawaan Kumar Tak's romantic drama *Dil Pardesi Ho Gayaa*, and in 2019 she earned a Lifetime Achievement trophy at the eleventh Mirchi Music Awards in Mumbai.

'The thing about Indian film-makers,' says A. R. Rahman, one of the best-known composers in the world, 'is that they never aspired to become international film-makers. Because there's 1.3 billion people in the country, there's a sense of satisfaction; "We don't need anything else, this is enough for us." Even *within* India, you had North Indian cinema, South Indian cinema – everything stayed within its own region.'

For Rahman, whom I interviewed for BBC Radio 4's *Screenshot*, that sense of self-sufficiency goes some way to explaining why the films on which composers like Usha Khanna worked often remained overlooked by international film commentators – the film-makers simply didn't need the approval of Western critics, and so they largely didn't get it.

'There is an international language of film-making, with iconic directors like Satyajit Ray and, of course, my mentor, Mani Ratnam,' Rahman continued. 'But for a long time there was a sense that these films are made mainly for Indians. When the non-resident Indians began moving out to other countries, then that market became bigger. But it was only really after *Lagaan* [2001] and those kind of movies that it expanded more. India is unique; there are so many different languages and so many different states, and each state has got its own dances and food and language and ways of dressing. Personally, I always feel that the world needs to celebrate each other's cultures, because then there's more peace, and more mutual admiration.'

That philosophy of 'mutual admiration' has led Rahman to become not only India's most successful film composer, but also an Academy Award-winner who now works across the full spectrum of world cinema. We will return to his career in Chapter 4, 'How Did We Get Here? Part 2', but for now let us simply note that on the eve of his double victory at the 2009 Oscars, Rahman was profiled in the *Los Angeles Times*, where writer Monya De noted that his score for Danny Boyle's *Slumdog Millionaire* included 'a mad pursuit through the slums [in which] his violins slice like Bernard Herrmann's in *Psycho*'. Meanwhile, at around the same time, the website of the PRX radio show *Sound Opinions* referred to Rahman as 'a giant in the Bollywood world [whom] many people are comparing to mainstream giants like Bernard Herrmann'.

A real composer's composer, and one who's often cited as an inspiration by music-makers today, Bernard Herrmann led the move away from music that directly illustrated the onscreen action, preferring instead to experiment with rhythms and harmonies that enhanced the atmosphere and sensory tone of a film. Described as a master of orchestration, with the ability to create complex yet instantly memorable scores, Herrmann provided the music for over two hundred movies. His CV starts and ends with two masterpieces: Orson Welles's *Citizen Kane* (1941), for which he received his first Oscar nomination (beating *himself* to the statuette with his own subsequent score for William Dieterle's *The Devil and Daniel Webster/All that Money Can Buy*), and Martin Scorsese's *Taxi Driver* (1976), which earned Herrmann one of *two* posthumous Academy Award nominations, the other being for Brian De Palma's *Obsession* (1976).

Herrmann's entry into the world of cinema came via radio, for which he wrote and conducted a large amount of narrative music, often broadcast live. His collaborations with Orson Welles on various radio plays, including the infamous 1938 production of *The War of the Worlds*, led to the director inviting the composer to Hollywood to score what would become Welles's feature debut and cinematic magnum opus. Not only did Welles kick back against the studio's attempts to pay this little-known composer a low fee, ensuring that Herrmann received the same salary as established names like Max Steiner, but the director also gave him artistic freedom. Keen to flex his creative chops on his first film score, Herrmann experimented with twelve flutes for the opening of the film rather than sticking to a standard symphony orchestra. Welles even proved amenable to being guided by Herrmann's music in the edit: as Herrmann recalled, *Citizen Kane* 'abounded in montages, which were long enough to permit me to compose complete musical numbers, rather than mere cues to fit them. Mr Welles was extremely cooperative in this respect, and in many cases cut his film to suit these complete numbers, rather than doing what is ordinarily done – cut the music to suit the film.'

Herrmann's work with Alfred Hitchcock on *Psycho* (1960) will be examined in Chapter 9, 'A Frightful Noise', but it's hard to overstate the influence of their collaboration. The 'Master of Suspense' (Hitchcock was one of the very few directors whose name alone could sell a movie) and 'Benny', as he was known to his friends, worked on eight films together, from *The Trouble with Harry* (1945) through to *Marnie* (1964). Their projects included *The Birds* (1963), which didn't have a typical score but on which the composer was credited as sound consultant, a telling indicator of his skills not just in making music, but in shaping the sound and therefore the filmgoing experience.

One of the pair's most significant and enduring collaborations was *Vertigo* (1958), voted the greatest movie of all time in *Sight and Sound*'s 2018 poll. Herrmann's score, which swings between the romantic and the unsettling, adds a sense of emotional depth to Hitchcock's perfectly conjured suspense. Just as Wagner's leit-motifs had influenced Korngold, so his opera *Tristan and Isolde*, with its anguished 'Liebestod' ('Love Death'), proved inspirational to Herrmann for the 'Scene d'amour', reflecting a darker side of love as it tips over into obsession. This was Herrmann and Hitchcock's fourth project together and, by this stage in their creative partnership, the director had full faith in the composer's abilities and talent. When Hitchcock gave his usual meticulous directions to the film's sound department, he would keep the notes about some of the scenes vague, stating that the sound requirements would be dependent upon Herrmann's score.

Again, in a manner similar to Korngold, and indeed many film composers across the decades, Herrmann reused elements of his own work in different projects. He was a fan of a particular three-note motif that captured a sense of ominous dread. This first appeared in his Sinfonietta, written in the mid-1930s, and you can hear it resurfacing in his score for *Psycho*, nearly twenty-five years later, as a representation of Norman Bates's fractured state of mind. He also included it in *Taxi Driver*, and John Williams paid tribute to Herrmann by incorporating it in one of his most influential scores, 1977's *Star Wars*.

Herrmann was also a fan of the ostinato – a short span of music that is repeated many times but has no fixed beginning or end, so can be broken off at any point to fit the scene. Ostinatos can be found in several of Herrmann's film scores, and he appreciated their comparative formlessness in contrast to a traditional melody. 'You know, the reason I don't like this tune business', he once said, 'is that a tune has to have eight or sixteen bars, which limits you as a composer'. He described it as 'putting handcuffs on yourself'. By going against the accepted idea of a traditional melody, Herrmann helped to make space for composers to have more creative freedom, placing more impetus on what film music can achieve and how it can affect the film and the audience.

It's interesting to compare Herrmann's film music with that of the British composer Elisabeth Lutyens, who serves as an intriguing counterpart in terms of musical experimentation, atmospheric creation and exploiting the more discomfiting side of film scoring. Lutyens enjoyed working with sparse aural textures and was the first female British composer to use Arnold Schoenberg's twelve-tone technique (in which all twelve notes of the chromatic scale are given equal emphasis), sometimes expanding into a self-created *fourteen*-tone scale. With four children to support, she composed for film, radio, television and theatre primarily for the income, and her first feature film score was in 1948 for the mystery *Penny and the Pownall Case*.

I first encountered Lutyens's work as a child, when I would

sneak downstairs after my parents had gone to bed, to watch the Hammer reruns that became a staple of late-night television in the early seventies. I had to watch the movies with the volume turned right down, so as not to waken anyone else in the house. Even with the speaker of our tiny kitchen-worktop portable TV set barely troubling the air in the room, I was still aware of (and, frankly, creeped out by) the music of films like *Never Take Sweets from a Stranger* (1960), the tagline for which boasted 'A Nightmare Manhunt for Maniac Prowler!'. Lutyens also provided memorably strange music for several films by Hammer rivals Amicus Productions, including the bone-chiller *The Skull* (1965), brilliantly directed by Freddie Francis, with genre legends Peter Cushing and Christopher Lee helping to ensure that 'When The Skull Strikes YOU'LL SCREAM!'. Although in my case, due to the covert circumstances under which I was watching these deeply corrupting films, it was a pre-*Alien* case of: 'In the kitchen, no one can hear you scream'.

The Oscar-winning composer Anne Dudley cites Lutyens' singular, uncompromising scores as significantly influential, a quality evident in a 2004 recording of a suite of Lutyens' music from *The Skull*, performed by the BBC Symphony Orchestra. Lutyens didn't consider her screen work as 'artistic music' compared to her concert pieces, but she appeared to enjoy her insight into the machinations of the industry and is remembered for her wry riposte: 'Do you want it good or do you want it Wednesday?' when asked to compose a score.

*

Bernard Herrmann's relationship with Alfred Hitchcock ended on a somewhat sour note when his score for the 1966 thriller *Torn Curtain* was rejected in favour of rather more 'crowd-friendly' fare by John Addison (although Herrmann's original score for *Torn Curtain* is now considered something of an overlooked classic, having been recorded and reissued several times since the film's original release). This was a time when film music was evolving to reflect the pop charts of the day. An accompanying hit single was seen as the key to a film's success with young audiences, and studios wanted more of a poppy, rhythmic score such as those composed by John Barry or Henry Mancini. The hit soundtrack song had become a matter of significance to film studios in the early fifties when Tex Ritter's recording of Tiomkin's earworm theme 'Do Not Forsake Me (Oh My Darlin')' from *High Noon* proved to be a key factor in the film's commercial success. Unsurprisingly, studios began asking composers to pen a lead single to accompany their scores, with soundtrack albums emerging a little later as studios acknowledged not only the power of radio cross-promotion, but also the potential of soundtrack LP sales to buoy up diminishing box-office revenues.

Amid these shifts, Herrmann found himself out of favour due to his perceived lack of commercial pop sparkle – or, more pertinently, his unwillingness to provide it. The innovator was no longer seen as innovative. As his wife Norma Herrmann recalled, when Bernard contacted 20th Century Fox to tell them he was available for work in the mid-sixties, musical director Lionel Newman replied, 'Sorry, Benny, we decided to run with the kids' – meaning that they were looking for younger composers with a more popular ear. 'This rankled,' Norma remembered. 'It hurt him!'

Herrmann returned to composing for the concert hall but (as we shall see in Chapter 9) enjoyed a movie career resurgence in the early 1970s as a new generation of directors like François

Truffaut, Brian De Palma and Martin Scorsese sought out the musical genius who had shaped their formative film-viewing experiences. He died in 1975, hours after completing his jazzy, dissonant score for *Taxi Driver*. Apparently, he had been in talks with Steven Spielberg and was due to meet him to discuss his next project on the day he died, delighted that his music was appreciated by these younger film-makers. According to Norma Herrmann, when Lionel Newman (who had snubbed the composer years earlier) called him during this late-career renaissance to ask him to work on a big Fox film, Herrmann had payback: 'Benny said, and I was there, "Sorry, I've decided to run with the kids!" and he put the phone down. And he was so happy. He was shaking with laughter!'

While the prospect of Bernard Herrmann collaborating with Steven Spielberg may sound intriguing, it's hard to imagine anyone other than John Williams becoming Spielberg's long-time musical muse. The creator of so many classic cinematic tunes, Williams has done more than most to shape modern filmgoers' experiences and memories. And while the emotional heft of his music may sometimes seem too wholesome for those of a darker soundtrack persuasion, his contribution to mainstream film scoring cannot be understated.

In the fifties and sixties, Williams worked with Golden Age greats like Herrmann, Alfred Newman and Franz Waxman. He was influenced by Korngold, whom he credits with bringing 'the Vienna Opera House to the American West', and also by Wagner's concept of creating the *Gesamtkunstwerk*, or 'total work of art'. For Wagner, this meant fusing all elements of a theatrical experience such as music, drama and visuals in order to create something truly immersive, and Williams has carried these principles into the cinema. Crucially, the key to Williams' success, and perhaps his greatest field of influence, is in creating music that gets straight to the heart of the film. He has an uncanny ability to translate emotion into melody, and with that he has given us a wealth of instantly recognizable tunes and memories.

In 2023, at a special celebration of John Williams and Steven Spielberg's impressive fifty-year collaboration held at the Writers Guild Theater in Beverly Hills, the director described his creative partnership with 'Johnny' (the name under which he originally worked) as an ideal marriage, while the composer called Spielberg his muse. In the 2024 documentary *Music by John Williams*, the composer refers to his first meeting with the young Spielberg as 'probably the luckiest day of my life'.

However, their collaborations are just one part of a much wider career. Williams was in his forties when he first sat down to lunch with the twenty-something Spielberg, and he'd already established himself as a composer of note. As a young thrill-hungry cinemagoer, I had first encountered Williams' work through a swathe of seventies disaster pictures that were such a core part of my own early cinema-going experiences; films like *The Poseidon Adventure* (1972), *The Towering Inferno* (1974) and *Earthquake* (1974), the last of which was released in 'Sensurround' – a low bass rumble designed to give the audience the impression that the entire theatre was shaking. Williams also scored Hitchcock's last feature film, *Family Plot* (1976), horror films like Brian De Palma's *The Fury* (1978) and John Badham's *Dracula* (1979), and a number of projects for Mark Rydell (*The Reivers*, 1969; *The Cowboys*, 1972; *Cinderella Liberty*, 1973). *The Reivers* had introduced Williams' music to the young cinephile Steven Spielberg, who listened to the soundtrack on repeat and told himself that if he ever made a feature film, he'd enlist the talents of this composer, whom he blithely presumed to be English.

With Japanese percussionist and keyboardist Stomu Yamashta, Williams also conjured an impressively experimental score for Robert Altman's *Images* (1972), and he lent stirring musical backbones to such typically bombastic Oliver Stone fare as *Born on the Fourth of July* (1989) and *JFK* (1991). While everyone knows Williams' infectiously hummable tunes for the *Harry Potter* franchise, not to mention his genre-defining theme from the 1978 hit *Superman*, how many recall that it was Williams who provided the offbeat score to Alan Arkush's 1981 robot romance *Heartbeeps*, starring Andy Kaufman and Bernadette Peters?

Classically trained at Juilliard in New York, the young Williams became a keen pianist, often practising for five or six hours a day. He turned his attention to film scores when his drummer dad started working in film studio orchestras – he'd accompany him to recording sessions and observe the making of such scores as *On the Waterfront* (1954) by Leonard Bernstein. But as an accomplished jazz keyboardist (he played on several studio albums in the fifties), Williams admits that he only really became interested in film music as a method of employment, serving time in Hollywood studio orchestras for many years before turning to orchestration and composition.

During this period, Williams tinkled the ivories on such seminal soundtracks as *The Big Country* (1958) by Jerome Moross, *Breakfast at Tiffany's* (1962) by Henry Mancini, *To Kill a Mockingbird* (1962) by Elmer Bernstein, and *The Apartment* (1960) and *Some Like It Hot* (1959), both by Adolph Deutsch. For the last of these, Williams accompanied Marilyn Monroe in her headset when she performed her songs. You can also hear him on the soundtrack of the original 1961 *West Side Story* – a film Spielberg would remake with Williams as 'musical consultant' in 2021.

On his early film scores, the composer was credited as 'Johnny Williams', becoming 'John' only when a colleague told him he needed a name that people would take seriously. And take him seriously they did; to date, Williams has racked up five Academy Award wins and a whopping *fifty-four* nominations, most recently for *Indiana Jones and the Dial of Destiny* (2023) at the age of ninety-one, making him the oldest nominee in any competitive category in the awards' history.

Among many other monickers, Williams has been described as the 'Master of the March' due to his extraordinary skill at creating rousing, celebratory anthems. 'The Raiders March', 'The Imperial March', the 'March' from *1941* (1979), or (digging a bit deeper) the 'Midway March' from *Midway/Battle of Midway* (1976), another mid-seventies adventure released in stomach-rumbling 'Sensurround' – all of these are stirring fun, channelling Korngold's spirit of symphonic adventure, and creating the sort of nostalgic yet timeless tunes that popular cinema loves.

Two scores from Williams' remarkable career wield the most influence on film music and composers today. First, the defining sound of fear from the 1975 hit thriller *Jaws*. Everyone knows the *Jaws* theme. Its effect is simple and its legacy is outstanding. The shark may spend most of its time off screen (Spielberg was hindered by the constant mechanical failures of the beast he nicknamed 'Bruce', after his lawyer) but Williams ratchets up the tension with those repeated low notes, taking Herrmann's lead by utilizing ostinato to full effect.

Jaws was Williams' second collaboration with Steven Spielberg, following *The Sugarland Express* (1974). Famously, when

Williams played Spielberg his deceptively simple musical identifier for the character of the shark at the piano, the director thought he was joking. It was only after Williams played the opening over and over that Spielberg understood he was serious, and he started to appreciate the power of the notes' simplicity. The composer explained to him that cellos and basses would make the music even more menacing, and that a sense of panic would be created by speeding up the repeated notes and bringing up the volume. Spielberg reflected in 2000 that 'To this day, I think that his score was clearly responsible for half the success of the film.'

That theme possesses a universal power. The Indian composer and producer M. M. Keeravani, who won a Best Original Song Oscar in 2023 for the brilliantly bombastic 'Naatu Naatu' from the epic Indian action film *RRR* (2022), credited Williams when he received the Los Angeles Film Critics Association (LAFCA) award for music: 'Thank you very much, John Williams, sir, for teaching me the lesson of simplicity and humbleness and being my inspiration for all these years.' (Anna Meredith had a similar Damascene moment with Williams' *Jaws* theme, as we shall see in Chapter 6, 'Switched-On Electronica'.) To this day, the *Jaws* theme remains a shorthand for menace, a theme so familiar that it was parodied by Elmer Bernstein in his opening to the 1980 disaster movie spoof *Airplane!* as the tail-fin of a plane is seen slicing through clouds, like a shark through water.

Another Williams masterpiece of particular significance to the evolution of film scoring is his music for a galaxy far, far away. Not only did *Star Wars* (1977) continue the legacy of Korngold's romping themes for Golden Age action-adventure films and introduce the sound to a new generation of filmgoers, it also defied the ubiquitous need for a pop hit to sell a movie, becoming an orchestral soundtrack smash in its own right. Less than two months after the film's original release, the score (which was a two-LP set – a rarity for a soundtrack at the time) was certified gold. A month later it went platinum, selling over four million copies, demonstrating the might of movie music and leading to a resurgence of orchestral film scores rather than pop or rock soundtracks. If cinema's role is to provide escapism for the audience, few opening bars are more effective than the sparkling, jubilant, brassy fanfare in Williams' 'Main Titles' from *Star Wars* – which was actually the last piece of music he wrote for the film.

Williams nearly didn't score *Star Wars*. Around the same time, he was asked to compose the music for Richard Attenborough's war epic *A Bridge Too Far* (1977), which boasted an impressive cast – not something that could be said about George Lucas's hokey-looking space project. Spielberg had been the one to recommend the composer to Lucas, who was keen to have an orchestral score and, while Williams hadn't seen the young director's previous film, *American Graffiti* (1973), Spielberg persuaded him that this was going to be a special project – although as Williams recalls, 'it didn't take much pushing'.

Star Wars was Williams' first opportunity to record a film soundtrack with a symphony orchestra, and he was over the moon at Lionel Newman's suggestion of hiring the London Symphony Orchestra. His ambition was to 'produce a beautifully set symphonic sound that struck late-nineteenth-century emotional and maybe even intellectual chords in some way with the listener', so it felt 'very familiar in the sense that its ethos is familiar for many'. By composing music that harked back to earlier decades, Williams created a timeless sound. He drew upon classical composers like Holst, Dvořák and Stravinsky, and he would discuss Prokofiev's *Peter and the Wolf* with George Lucas because the director was keen to adopt a similar approach of each character having their own theme, or leitmotif.

By incorporating influences from classical composers and Golden Age scores by Steiner and Korngold, and then adding in choral music with occasional references to earlier eras, Williams created a rich and colourful sound world upon which he has been able to expand throughout the series. 'Duel of the Fates' from *Episode I: The Phantom Menace* (1999), 'Across the Universe' from *Episode II: Attack of the Clones* (2002), 'Battle of the Heroes' from *Episode III: Revenge of the Sith* (2005), 'Rey's Theme' from *Episode VII: The Force Awakens* (2015) – the music is masterful and somehow feels effortless, something you can't always say about the films themselves.

As the *Star Wars* universe continues to grow through films, TV series and video games, so an ever-growing list of modern composers have found themselves harnessing musical familiarity and nostalgia from Williams' original film score into their work. Natalie Holt (*Obi-Wan Kenobi*, 2022), Michael Abels (*The Acolyte*, 2024), Ludwig Göransson (*The Mandalorian*, 2019–23), John Powell (*Solo*, 2018), Michael Giacchino (*Rogue One*, 2016) and Stephen Barton and Gordy Haab (*Star Wars Jedi: Fallen Order*, 2019, and *Star Wars Jedi: Survivor*, 2023) are among the composers who have been invited to experiment and play with the palette he created.

When working with Steven Spielberg, Williams tends not to read the script but waits until he can watch footage of the film. He'll view a rough cut and then the two will discuss where the music should go during what's called a spotting session. They clearly both have the same ideas and ideals about the role that music plays within a film, and equally the power of silence – as demonstrated to striking effect in the opening scene of *Saving Private Ryan* (1998).

At times Spielberg has allowed the music to dictate, or at least inform, the final edit of his films. In his 1982 masterpiece *E.T. the Extra-Terrestrial*, Williams had written music for the closing scenes and was struggling to cut it down to fit. The director suggested he stop looking at the film and instead 'conduct the orchestra the way you would want to conduct it in a concert so that the performance is just completely uninhibited by any considerations of mathematics and measurement'. Which is how the thrilling, magical final scenes of *E.T.* were born – simply because the composer wasn't restricted by the visuals.

The year 1993 was a significant one for both Williams and Spielberg's creative partnership and as a representation of their individual talents because they worked on two exceptional – and exceptionally different – films: *Jurassic Park*, which boasts a score that can transform grown adults into wistful and wide-eyed children, and *Schindler's List*, with its powerful theme which reduced Spielberg and his wife Kate Capshaw to tears when Williams first played it to them at the piano. The oft-told story is that when the composer first watched footage of *Schindler's List*, he was overwhelmed to the point of speechlessness. After taking a short walk to gather his thoughts, he told the director that he'd need to find a better composer for the film – to which Spielberg replied, 'I know, but they're all dead!'

'I owe a tremendous debt of gratitude to John Williams,' Christopher Reeve once said. He was talking about his breakout role as the man of steel in Richard Donner's 1978 superhero movie, the tagline for which declared that 'You'll believe a man can fly'. Yet, as Reeve astutely observed, 'Without [Williams'] music, Superman's powers are greatly diminished.'

I think that perfectly sums up Williams' screen work – creating music that, at its best, can lift the soul and make it soar. As well as soundtracking the childhoods and filmgoing memories of millions of people around the world, Williams' lasting legacy will doubtless be his respect for, and love of, the orchestra. By championing big, symphonic orchestras, Williams has inspired generations of performers and film fans.

Reflecting on his career, the composer describes himself as 'impossibly lucky'. Yet it's hard for us to imagine film scores from the last sixty or so years without the John Williams touch.

Luck has nothing to do with it.

Soundtrack Selection:
Eyes Wide Shut (1999)

First things first: Stanley Kubrick's final film is not universally hailed as one of his best. On the contrary, the septuagenarian's long-gestating foray into the erotic thriller genre is, for some, one of the few false steps of his otherwise extraordinary directorial career.

Adapted from Arthur Schnitzler's 1926 novella *Traumnovelle* (literally 'Dream Story'), *Eyes Wide Shut* (1999) featured Hollywood hot couple Tom Cruise and Nicole Kidman as upmarket doctor Bill Harford and his glamorous wife Alice, whose marriage is thrown into disarray by Alice's revelation of a contemplated (but crucially unconsummated) affair. Riven with jealousy, Bill embarks upon a sexual odyssey that takes him to a cult-like orgy in a grand mansion outside New York where strange ceremonies and uncomfortable discoveries await.

Granted unbridled artistic freedom by his regular studio, Warner Brothers, Kubrick shot *Eyes Wide Shut* over a record-breaking period of forty-six consecutive weeks – a schedule so elongated that key cast members like Harvey Keitel and Jennifer Jason Leigh had to drop out mid-shoot because they were no longer available to work. Stories of Kubrick demanding over ninety-five takes of either Cruise or Keitel walking through a door proliferated around the industry, with cast and crew apparently exhausted by what was politely referred to as the director's 'perfectionism'. An equally prolonged editing period followed, with Kubrick finally showing a cut of the movie to Cruise and Kidman just a few days before his death on 7 March 1999.

Heated debate about just how 'complete' Kubrick's cut was has bubbled away over the years, with detractors insisting that Cruise and Kidman effectively took over the edit from their director (R. Lee Ermey, who starred in *Full Metal Jacket* [1987], was quoted as saying that Kubrick had phoned him shortly before he died to complain that Cruise and Kidman 'had their way with him' – a claim that has been pretty thoroughly debunked by Kubrick's friends and family). Yet it seems unlikely that the film which opened four months after Kubrick's death departed substantially from his singular vision, meaning that the praise and derision it received in equal measure is ultimately down to its director. Like it or not, *Eyes Wide Shut* is most definitely 'un film de' Stanley Kubrick.

One area in which critics agree that Kubrick *did* most definitely hit the right note was in his choice of music – although it's worth stating that there actually *isn't* a huge amount of music in *Eyes Wide Shut*. Silence does a lot of work and, as a result, so does the sparsely used soundtrack.

Having served as composer on *Full Metal Jacket* under the pseudonym Abigail Mead, Stanley's daughter Vivian Kubrick was initially earmarked to provide music for *Eyes Wide Shut*, although that proposed collaboration did not bear fruit. Instead, the director turned to Jocelyn Pook, a young British musician working across stage and screen who was about to emerge as one of the most exciting screen composers of her generation.

A viola player by trade, Pook had toured for years with The Communards and recorded and performed with the likes of PJ Harvey and Peter Gabriel. Her first film score was *Strange Fish* (1993), which started life as a stage production and went on to win the 1994 Prix Italia. But she called *Eyes Wide Shut* her 'first proper feature film' in a 1999 interview with the legendary soundtracks magazine *Film Score Monthly*, in which she described her signature sound as 'kind of a new tonal music, slightly minimal, and some of it definitely has a medieval or religious element'.

Pook came to Kubrick's attention through her 1997 album *Deluge*, specifically the brilliant track 'Backwards Priests', in which Pook reverses a recording of singing from a Romanian Orthodox church service to ominous and incredibly eerie effect. Choreographer Yolande Snaith had been playing it as she worked on *Eyes Wide Shut*'s extravagant masked-ball scenes. Kubrick was so impressed that he contacted the composer, who told a panel at Abbey Road's Equalise festival in 2023 (chaired by Jenny Nelson), 'He asked me to give him a compilation of other stuff that I'd done, and literally two hours after our phone call, a car came to collect the cassette that I'd made. This big car took this little cassette away, and then the next day the car came back for me and I went to meet him!'

'It was very easy to have a dialogue with him about the score,' Pook said. 'He was good at providing references, at giving ideas about what other composers he liked.' Kubrick played Pook specific pieces that would end up in the final film, including a solo piano work by Franz Liszt called *Grey Clouds*, and music by the Hungarian-Austrian composer György Ligeti, whose work Kubrick had previously used to memorable effect in his 1968 sci-fi epic *2001: A Space Odyssey*, and again (briefly) in *The Shining* (1980).

Initially, Kubrick asked Pook to compose just two pieces, for the masked-ball section and the orgy scene. Later, he came back and requested more original music for the rest of the film. 'Backwards Priests' would become 'Masked Ball', the singular tone of which is heard as soon as Bill arrives at the Somerton stately home, the location of the orgy. 'It's really the one that everyone mentions,' admits Pook in an interview with another influential film music publication, *Soundtrack! The Collector's Quarterly*. Unsurprising, since the music is right upfront in this scene, whereas elsewhere in the film it is used more sparingly – lower back in the soundmix.

Crucially, some of the music Pook wrote for *Eyes Wide Shut* was composed before the scenes were shot, allowing Kubrick to use her tracks on set during filming, setting the tone. According to Pook, Kubrick 'would describe the atmosphere of the scene to me', providing only a few specific details, after which she would go away and compose. A demo would be produced, and Kubrick and Pook would meet again to discuss – and perhaps change – the work she had done. The composer recalls Kubrick as being an encouraging collaborator who welcomed dialogue and was 'very open to what I had to bring and offer'. He made himself very familiar with Pook's other music as well as the pieces she composed for the film, and helped steer her towards his vision: 'He might play a couple of things that he had on his mind, as references, or even to say "What do you think of this?" He was actually so passionate about music.'

Even when scenes *were* available for Pook to view in advance of composing, the secrecy surrounding the filming of *Eyes Wide*

Shut meant that *other* scenes that would allow the composer to get a sense of context or overview were withheld. Despite attempting to work within these strange confines, Pook soon found that she needed to know more about the overall dynamics of the entire movie in order to pitch an individual piece for a particular scene. 'I have to know the whole film,' she told Kubrick. 'I have to understand how loaded is this scene, you know?' Pook now laughs at how cloak and dagger – or should that be cloak and mask? – this process became, with the film company considering sending a man to come and sit in her house while she viewed sections of the film, and then to take them away at the end of the day. In the end, they relented, trusting her enough to keep the video without a constant bodyguard!

Pook wound up composing twenty-five minutes of music for *Eyes Wide Shut*, and an additional twenty minutes of sketches that didn't make the final cut. As well as the orgy scene, she created music to accompany Alice's fantasies of running off with a handsome naval officer, both when she recounts her erotic dream to her husband, and when Bill is tortured by visions of his wife's imagined sexual encounter. These textured string pieces, 'Naval Officer' and 'The Dream', were recorded at Abbey Road and feel yearning, anguished and, fittingly, dreamlike – at times discordant and other times sensual.

Of the existing classical pieces featured in *Eyes Wide Shut*, the most prominent by far is the second movement of Ligeti's *Musica ricercata* – a repetitive semitonal piano dirge, played in stentorian fashion by Dominic Harlan. The director discussed the placement of this and Shostakovich's Waltz 2 from his *Jazz Suite* with Pook, who felt that she needed to understand where and how the director was deploying other music, in order for her own contributions to reflect, refer to, or perhaps counter-balance those pieces.

The Shostakovich appears over the film's title credits and plays into the opening scene, where it is revealed to be diegetic (occurring within the action of the film itself) as Bill switches it off from the stereo when the couple leave their bedroom to go to a party. The waltz then recurs throughout the film, as does Ligeti's *Musica ricercata*, which becomes increasingly prevalent as Bill descends further down a psychodramatic rabbit hole. It pops up when he returns to Somerton, when he's followed on the streets of New York, when he reads about the death of an ex-beauty queen and, ultimately, when he comes home to find his mask from the orgy on his pillow next to his sleeping wife. What starts as a creepy callback becomes incessant, with Pook's layered strings offering a fitting respite. While the Ligeti may be the most memorable piece in the film due to its overuse, Pook's score opens the door into the world of fantasies, both fulfilled and unfulfilled.

Looking back on the scoring process, Pook describes it as like 'jumping off a cliff', admitting to feeling 'out of my depth', but reflecting that in the end, an element of uncertainty – and even occasional panic – probably aided the momentum of the creative process. It's a bold score for a composer who would go on to provide memorable accompaniments to such varied films as *The Merchant of Venice* (2004), *Brick Lane* (2007), *The Wife* (2017), *The Kingmaker* (2019) and *Tin & Tina* (2020). But given that Pook was already composing such audacious music, it's not surprising that Kubrick trusted a relative unknown to deliver the goods for what would become his final film.

'I was aware that my music might not be used,' says Pook, acknowledging the fate of composers like Alex North, who famously wrote and recorded a ditched score for Kubrick's *2001: A Space Odyssey*, and who did not know that his music had been replaced by pre-existing tracks until the curtains went back on the film's first screening in 1968. As far as Pook was concerned, she didn't believe that her name and music would be in the film until she actually saw it.

It's a credit to Pook's genius that, whether one loves or hates *Eyes Wide Shut*, it is impossible to imagine the film without her music. It really is the very best thing about Kubrick's flawed swansong. Without it, the movie would simply fall apart.

CHAPTER 3

The Director's Vision

'It's helpful to remember that the director's job is harder than yours,' observed composer Michael Abels when interviewed for this book, adding that 'it certainly has more stakes than yours does.' Sage advice from comedian-turned-director Jordan Peele's regular musical collaborator, starting with the Oscar-winning *Get Out* (2017) – Peele's feature directorial debut and Abels's first feature film score – the soundtrack of which boasted a fascinating blend of Swahili vocals and unsettling orchestration, perfect for the racially charged body-horror of the movie.

By acknowledging that the director has the tougher challenge, Abels makes it clear that his role as composer is to help, not hinder, the film and the film-making process. And as British film composer David Arnold – whose credits include five James Bond films, science fiction favourite *Stargate* (1994) and Edgar Wright's hugely popular cop comedy *Hot Fuzz* (2007) – says: 'The trick of film composition is that you don't want to sound like yourself. You need to sound like the director.' But how does a composer create a score that works for their director, and how does the director get them to conjure the sounds they are looking for? To find out, let's take a look at some of the most significant composer–director partnerships and explore the key ingredients to a successful working relationship – one that fuses sound and vision so seamlessly that the composer's work becomes instinctive. Their aim is to bring to life what the director wants, even if the director doesn't know it yet.

For the relatively solitary job of composing, an essential skill is being open to collaboration. To listening. A willingness to try out new things, and to be aware of the bigger picture, literally. As Abels puts it, 'You may be the creator, but the director is the *curator*, the one who picks what's going to work.' Things become complicated if the director doesn't know what they want from a score, or doesn't have the words to articulate it. A crucial early stage in the scoring process is the spotting session, when the director and composer watch a rough cut of the film and discuss the placement of the music – when it should be prominent and when it should hang back or fall silent. This conversation tends to cover the overall ambitions for the score. The director may be comfortable talking for hours about the visuals, characters and script, but music is another language. So how can they truly convey their sonic vision if they aren't fluent in musical terminology?

'There's a real language that you develop with different directors,' notes Jocelyn Pook. 'It's always a different dynamic but you get to know each other's way of working.' Not only does the composer have to be musically adept but, depending on the director, they may also need to be a mind reader, or at the very least an intuitive communicator.

'That dialogue is really important,' insists Warren Ellis, whose film score CV includes numerous collaborations with Nick Cave on features such as Andrew Dominik's sublime *The Assassination of Jesse James by the Coward Robert Ford* (2007) and more recently *Blonde* (2022), alongside solo compositions for films like Deniz Gamze Ergüven's *Mustang* (2015) and more recently Walter Salles's Oscar-winning *I'm Still Here* (2024). As Ellis told me, working with a director who is able to state clearly what they like, and what they *don't* like, is a major boost, but it's not always that simple. 'I have a hard time explaining aspects of films, and directors can have a hard time with music,' says Ellis. 'And to be honest, *I* have a hard time with music, trying to explain stuff; what may or may not work, or what's a problem with a cue. The best thing is when the director is engaged from the beginning, like Andrew [Dominik] was on *The Assassination of Jesse James*. He *knew* what did and didn't work for him, which meant we were really able to narrow things down.'

Of course, it helps when the director knows how to talk about music. Anne Dudley has a long-standing and extremely productive relationship with Dutch director Paul Verhoeven, providing scores for the intense Second World War drama *Black Book/Zwartboek* (2006), the provocative psychodrama *Elle* (2016) and the wonderfully overcooked nunsploitation romp *Benedetta* (2021). She was initially keen to meet him to find out about his past collaborations with her screen music hero Jerry Goldsmith, in particular his score for *Basic Instinct* (1992). But the conversation didn't go quite as expected . . .

'We started talking about our favourite twentieth-century composers,' she remembers. 'Paul said, "Oh I'm not interested in film composers, I'm interested in classical composers like Shostakovich and Bartók and Stravinsky. I think Shostakovich's orchestration is fantastic!"' And with that, the pair embarked on a detailed and fairly in-depth conversation about the merits (or otherwise) of twentieth-century composers' orchestration techniques! As Dudley says, 'I thought "This is quite unusual, I don't usually get into this detail with a director about music."'

Verhoeven's knowledge of classical music and his passion for discussing it allows for a shorthand between him and his now-regular composer. He doesn't need Dudley to make elaborately produced demos but is instead happy to hear her play her ideas at the piano, which makes for 'a really wonderful, traditional, straightforward scoring experience', one that can only happen when the director has an innate understanding of how the final score will integrate into the film.

Some directors may have a better idea of where a cue will fit within the movie than their composers do. Michael Abels no longer tells Jordan Peele what scene a particular piece is written for because 'Often, it works for him in a scene that I wasn't considering. Or even if it does work in the scene I'm considering, he still wants to try it out in a *different* scene, so I end up learning about how he sees the character by where he chooses to try the music.' Leaning into the collaboration and operating with flexibility is crucial for the composer. Anne Dudley notes that 'You can't fall in love with your own themes because it may be that nobody else has fallen in love with them, so you need to adjust.' For Dudley, the key lies in being able to rework material – to allow pieces to improve and develop through the process of discussion and revision. 'They almost always get better,' she says, adding that such discussions allow the composer to 'hear your own music in a different light'.

*

Speaking in 1999 about his work with Spike Lee – a collaboration that has garnered two Academy Award nominations for the composer, for *BlackKklansman* (2018) and *Da 5 Bloods*

(2020) – Terence Blanchard described the director as 'very detailed in terms of the melodic material for the music', and yet, 'once all of that is done, he lets me go. He doesn't even want to talk to me until we get to the session. I feel good that he has that much confidence in me.'

When asked if she prefers working with directors who are musically literate, Jocelyn Pook observes that 'It's more to do with them being confident about when they hear the right thing.' Germaine Franco, the first Latina composer to receive a scoring nomination at the Academy Awards, for the 2021 Disney animation *Encanto*, doesn't see it as a problem if the director can't 'speak' music because the composer can gather all they need from the plot and characters: 'You just keeping talking to them about the *story*,' she says, keenly aware that film-makers can get nervous if a composer starts focusing in on overly detailed musical specifics which they may not understand. 'You have to meet them on their own ground in their own language,' Franco argues. For her, that means building a good relationship with directors by finding out what they like and what inspires them. She's also quick to point out that (as Ellis noted) it's just as useful to learn what they *don't* like, in order to avoid wasting time, not least because 'you're always on a deadline.'

For Oscar-winner Rachel Portman, whose celebrated scores include *The Cider House Rules* (1999) and *Chocolat* (2000), both of which earned Academy Award nominations, it can be a case of deciphering what the director says, what they *mean*, and what they actually *want* or *need*. Having worked with a lot of very articulate directors, Portman has discovered that it's entirely possible to collaborate on a project for a month or so, only to discover that despite intense discussions with the director: 'It's all nothing. It's air.'

Portman has a simple but fascinating exercise that she uses with directors to get swiftly to the core of any given scene: asking for three adjectives to describe the scene in question. 'It's amazing how hard some directors find it to be able to answer that,' she reveals. 'Because they actually don't *know* – they just want you to try something and then they can say "No".' Portman's method breaks the cycle of a composer bringing something to the table only for the director to discard it, over and over again. When I ask her on the spot to provide an example of three adjectives, she picks 'Angry, amusing and compelling. I would know what to do then. I'd know how to be angry, and it needs to be compelling so it's going to have to have some movement, but it's also comedic – OK great! I'd fire off on that.'

James Newton Howard, a prolific composer whose credits include Barbra Streisand's *The Prince of Tides* (1991), several M. Night Shyamalan films including *The Sixth Sense* (1999) and *The Village* (2004), and more recently the *Fantastic Beasts* franchise (2016–22), has experienced the challenge of attempting to put words into music, or music into words: 'I've had one director describe what he wanted from this piece by saying that it has to be more "floral". You have to say, "OK, more floral." I don't say, "I have no idea what you're talking about," but I figure it out.' And according to Howard, the solution to the knottiest problems can often be deceptively simple. 'Sometimes the smallest change can make a big difference,' he explains. 'Like the instrument: some directors don't want to hear an oboe, they think it's too sweet. I had one director say "no bassoons in this score" – which I still think is hilarious.'

While feedback from the director is vital, it's important for the composer to avoid getting stuck in that familiar loop of following one set of steers from the film-maker, only for them to reject it, and then feeling compelled to rip it up and start again. As Anne Dudley admits, hearing 'No' from the director may make a composer feel combative or disheartened, but it's important to try to understand *exactly* what it is that the film-maker doesn't like – even if they don't yet know it themselves. 'I've had instances when people say, "Oh that's completely wrong,"' she recalls, 'and it's actually not *completely* wrong – there's just *one* thing about it they don't like. It might be the instrument that's playing it [as James Newton Howard observed], or the speed of it, or even that it's being played too loud against the picture. It can be something that you can deal with.'

*

For many directors, one quick way to communicate what they are looking for musically is to use a 'temp score' – two words that strike dread into the heart of many a composer. In short, the director finds pre-existing music to lay over the rough edit of their film in an attempt to show their composer what they are aiming for. It sounds helpful, but according to British composer Isobel Waller-Bridge, whose film scores include *Vita & Virginia* (2018), *Emma.* (2020) and *Wicked Little Letters* (2023), 'It's really challenging and I will do anything to avoid it.' As David Arnold sardonically observed of the writing of this book: 'For the true film scoring experience, I hope the publishers told you to base it on some other books that they really liked . . .'

The temp track can be problematic, not least because a director can become so wedded to it that nothing the composer writes will match it. A good example is the case of *Manchester by the Sea* (2016), Kenneth Lonergan's angst-ridden drama for which he won the Best Original Screenplay Oscar, while Casey Affleck (controversially) won Best Actor. Canadian composer

Lesley Barber wrote the haunting score, which includes the spine-tingling 'Manchester by the Sea Chorale', an instantly recognizable cue that has developed a life of its own outside of the film. But for the movie's most dramatic sequence, Lonergan used Albinoni's Adagio in G Minor – a piece of music that, as we noted, had previously appeared in everything from *Rollerball* to 1981's *Gallipoli* (not to mention the BBC sitcom *Butterflies*, which ran for four seasons from 1978), becoming something of a screen cliché. Lonergan's intention was always to replace the Albinoni with something else, presumably penned by Barber. But after spending months in the edit, he simply became wedded to that Adagio, and nothing could sway him from keeping it in the film. The result is disastrous – a moment of cheesy familiarity in a scene which should be full of dread and shock.

The reliance on temp tracks led to the overuse of Hans Zimmer's 'Journey to the Line' from Terrence Malick's *The Thin Red Line* (1998), both as a guide for feature film composers, but also in trailers, video games and other visual media. Zimmer ended up dubbing it the 'forbidden cue' because directors were even giving it to *him* to demonstrate the sort of thing they were after, and he didn't fancy trying to emulate the emotional heft of his own piece. It became a reductive task, with various composers all trying to create a musical successor to one particular piece. As Waller-Bridge observes, 'It's really tough because people fall in love with the temp, then your identity is swallowed a bit by the temp, and you have to claw it back!' She tries to work through these issues by digging deeper – by analysing the shape, texture and melodic tone of the temp track rather than simply attempting to mimic its key motifs. She then refashions these into a piece in which 'none of the instrumentation will be the same', making her own piece 'as different as possible' from the temp track while still retaining the key elements that first attracted the director's attention.

The Icelandic composer Hildur Guðnadóttir, winner of a Primetime Emmy Award and Grammy Award for the miniseries *Chernobyl* (2019), and the third (and, at the time of going to print, most recent) woman to win a scoring Oscar, for 2019's *Joker*, came to film composing later in her career after spending years crafting her own sound, style and creative working methods. As such, she doesn't feel the need to rely on temp tracks, although she is generous about those who find them useful. 'If you're someone who has really been putting your full focus on film music and nothing but film music,' she explains, 'I guess you're maybe more influenced by the screen itself. Because I've never thought in that way, I like to have the space to make up my own mind.'

Waller-Bridge tries to avoid getting stuck in a temp score cul-de-sac by composing a large selection of cues up front, ensuring that 'by the time they've started editing, they just have lots of music'. It's a simple but effective ploy to circumnavigate the potential creative pitfalls by effectively making *your* music the temp track. James Newton Howard prides himself on making demos to a high standard, so that when he plays them to the director early on in the process, he can encourage them to use these bespoke demos as the temp. It's undoubtedly more labour intensive for the composer – Howard wrote roughly two hours and twenty minutes of music for the *Hunger Games* prequel, *The Ballad of Songbirds and Snakes* (2023) – but he finds it beneficial for everyone involved because the score becomes embedded within the film and the director's mind as 'they really get addicted to *my* music.'

Some composers do find temp scores helpful, appreciating

the tangible musical steers from the director. Amelia Warner, the British composer for films like Niall Johnson's *Mum's List* (2016), Haifaa al-Mansour's *Mary Shelley* (2017) and Joachim Rønning's *Young Woman and the Sea* (2024), provides a useful counterbalance, declaring that the temp can be 'a tool to understand why something works,' because 'then I feel like I've got something to go from, rather than just having this frightening blank space.' Better to have something to dissect, especially if the director doesn't feel confident using musical terminology.

Some directors will put the composer's earlier music into the temp, as Julio Medem has when working with Jocelyn Pook, who very diplomatically sees both the pros and cons of a temp track – not least because she's experienced the perks when it ends up staying in the final cut. 'That's partly how I was on the score for [2002's] *Gangs of New York*,' she recalls. 'Apparently Scorsese got very attached to the track ['Dionysus'] that they were using as the temp, so I benefited actually!'

Another example of a temp score helpfully paving the way for a composer to expand their reach came with the underrated 2017 British war film *Journey's End*. The director, Saul Dibb, had temped it with music by Hildur Guðnadóttir, so when Natalie Holt joined the project to score the film she was instructed to work with the tracks to which Dibb had become wedded. A trained violist, Holt was confident writing and performing for strings, so 'I did something "Hildur-ish"' and 'kind of co-wrote the score with Hildur's work'. In the end, they were able to license Guðnadóttir's music in order for both composers to receive a credit. This worked out well, not only for Dibb – who was so attached to the temp score – but also for Holt, who laughingly admits that Guðnadóttir's agent was so impressed with *her* work that it led to commissions for projects that the Icelander had turned down.

*

Whether the director's vision is communicated to the composer in words, footage from the film or – in the case of the temp – other music, the composer's challenge is to make that vision an original musical reality. Listening is key, but equally important is leaving the ego at the door. As James Newton Howard says, 'I certainly have my ideas, but always in mind is the director – they are my boss. My job is to fulfil *their* vision, and maybe to make it even better or bigger than they thought it could be.' Michael Abels echoes this, reminding composers they have to walk a fine line: 'You have to be really excited and passionate to create great music *and* be completely detached from the idea that the music is great, because maybe it's not great for the film.'

Demonstrating enthusiasm about the project can go a long way in earning the director's trust, or simply conveying confidence. As Anne Dudley puts it, 'You need to give this impression that if there's a problem, I can deal with it. I can be a part of the solution, I'm not the problem, we will get through this together.' The composer needs to be a people-pleaser of sorts, especially on bigger budget projects where they also need to juggle feedback and opinions from other key players. Natalie Holt observes that with studio films, 'You go on a call and it's not a relationship that's just between you and a director. Sometimes the director is gone and it's between you and a team of producers and a music supervisor or two, and the editor will chip in on stuff, and suddenly you've got about twenty people weighing in opinions on how the score should sound.' Holt admits that in the past she has felt stifled by this level of input, having to find a balance between not being precious about her compositions while still knowing when to stand firm. As she puts it, 'You have to kind of be quite aggressive in protecting your vision at that point.'

A. R. Rahman notes that in Hollywood he tends to be given more time to work on individual projects, but that time comes with the caveat of more external input (or interference) than he would get while working in India. 'When I work on a Hollywood movie, it's undivided attention for like three or four months. You score the first cut, and then there's a *lot* of back and forth – a lot of people supervising your work.' This is in stark contrast to Rahman's experience of working with Danny Boyle on the British Oscar-winner *Slumdog Millionaire*, during which his contact was one-on-one with the director, with little or no external interference. 'But generally doing studio movies you have twelve different people coming in and telling you how it sounds or how the test-shows went. There's so much pressure.'

It's worth bearing in mind that directors (unless they are Stanley Kubrick – or perhaps Danny Boyle) may also be working to committee and needing to respond to the studio's demands. Understanding the pressures faced by the director can lead the composer to take on a more supportive and problem-solving role. James Newton Howard admits that his advice to young composers includes encouraging them to pity the film-maker when things get tough. 'I tell them, "If you're going to succeed as a film composer, you have to feel sorry for the director in a way, because it's a horrible job". Once they get to the point where the studio's intervening, it can be very difficult.'

*

When creative partnerships between directors and composers work, the results can be extraordinary, as with the half-century of cinematic magic that has sparked between John Williams and Steven Spielberg. Joe Hisaishi has been dubbed 'the John Williams of Japan', in part due to his forty-year collaboration with animator and Studio Ghibli co-founder Hayao Miyazaki. Together they have created so much colour, intensity and life with the likes of *My Neighbour Totoro* (1988), *Princess Mononoke* (1997) and *Spirited Away* (2001). The composer, who has also worked on a number of projects with another legendary Japanese film-maker, Kitano 'Beat' Takeshi, has scored Miyazaki's films since 1984, starting with the technically pre-Ghibli *Nausicaä of the Valley of the Wind* and staying with him right up until his most recent feature *The Boy and the Heron* (2023), for which he created another typically sumptuous score. Throughout Miyazaki's career, Hisaishi has breathed musical life into his animated fables, creating scores that have proved every bit as enchanting to younger viewers as they are to the battle-scarred adults who find solace in the melodic melancholia.

When working for Ghibli, Hisaishi was typically brought on board at a very early stage in the creative process so that his musical contributions could help shape the direction and writing of the film. Things were different, however, for the swansong surprise *The Boy and the Heron* (Miyazaki had announced his retirement from feature films after 2013's *The Wind Rises*). Here, for the first time, Miyazaki didn't want his composer to have any knowledge or preconceptions about the story. Instead, he simply showed him the final cut and told Hisaishi 'I leave it all up to you.'

The timing of a score's creation during the film-making process can be a simple matter of the composer's availability, or it can be the choice of the director or the studio. The great Ennio Morricone worked on the music for Sergio Leone's *For a Few Dollars More* (1965) from the script alone, and delivered the music in time for it to be played to the actors on set. As Morricone told *The Observer* in 2007, Leone 'often kept the scenes longer simply because he didn't want the music to end'.

Sometimes the director prefers the composer not to stick too closely to the script. When Francis Ford Coppola and David Shire were working on *The Conversation* (1974), the director knew he wanted a piano-driven score and gave the composer a list of subjects to write pieces about – none of which featured in the film. According to Shire, Coppola said, 'I want you to loosen up and not think about it on the nose', because 'he wanted me to explore the whole emotional world of the movie and of the particular theme that the score was about'. This broader experimentation made space for the creation of cues under titles like 'Harry Picks up His Laundry', with Shire suggesting melodies that might catch Coppola's ear, and then developing and experimenting with them in conjunction with the director. The method may have been meandering, but for Shire it was necessary to explore a few side roads (some with dead ends) before getting to the elusive final destination.

Very occasionally, a composer's original music can be an influence on a film even before a first draft script is written. That was the case with *Interstellar* (2014), a product of the blockbuster partnership between Hans Zimmer and Christopher Nolan. *Interstellar* has a big score with added organ, although the overall effect is nuanced due to the inclusion of softer cues. The director asked the composer to spend a day writing a piece of music based on a father's love for his son – not daughter, as is the scenario in the finished film. Zimmer has recalled in interviews that he received a letter from Nolan with this simple instruction and that's all he had to work with. He came up with 'Day One', an intensely personal piece, and when he played it to the director, Nolan responded, 'Well I suppose I'd better make the movie now.' The composer exclaimed that he was still none the wiser about the story (he didn't even know that it was to be a science fiction picture), but that piece went on to become a central part of the film's planet-hopping, time-spanning tale. This intimate cue was, as Nolan put it, the heart of the story, and he listened to it while writing the script.

One of the most creative and exciting director–composer collaborations today is the deliciously surprising and inventive partnership between Paul Thomas Anderson and Radiohead's Jonny Greenwood. This feels like a meaningful meeting of creative minds, with a composer who's willing to listen and experiment according to the needs of each project. Awards are subjective and frequently wrong, and arguably one of the biggest travesties in recent Academy Awards history was when Greenwood's menacing, multilayered music for the pair's first project together, *There Will Be Blood* (2007), was disqualified from the Best Original Score category because it contained pre-existing music: one of the key cues, 'Henry Plainview', features an excerpt from an earlier piece by Greenwood, the BBC-commissioned 'Popcorn Superhet Receiver'.

As Greenwood recalled when I talked to him about his work with Anderson, the director had found it online 'and started using it. And then he wrote to me to say, "Can you write more music like this?" And suddenly I was doing *that* score.' With Greenwood on board, Anderson revelled in the chance to use his music. 'I remember seeing an early version of it, and he had even more of my music in. It was stupid! He just left it running and running and running. Even when people started talking, there was still music going on. He gets kind of over-enthusiastic about things and eventually calms down. So that was very weird. And then I remember meeting some other film composers and them explaining that this is not normal and that I was very lucky to have that as a way in.'

There Will Be Blood is remarkable for its unique pacing (I described it in my original review as 'redefining the grammar of cinema'), which is enhanced by the score. 'I just thought of it in terms of "close-up" and "landscape" for the music,' says Greenwood. 'I'm quite – what's the word? – *sentimental*. So I really responded to the kid and *that* side of the story.'

Clearly Anderson and Greenwood have a great affection for each other as people, as well as artists. 'Paul is so amusing and entertaining, and he makes me laugh so much, as well as being *so* committed to what he's doing,' notes Greenwood. 'You'll talk to him, and you're watching the rough cuts of the film with him. And he's laughing all the way through every single film – he finds his own films *really* hilarious. And then there'll suddenly be a kind of click, and it's like he's seriously focused on the music and what it needs to do.'

Greenwood, who was Oscar nominated for his work on Anderson's 2017 masterpiece *Phantom Thread*, admits that he prefers not to receive too many details in terms of musical steers. 'Whenever we've had those conversations,' he says, 'I feel like I'm just kind of drifting off in class and not really listening. Instead, I just end up saying, "Listen, can't I just write you two hours of music and *you* deal with the problem, you work it out?" And we've mostly got away with that. There's still a few scenes where he'll say, "I need something specific for these three minutes that does *this*." But quite often, it's just "Here's a whole suite of romantic music, that's all based around the costume and the colours and the story. And you've got this all to play with."'

I had the pleasure of introducing Greenwood and Anderson on stage before a screening of *Phantom Thread* accompanied by a live score performance at London's Southbank Centre in January 2018. The Oscar nominations had just been announced, and Anderson told me how much he wanted Jonny to win, not least for the awkwardness that would ensue from the famously shy and retiring musician having to accept the accolade in front of Hollywood's great and good. Greenwood explains the relationship best when he reflects on his work with Anderson alongside his role in Radiohead: 'You're in a band with the film director as well, which is really nice! It's like a partnership that you can completely rely on.'

*

Another landmark collaboration in terms of sheer creativity, and of capturing the story within the score, is the long-standing partnership between David Cronenberg and Howard Shore. The composer may be more familiar to mainstream moviegoers for his multi-award-winning work on *The Lord of the Rings* and *The Hobbit* trilogies, or for his six collaborations with Martin Scorsese. But, to my ears, his best work has been written for Cronenberg. Shore has scored all but one of the Canadian auteur's films since *The Brood* in 1979, working with him on body-horror projects like *Videodrome* (1983) and *The Fly* (1986), the graphic novel adaptation *A History of Violence* (2005), the tattooed London-set thriller *Eastern Promises* (2007) and the grief-stricken fable *The Shrouds* (2024).

According to Shore, the working relationship he has developed with Cronenberg over four decades has been remarkably consistent. 'David and I don't have a lot of discussion,' he tells me. 'It's a very intuitive process. He lets me read his scripts when they're in the screenplay stage, and I really start to work from the ideas, from his writing. So it's a kind of internal process. It doesn't really involve the film right away, it's more about the ideas, and we've built up a great trust over the years. He really gives me a lot of creative freedom to create interesting scores for his films.'

Later in this book, you will find a deep dive into Shore's score for Cronenberg's note-perfect adaptation of J. G. Ballard's *Crash*, my favourite film score of 1996. But for other highlights of the pair's collaborations, check out the William Burroughs adaptation *Naked Lunch* (1991), in which Shore teamed up with free-jazz maestro Ornette Coleman to create a work that is truly unpredictable; and *Dead Ringers* (1988), which takes the musical tropes of a gothic melodrama and reins them in with clinical restraint.

According to Shore, the main theme to *Dead Ringers* came to him through a process of post-script-reading 'free association' at the piano and electronic keyboard. 'I would just think about the scene and put my hands down and start to work in a very tactile way without the pencil.' Hours of music were recorded in this fashion, which Shore would then review and revisit, searching for the seeds of the film's score. 'I would find these little kernels,' he recalls, 'and the little kernel I found one day was that theme to *Dead Ringers*. It was just there, waiting to be found.'

Unlike his work on Peter Jackson's Tolkien films, which use leitmotifs to guide the audience through the expansive action, Shore says that with Cronenberg 'we're not interested in clarity of storytelling. I'm working around the edges of the frame.

I'm trying to deepen the story, add subtext to it, not try to explain to somebody who this character is, or what they're doing – that's for you as the audience to experience, not for me to explain.'

A relatively recent match made in film music heaven is the partnership between Greek director Yorgos Lanthimos and British composer/musician Jerskin Fendrix. Their first collaboration, *Poor Things*, produced the most adventurously inventive score of 2023, an Oscar-nominated work featuring a plethora of playful boings amidst more intricately melodic oddities. Lanthimos used to film dancers early in his career, and this experience has clearly gifted him with a visual talent for rhythm and physicality. The director first approached Fendrix after listening to his 2020 album *Winterreise* and sensing that the musician would be able to deliver the necessary musical goods for his film. As Lanthimos told me in December 2023, when he played the album to *Poor Things* star Emma Stone, 'She said, "It's like everything in your head exploded into music"' – the perfect description of Fendrix's work.

Lanthimos asked Fendrix to deliver the music for *Poor Things* before the film was shot, so that he had it for the edit. What followed was a back and forth between the two in which the director showed Fendrix the script and would give regular feedback about the music based on what he thought he might require. As a result, around 95 per cent of what Fendrix composed made it into the finished film. It's a lean way of working in which the director doesn't show the composer any of the footage 'so he doesn't become too literal about how he composes', ensuring that the music runs parallel to, but doesn't ape, the onscreen action. As both Lanthimos and Fendrix independently told me, the composer happily adhered to these working practices, and the director was able to declare with great satisfaction, 'I have finally found someone that I can work with in terms of music.'

*

Some directors choose to cut out the middleman and simply take the score into their own hands. It's fairly common for directors to write, edit and produce their films, and even to act in them, yet there are more than you might think who also compose the music. I personally cherish my vinyl copy of Mark Jenkin's lo-fi score for *Bait* (2019), full of drones, eerie sound-scapes and ambient noises that perfectly encapsulate the tension and dread created by the meticulous director, writer, producer, editor and cinematographer. An early example of a director creating the music for their films is pioneer Charles Chaplin, whose only competitive Academy Award win was for his score for *Limelight*, made in 1952, but not properly released in the US in line with Academy qualifications for another twenty years.

Chaplin famously couldn't read or notate music. Instead, he worked closely with transcribers, arrangers and orchestrators to bring his musical visions to life. As cinema transitioned from silent films to talkies, the actor and film-maker was keen to assert his musical identity in his work, writing in his 1964 autobiography about the crucial need for a comedy score *not* to sound funny: 'I tried to compose elegant and romantic music to frame my comedies in contrast to the tramp character, for elegant music gave my comedies an emotional dimension. Musical arrangers rarely understood this. They wanted the music to be funny.'

Despite his lack of musical training, Chaplin had a keen ear and a sense of rhythm (similar to Yorgos Lanthimos's appreciation for dance and choreography) which filtered into his directing and editing processes. Chaplin even conducted the studio orchestra during some recordings, adding an extra 'Chaplin-esque' quality to the sound of his music, despite the fact that it was arranged and orchestrated by 'real' musicians.

Another multi-hyphenate talent, the British artist Sally Potter is a musician as well as a director, writer and actor. She ran her own dance ensemble, the Limited Dance Company, and her work as composer involves collaborating on the scores for her films, most notably co-composing *Orlando* (1992) with David Motion. As she told *Sight and Sound* magazine in 1993, her original intention was to use a pre-existing piece, *Cantus*, by the Estonian minimalist composer Arvo Pärt. She went so far as to obtain official permission for it, but 'it was a piece in its own right that couldn't be cut or repeated', so she 'started on a journey to find out what it was about that piece of music that was appropriate to the film, and then to look for another way of achieving this'. Potter explored specific keys and triads as a way of pinning down the music she wanted to create, and then went into a studio to record, using her own voice. Motion wrote instrumental cues to emulate or fit around these recordings, and Fred Frith improvised additional guitar lines. The resulting score features moments of majestic grandeur along with these breathier, transcendental vocal samples.

Perhaps the most famous composer-director of modern cinema is John Carpenter, director of such influential horror hits as *Halloween* (1978) and *The Fog* (1980). Introduced to classical music by his father, who was a music professor, composer and concert violinist, Carpenter tried the violin to little success, so turned instead to the piano, guitar and bass guitar. When studying at film school, budgetary constraints led Carpenter to start scoring his own films. Citing his inspirations as Golden Age greats like Dimitri Tiomkin and Bernard Herrmann, Carpenter was also influenced by the synth sounds of Tangerine Dream and Goblin, the latter of whom provided nerve-jangling scores for the *giallo* nightmares of Italian director Dario Argento. Despite minimal funding, Carpenter wanted his scores to sound big, so he began using synthesizers to create this sonic sense of scale. His first feature score was for *Dark Star* in 1974, followed by *Assault on Precinct 13* (1976) and the propulsive, chilling and instantly recognizable *Halloween* (1978), into which we shall delve deeper in Chapter 9, 'A Frightful Noise'.

Collaborating over the years with Alan Howarth on films like *Escape from New York* (1981), *Big Trouble in Little China* (1986) and *They Live* (1988), Carpenter has also worked with his son Cody and his godson Daniel Davies on more recent horror scores, notably for David Gordon Green's *Halloween* reboot sequels (2018–22). His musical passions have added a new dimension to his directing career, and in 2015 he released his first non-soundtrack album, *Lost Themes*, with the fourth iteration in the series, *Noir*, appearing in 2024.

*

While film-makers who write and/or perform their own scores may bypass the possible pitfalls of working with composers with whom they may not be perfectly in tune, there are occasions on which a director and their composer become so creatively unified that they appear to become *one* mind, with one singular vision. Take British composer Clint Mansell and British director Carol Morley. Mansell first rose to prominence in the alternative rock band Pop Will Eat Itself. Best known to some as the composer for Duncan Jones's feature debut *Moon* (2009, more of which later), Mansell has scored several films for American auteur Darren Aronofsky (including *Requiem for a Dream*, 2000, *Black Swan*, 2010, and *Noah*, 2014) and British upsetter Ben Wheatley (from *High-Rise*, 2015, to *In the Earth*, 2021). More recently, Mansell provided the music for Rose Glass's electrifying sophomore feature *Love Lies Bleeding* (2024). But it's his collaboration with Carol Morley on her misunderstood 2018 masterpiece *Out of Blue* that produced something genuinely out of this world.

A neo-noir murder mystery that turns into a quasi-metaphysical rumination upon life, the universe and everything, *Out of Blue* was nominally adapted from Martin Amis's 1997 novel *Night Train*, although Morley, who had earned plaudits for her 2014 psychodrama *The Falling*, has described her film as an attempt to 'rescue the characters from the pages' of the book. The movie is breathtakingly complex and enigmatic, juggling realities as it tells its star-crossed tale. Underpinning it all is Mansell's superb score, in which electrifying ambient tones and falling notes cross with splashy jazz beats, counterpointing Alex Mackie's evocative editing of Conrad W. Hall's handsome cinematography.

As with so many of my favourite scores, I own Mansell's music for *Out of Blue* on 12-inch vinyl, and I played it to death on Jenny's and my Scala show. For me, the film offers the perfect union of film-maker and music-maker. But despite my enthusiasm (I gave the film a five-star rave in *The Observer*) it performed badly at the box office after most critics turned their noses up at its cosmic ambitions. 'Over the years I've become accustomed to the possibility that disappointment is always around the corner,' Mansell tells me. 'After more than one film I'd scored (and loved) had taken a beating by critics, particularly *The Fountain* [Darren Aronofsky's similarly mind-boggling 2006 sci-fi romance], which I felt was my best work to that point, I realized that in order not to have a life full of these disappointments I must focus on the elements of scoring with which I have influence.'

For Mansell, what's most important when scoring a film isn't worrying about critical or popular acclaim, but instead focusing solely on 'my writing, my imagination, my curiosity, my sensitivity to the material, my collaboration with the director. The only result that matters is that we, the creative team making the film, are happy with what we've achieved. After that, anything else will be gravy. *Out of Blue* was a perfect example of the kind of film I like to watch and I love to score. Its abstract nature, its slightly surreal, dreamlike feel allowed me to get lost in the world of the film. When Carol Morley contacted me to work with her I had no hesitation as I'd really liked her previous films, particularly *The Alcohol Years* [2000] and *Dreams of a Life* [2011].'

For Mansell, an appreciation of Morley's previous films dovetailed with a shared love of the directors who inspired *her*, meaning that the pair's creative collaboration was built upon common ground. 'Nicolas Roeg, Peter Weir, Ken Russell, Lindsay Anderson are directors that come to mind who have made films that are challenging, questioning, and not formulaic,' Mansell enthuses. 'I *love* films like this, and while I understand that they're not to everyone's taste, for me, they're inspiring, freeing.'

That shared heritage of cinema reaped benefits when it came to composing music for Morley's most ambitious project. 'When Carol came to my studio to hear demos for *Out of Blue*, I played her the opening titles and she cried! Which is such a wonderful response. To connect with the film musically such that it elicits a response from the director who has invested so much in the work is a moving experience. And those are worth more than whether a film finds its audience or not. To me, anyway. We wish all our films were seen and adored by millions but that's not our choice. When music meets image, a magical third element is created, a feeling that is only present when the two come together – *that* is the reward. The work itself has got to be the most rewarding part.'

At its best, that work involves an essential meeting of minds between a director and their composer, both striving for the same goal. The director needs to trust the composer's ability and the composer needs to acknowledge that the director is in the driving seat, holding everything together. As Michael Abels says, the key to forming a fertile collaboration with a director is to 'give them good things to choose from, but know that the choice is theirs, and trust the process'.

'I've had some scores where I knew the director didn't understand what the hell I was doing,' recalls Howard Shore. 'Because music can be very mysterious. It's a difficult process to understand how it's created. But they went with it. And then the film came out. And then three or four months later, I get a call from the director going, "Oh, *now* I understand – now that the film is successful!" It's as if they're really seeing it and *understanding* it for the first time.'

*

Let's close this chapter with an anecdote from Scottish director Bill Forsyth, writer-director of one of my favourite films, *Local Hero* (1983). A bittersweet tale of an American oil executive who falls in love with a remote Scottish village, *Local Hero* has been described by Forsyth as '*Brigadoon* meets *Apocalypse Now*'. The music for the film was provided by Dire Straits frontman Mark Knopfler, who was originally brought in to oversee the ceilidh sequences, and ended up scoring the entire movie. His music is superb – evocative, touching, tender, and brilliantly catchy. The main theme, 'Going Home', has become a football anthem, while the soundtrack album is a staple of every discerning film fan's library.

One day, in 2008, I found myself with Forsyth, sitting on the quay in Pennan, the Scottish village in which much of the film was shot. We'd gone there to film a piece for BBC Two's *The Culture Show* and I was in heaven – on the set of one of my favourite movies, with one of my favourite film-makers, humming one of my favourite film scores to myself.

'You really love that music, don't you?' said Bill.

'I do,' I replied. 'I think it's just . . . wonderful.'

'Ah, that kind of makes me sad,' said Bill, ruefully.

I was surprised. 'Why on earth would that make you sad?'

Bill looked off into the distance, over the sea, and then turned to me and said something unexpected.

'The thing is,' he mused, 'I've always been of the opinion that a really good film should work *without* music. You know, on its own. I think that quite often the music is there to cover over the director's failures. And so when you say that you love the music to *Local Hero*, it makes me think that I failed as a film-maker.'

I looked at him in astonishment.

'But Bill,' I said. 'I thought *you* loved the music too.'

He looked back out over the bay.

'Aye,' he replied. 'I do. That's the problem . . .'

Soundtrack Selection:
Under the Skin (2013)

One of the strangest 12-inch vinyl albums I own is the sound-track to Colombian-Ecuadorian film-maker Alejandro Landes's dizzying fable of child soldiery, *Monos* (2019). The film is aston-ishing: a hallucinogenic work set on a remote mountaintop that has drawn comparisons with Herzog's *Aguirre, Wrath of God* (1972) and Coppola's *Apocalypse Now* (1979). Landes has said that he and his co-writer watched Elem Klimov's traumatizing *Come and See* (1985) while writing the script, although there's a strong strain of Brothers Grimm fairytale about this account of children lost in the woods, searching for themselves in abstract environments.

If Landes's film is unusual, then British composer Mica Levi's score is unprecedented. At the top end of its strange frequen-cies, we find whistles that echo the handmade bird calls of the teenagers, but which also sound to me like lonely radio signals or sonar, highlighting the sense of isolation. Underneath, we find a cacophony of timpani and electronica, producing sonic landscapes that tremble with the thunderous experience of a first kiss, and rumble like a volcano waiting to erupt.

It is genuinely astonishing.

Playing that soundtrack album to *Monos* away from the film is a very peculiar experience, since Levi's music is almost incomprehensible when detached from the images for which it was created. But we should expect nothing less from one of modern cinema's most exploratory composers – a fiercely creative musician who was Oscar nominated for their superbly emotive orchestral work on Chilean director Pablo Larraín's *Jackie* (2016), and whose eclectic CV ranges from Michael Almereyda's shimmeringly melancholic adaptation of Jordan Harrison's science fiction play *Marjorie Prime* (2017) to British director Jonathan Glazer's quietly stunning Holocaust drama *The Zone of Interest* (2023).

Having first gained popular acclaim in the experimental pop band Micachu and the Shapes, Levi was enlisted by Glazer to make their feature film compositional debut with 2013's *Under the Skin* – a bold, flawed and admirably out-there adaptation of Michel Faber's 2000 novel about an extraterrestrial stalker. An eerie tale of a space traveller inhabiting human form, prowling the streets of Glasgow in search of raw flesh, *Under the Skin* stars Scarlett Johansson as an initially predatory presence, her clipped English vowels and thousand-yard stare effectively suggesting an imitation of life, an act refined to lure male prey. But time spent inhabiting human form appears to have a price and, as alienation turns to something resembling empathy, so vulnerability rears its head, and our voracious visitor begins to lose her mission control.

Beneath it all is Levi's music, which inhabits that strange *musique concrète* netherworld between score and sound effects. Working closely with Oscar-winning sound designer Johnnie Burn, Levi creates percussive, scraping, buzzing accompaniments that nod towards the avant-garde strains of John Cage and György Ligeti (and arguably the film scores of Jonny Greenwood), while groaning fragments of what sounds like an alien language recall the industrial soundscapes of David Lynch and Alan Splet. Much of the music is led by the strains of viola and violin, with notes stretched and bent partly by altering the pitch and tempo of the original audio recordings, creating a sound that is inherently unsettling and at times alarming. But those same stretched sounds (which have been performed by the London Sinfonietta on several memorable live score renditions of *Under the Skin*) also find a more empathetic home in the film's main theme, 'Love', in which alien noises morph into something unexpectedly tender and yearning.

The overall effect is dazzling, lending cohesion to a film that occasionally threatens to fall apart, the disparate elements of the visuals locked together at a genetic level by the firm foundation of sound. As for the soundtrack album to *Under the Skin*, impressively it also works as a standalone symphony, although it could hardly be described as easy listening.

'With *Under the Skin* I was relating it to being a teenager,' Levi told American composer Daniel Lopatin on the excellent A24 podcast in December 2018. For Levi, the film's central character is 'a rebel, basically', someone who is 'working for an organization of some kind, and because she starts to discover her feelings – and herself – she takes a risk and cuts out of that whole life'. Levi's description rings true, suggesting that the key to the brilliance of the score lies in an understanding of the narrative's mix of the down-to-earth and the out-of-this-world. Yes, this is an outlandish story of an extraterrestrial arriving on Earth to feed upon human flesh. But it's also a relatable tale of someone finding themselves in an alien skin and trying to figure out how (and *if*) to fit in. No wonder Levi's music, for all its swooning strangeness, is also contradictorily compelling.

In their discussion with Lopatin about the creative process of scoring a film, Levi raises the subject of 'method' composing – an idealized situation in which the composer would be 'living the life' of the film, wearing its clothes, breathing its air, inhabiting its set. They also talk about wondering what the characters in the film would think of the music, with Levi revealing that the score for *Jackie* was led by a desire to understand what Jaqueline Kennedy would have listened to, and an admission that Levi loves Giorgio Moroder's score for Brian De Palma's *Scarface* (1983) partly because Tony Montana himself would have approved of it.

There's also a discussion about the innate artificiality of film music, and the way it can break the illusion of 'reality'. As Levi states, films that feature no music at all can often feel 'more real' than their heavily orchestrated counterparts. This would become an issue of paramount importance in the creation of *The Zone of Interest*, for which Levi wrote sections of music that the composer then argued should be left *out* of the film – a very rare occurrence in film scoring!

For Levi, the addition of music is a fundamentally 'surreal' experience which 'heightens dramatic possibilities' and 'can let you access an arena of non-reality which can make things a bit more extreme'. Perhaps this is why Levi's score for *Under the Skin* works so well – because it captures the surreal nature of the story, taking the viewer to another level, elevating them into the realm of the *un*-real, while still tugging at their all-too-human emotions.

CHAPTER 4

How Did We Get Here?

Part 2 – From Goldsmith to Guðnadóttir

So, where were we?

Ah yes, we were talking about John Williams, surely the most successful and influential composer of the modern age. His place at the top of the film composition tree is unassailable; the scope of his awards and accolades unmatchable. Yet, looking through my own soundtrack collection, I find that the number of Williams LPs I own is overshadowed by those of one of his contemporaries – one who tends to appeal to those with an interest in the more outlandish (and arguably garish) forms of film music.

While Williams' achievements may be matchless, my own personal preference has always been for an American composer whose career similarly flourished in the second half of the twentieth century across an equally impressive range of movies. Jerry Goldsmith was a real shape-shifter in terms of the creative variety of his scores, some of which were far superior to the cinematic source material. While Williams scored *Superman*, Goldsmith had *Supergirl* (1984) – a huge flop, certainly, yet boasting a main theme that is one of the best in the superhero canon, a note-perfect example of 'Great music, shame about the film'.

It's genuinely impossible to define a 'typical' Goldsmith score since his work was so varied. He possessed a real versatility and an ability to compose for multiple genres. After the news of Goldsmith's death on 21 July 2004, Williams praised his contemporary's 'freshness' and 'chameleon adaptability' – a phrase that exactly captures his wide-ranging style. Like Williams, Goldsmith could get to the emotional heart of a film, often challenging our expectations of what a score should and *could* do. His work in the horror genre includes memorable scores for Richard Donner's *The Omen* (1976 – for which Goldsmith earned two Oscar nominations and one statuette) and Tobe Hooper's *Poltergeist* (1982), while the sound of science fiction would be blander without his work on Michael Anderson's *Logan's Run* (1976), Robert Wise's *Star Trek: The Motion Picture* (1979) and Ridley Scott's *Alien* (1979).

Most significantly, Goldsmith displayed his love of experimentation and the avant-garde on Franklin J. Schaffner's original *Planet of the Apes* (1968) – the film which launched a series that taught me everything I know about politics. Really. Using a ram's horn, bowls and woodwind instruments played without mouthpieces, Goldsmith conjured otherworldly sounds that were created acoustically, without resort to electronics. If you've never heard his cue 'The Hunt' from *Planet of the Apes* being performed live, then you are missing out on one of the great orchestral experiences. I have vivid memories of presenting a programme of film music performed by the City of Birmingham Symphony Orchestra under the baton of Robert Ziegler in which the splendid cacophony of 'The Hunt' – with its frantic piano, blaring horns and thunderously inventive percussion – stunned the audience night after night. It really is an electrifying work. It's no surprise that Goldsmith is reported to have conducted part of the score wearing an ape mask!

Goldsmith's reputation for challenging both himself and the audience with his use of unexpected sounds and orchestrations was well rehearsed in Hollywood. On hearing a strange noise outside the scoring stage, his long-time orchestrator Arthur Morton quipped, 'Find out who that guy is and bring him in here. We can use that in Jerry's next picture.'

One of my favourite contemporary composers, Nainita Desai, credits Goldsmith's thirst for experimentation with paving the way for her contemporaries, broadening the creative avenues for people with her skillsets. 'I'm an early digital baby,' Desai tells me. 'If it wasn't for technology, I would not be able to be a composer in this day and age.' For Desai, the advent of electronic music has enabled her to realize experimental sounds and compositions that she would otherwise have struggled to conjure. She remains keenly aware of the constraints placed on her predecessors, for whom conventional instruments were the only tools available. 'But then you have people like Jerry Goldsmith with his score for *Planet of the Apes*, which just blew my mind! I hadn't heard anything like it. He was really pushing the boundaries of what the orchestra could do in terms of atonal music.'

Goldsmith's musical talent was evident from a young age. He started composing as a teenager, but he received his formal music education at the University of Southern California, where one of his teachers was the Golden Age great Miklós Rózsa, creator of epic scores like *Ben-Hur* (1959) and *El Cid* (1961) along with more experimental fare such as his theremin-led score for Hitchcock's 1945 thriller *Spellbound* (more of which in Chapter

6, 'Switched-On Electronica') that Goldsmith credited as igniting his love of film music. He started composing for radio and TV, conducting live shows and learning vital skills of on-the-spot improvisation before scoring his first feature, the 1957 Western *Black Patch*.

Goldsmith's big break, however, came in 1962 with John Huston's *Freud: The Secret Passion*, on which Jean-Paul Sartre was an uncredited writer (he had his name existentially removed from the film). Faced with a biographical drama about the godfather of psychoanalysis, Goldsmith experimented with dissonance and atonality, earning his first Academy Award nomination. He would go on to receive eighteen nominations in total across his career, for his work on such films as *Patton* (1970), *Papillon* (1973), *The Boys from Brazil* (1978) and *Hoosiers* (1986), with his final nomination being for Disney's 1998 animation *Mulan*.

Although *Alien* remains one of Goldsmith's most celebrated scores, his experience of working on Ridley Scott's science fiction/horror hybrid was bruising. During the edit, the composer saw elements of his music being hacked up or rejected (his preferred original romantic opening was ditched in favour of something more ambiently atmospheric), with cues being cut, rearranged, and occasionally augmented with existing music from Goldsmith's score for *Freud* which editor Terry Rawlings had used as a temp track. Worse still, a 1976 recording of American composer Howard Hanson's Adagio from the 1930 Symphony No. 2 ('The Romantic') was used to replace the bulk of Goldsmith's 'Out the Door' finale, and then reprised in the end credits. As Rawlings ruefully admitted, 'I don't think he ever forgave me for using Howard Hanson for the end of the film.'

Despite these indignities, however, Goldsmith's *Alien* score still creates a pervasive sense of eeriness bordering on all-out terror. A 2007 deluxe album release allowed fans to fully appreciate his work on this film, from his use of an Echoplex – a tape delay effects unit – to create unsettling reverberations, to the low-pitched early wind instrument called a serpent, to the solitary trumpet theme. It's a cold, angular, unforgiving score that delivers real chills.

While Goldsmith could encapsulate terror in a place where no one can hear you scream, he was also more than capable of turning his hand to playful fun, sounding like he was having a great time in the process. He worked on nine films with director Joe Dante, including *Gremlins* (1984), *The 'Burbs* (1989) and his final score, *Looney Tunes: Back in Action* (2003). Shortly after Goldsmith's death in 2004, Dante said, 'I don't know if I've worked with any geniuses in this business, but if I have, it would be Jerry. The scope and breadth of what Jerry achieved in his career is just phenomenal. He was the luckiest find I ever made in movies.'

From thrillers to war epics, fantasy, action, horror and romance, there were few genres in which Goldsmith did not excel. In 1974 he was drafted in at the last minute to replace Philip Lambro's rejected score for *Chinatown* and completed the assignment in just ten days. According to producer Robert Evans, he 'saved the picture'. There's only about twenty-five minutes of music in the whole film but through its haunting trumpet solo and avant-garde textures, Goldsmith's score lends a modern twist to the film noir sound and precisely evokes the dry Los Angeles landscape. He would return to the neo-noir genre in subsequent hits like Paul Verhoeven's *Basic Instinct* (1992) and Curtis Hanson's *L.A. Confidential* (1997), conjuring lush scores ripe with intrigue and uncertainty.

*

British composer Anne Dudley credits Goldsmith with sparking her interest in scoring, recalling that seeing films like *Chinatown* first made her sit up and take notice of the work of a film's composer. Like Goldsmith, Dudley's scores cannot be pigeonholed. Her credits include the TV series *Poldark* (2015–19) and *Jeeves and Wooster* (1990–93), while on the big screen her CV boasts such critically acclaimed hits as Neil Jordan's *The Crying Game* (1992), Tony Kaye's famously troubled *American History X* (1998) and Peter Cattaneo's phenomenally successful *The Full Monty* (1997), for which Dudley received an Academy Award, making her only the second woman to win a scoring Oscar. Yet Dudley's success is not limited to the screen. She's also hugely influential in the world of pop music, having worked as arranger or producer for the likes of George Michael, Paul McCartney, Pet Shop Boys, Liza Minnelli, Tom Jones, Debbie Harry, Alison Moyet, ABC, Tina Turner and more.

Dudley's music career began in the synth-pop group Art of Noise. 'I'd always really wanted to write film music but I had actually no idea at all about how you got into it,' she remembers. For Dudley, this period before the rise of film composition courses made it all seem 'pretty much a closed shop', and her entry into the world of film was more fortuitous than planned.

Art of Noise were asked to write music for some commercials, 'because this was the eighties, and there was a huge market for commercials, especially in Britain. We had people like Hugh Hudson and Adrian Lyne and Ridley Scott and Tony Kaye, all making these epic ninety-second little masterpieces of film. There was so much money in advertising then, I suppose because there were only four terrestrial channels that you could watch, so adverts would reach millions of people.'

Cinema came calling in the shape of *Disorderlies* (1987), a forgettable knockabout comedy starring rappers The Fat Boys, the soundtrack of which is packed with the upbeat poppy sounds of Art of Noise's 'Roller 1', Bananarama's 'I Heard a Rumour' and Bon Jovi's 'Edge of a Broken Heart'. 'It was really quite a casual process in those days: the director said, "Oh yeah, I think we need a bit of music here, a bit of music here." We didn't have any temp score, didn't have any music editor, didn't have any music supervisor, you know, it was just the way things were. You just sort of got on with the job. I really enjoyed it. I probably enjoyed it more than the rest of the band did, who couldn't understand why we had to keep watching this same bit of film over and over again! That was the start of it, really.'

From there, Dudley went on to score the British biographical comedy drama *Buster* (1988) and to collaborate with Jeff Beck on the music for *The Pope Must Die* (1991). But it was Neil Jordan's groundbreaking gender thriller *The Crying Game* (1992) that put Dudley on the international map, her orchestral tracks interweaving with a jukebox tapestry that included both Dave Berry and Boy George performing the title song.

Five years later, Dudley won her Oscar for *The Full Monty*, the lolloping reggae-skank of her infectiously catchy theme tune brilliantly mirroring the gait of Robert Carlyle's chancer anti-hero who convinces a group of his unemployed friends to become a male stripping troupe. Along with the original score, Dudley also commissioned and produced Tom Jones's cover of 'You Can Leave Your Hat On', a 1972 Randy Newman track that became a hit when Joe Cocker's cover version featured in the erotic drama *9½ Weeks* (1986), but which was promptly eclipsed by Jones and Dudley's altogether raunchier version.

Dudley also served a key role solving the numerous live vocal complications of Tom Hooper's Oscar-courting stage-musical adaptation *Les Misérables* (2012), and provided a gorgeous score for Ridley Scott's long-nurtured dream project *Tristan & Isolde* (2006). Of her collaborations with director Paul Verhoeven (explored in Chapter 3, 'The Director's Vision'), Dudley's score for *Elle* (2016) is a particular standout, the slithering strings and pulsing beats of her music amplifying the voyeuristic nods to *Rear Window* (1954) while retaining a thoroughly modern cutting-edge sensibility.

While citing Goldsmith as a key inspiration, Dudley also acknowledges Hans Zimmer's influence on contemporary film music. She first encountered the young synth enthusiast in the early eighties, after he'd appeared in TV promos for the Buggles' hit 'Video Killed the Radio Star' with her Art of Noise bandmate Trevor Horn. 'The thing about Hans is he keeps reinventing himself,' she enthuses. 'He's so creative and innovative, he's always trying to push the boundary. He doesn't have to do that, but he still does extraordinary things and his influence is immense.'

The current blockbuster composer of the day – or to give him proper credit, the past few decades – German composer Zimmer has scored over two hundred films in over forty years and is one of the few film composers to sell out stadiums with his live shows. He's something of a film music rock star, winning over audiences with his work on animations like *The Lion King* (1994), for which he won his first Academy Award, and bankable hits like *Thelma & Louise* (1991), *Gladiator* (2000) and *The Da Vinci Code* (2006 – great music, shame about the film). But for many, he is most cherished for his collaborations with director Christopher Nolan.

One of Zimmer's most influential scores is for Nolan's 2010 science fiction head-melter *Inception*. This ambitious story of 'dream stealers' required propulsive action riffs like the cue 'Mombasa', along with moments of intimacy which allowed for the creation of 'Time', a simple piece with real emotional heft. But when it comes to impact on the evolution of film music, it's in the opening track 'Half Remembered Dream' where we encounter the much-aped loud and low 'BRAAAM' sound that would come to define Zimmer and his imitators.

This call to attention – the time-stretched audio equivalent of being thwacked around the ears – was created by Zimmer after experimenting with the Edith Piaf song 'Non, Je Ne Regrette Rien', which Nolan had written into the script of *Inception* as a key motif. The ambition was to introduce a different slowed-down or stretched part of that song within each of the dream layers of the film, and to create a sound similar to distant horns. Encouraged to experiment by Nolan, Zimmer recorded brass players emulating a sustained echo sound that was made by a piano in a church with a book resting on its pedal. He took that recording, added some electronic effects and, in doing so, created 'braaams' (although it's worth noting that various people who worked on the pre-release trailers for *Inception* have since claimed credit for inventing that sound themselves). Zimmer has called himself the 'godfather of braaams', and given that the now-ubiquitous wallop of sound came from his experimentations elongating the Piaf song, that's a title he richly deserves.

Starting out as a performer, playing keyboards and synths, Zimmer broke into the world of scoring in the 1980s under the patronage of Stanley Myers on films like *Moonlighting* (1982) and *My Beautiful Laundrette* (1985). Over the years, Zimmer has taken on a mentorship role himself, developing the talents and careers of numerous composers who've worked through the ranks at his Remote Control studios – names like Rupert Gregson-Williams (*Wonder Woman*, 2017), Harry Gregson-Williams (*Gladiator II*, 2024), Lorne Balfe (*Black Widow*, 2021), John Powell (*How to Train Your Dragon* series, 2010–25), Ramin Djawadi (*Game of Thrones* TV series, 2011–19) and Pinar Toprak (*The Lost City*, 2022). Zimmer's love of the synth is still evident today in his scores and live shows. Most evident, though, is his love of cinema. It's infectious. Despite his monumental success, critical acclaim and two Academy Awards, Zimmer exudes a passion for his work and an 'I-can't-quite-believe-I'm-here' enthusiasm during interviews.

One of the many reasons Zimmer stands out is the fact he's pretty much self-taught. He had piano lessons when he was young but admits he wasn't a fan of being made to practise scales. He was more concerned with how the music made him *feel*, and he brought that emotional element with him into scoring for the screen, saying, 'I always write from a personal point of view and I love the directors that allow me to do that.' Getting to the heart of the score is his goal, and his ideal creative partnership is one involving a director with whom he can have a lively and creative collaboration, even if that involves calling them in the middle of the night to say: 'I have an idea, can we not go and turn it all upside down, and what if we tried *this*?'

He describes to me working on *Hannibal* in 2001. 'We'd just finished shooting, it was eleven o'clock at night and we were in the cutting room at Fox. There was [editor] Pietro Scalia, Ridley Scott and myself, and frozen on the screen is a shot of Clarice Starling and a tear running down her face. And I'm going,

"Well, it's because she's in love with him," and Ridley's saying "Oh no, it's a tear of disgust." I can't remember what Pietro said but we sort of got into it and we were arguing. Three grown men are standing on their feet and shouting at each other and I had this sort of camera-pulls-back out of body experience and thought, "Wow, only in film, would people, at eleven o'clock at night, be so passionate about what the meaning of a tear on a woman's face is. This is a great job, this is where I want to be. I want to have this discussion."'

Zimmer's keenness to push the limits of mainstream film scoring is nowhere more evident than in his second Oscar-winning score, for Denis Villeneuve's ambitious 2021 adaptation of Frank Herbert's classic science fiction novel *Dune*. The teenage Zimmer was a huge fan of the book and he grabbed the chance to score the film. Indeed, he was so excited to work on *Dune* that he chose it over another collaboration with Christopher Nolan when the two projects clashed, which is why *Tenet* (2020) was scored by Ludwig Göransson.

As you might expect from the godfather of braaams, Zimmer went big for *Dune*. This is a score on an epic scale by all definitions – volume, ambition and duration. There are no fewer than *three* album releases: the original soundtrack, *The Dune Sketchbook (Music from the Soundtrack)* and *The Art and Soul of Dune*, accompanying a book of the team's vision for adapting the story for the screen. So immersed was Zimmer in the sound world he'd created that he kept on writing after the first film had wrapped, and had an hour of music ready to help the film-makers prepare for *Dune: Part Two* (2024).

Female voices are at the forefront of the *Dune* soundtrack, most notably 'the cry of a banshee' for the standout motif that transports us straight onto the planet Arrakis. Zimmer also had new instruments made to create the distinctive desert sounds, such as a large-scale metal 'house' devised by musician and sculptor Chas Smith, which served as part of the impressive percussion section. Flute-like instruments were constructed from PVC pipes, and other instruments were created using synthesizers for a truly otherworldly sound. As Zimmer explained, 'There are sounds that are not of humanity. I mean, with some rhythms – there's no way a drummer could play that.'

*

If you're a fan of Hans Zimmer scores from the eighties and nineties – or the scores by Danny Elfman from that era too, for that matter – there's a strong chance you're also a fan of the work of Shirley Walker, even if you don't know it yet. Walker was an unassuming glass-ceiling breaker who helped lead the way for women composers in Hollywood. Working with Elfman, she orchestrated and conducted the scores for Tim Burton's *Beetlejuice* (1988) and *Batman* (1989), Warren Beatty's *Dick Tracy* (1990) and Sam Raimi's *Darkman* (1990). She did similar work with Zimmer on Tony Scott's *Days of Thunder* (1990), Ron Howard's *Backdraft* (1991) and Penny Marshall's *A League of Their Own* (1992). Zimmer describes her as 'truly one of the most incredible composers I've ever met', who 'didn't look down on me because I hadn't gone to music school'.

Acknowledging that Zimmer was the first 'major-star composer' who hired and – more importantly – *credited* her as orchestrator and conductor, Walker would in turn hire *him* as a synthesizer player for *her* recording sessions. Zimmer recalled, 'It was great to have Shirley boss me around, because I would learn a lot. And the way she fought for the rights of musicians – she was really nice but she could have a real edge to her. I loved the edge.'

Walker's first screen credit was playing synthesizers for Francis Ford Coppola's 1979 Vietnam war epic *Apocalypse Now*, and in 1992 she followed pioneers like *The Incredible Shrinking Woman* (1981) composer Suzanne Ciani to become one of the first women to score a major American feature, writing all of the music for John Carpenter's *Memoirs of an Invisible Man*. For years, Walker held the record for composing more original scores for major studio features than any other woman (including three *Final Destination* films, 2000–6, and 2003's psychological horror *Willard*) and she may be best remembered for her music for DC superheroes, with *The Flash* (1990–91) and various animated shows such as *Batman: The Animated Series* (1992–95) and *Batman Beyond* (1990–2001), both of which won her an Emmy award.

Although there aren't too many film or TV scores for which Walker has a solo credit, she was involved in numerous screen productions as a performer, orchestrator, arranger, conductor or co-composer, and often as a ghostwriter. As the last of these, it seems that magic touch – albeit behind the scenes – helped save many a score. Speaking frankly about her experiences in Hollywood in Michael Schelle's *The Score: Interviews with Film Composers*, she observed that when she started working in the industry, composers were financially incentivized not to talk about being ghostwriters 'and to support the illusion or delusion, whichever you prefer, that composer X was actually doing the work that they were being paid for'.

Walker was in her thirties when she started working in the world of film music, and she acknowledged that her life experience may have given her more self-belief – or rather, *less patience* with Hollywood's expectations of what a composer should be, and how they should behave. Realizing that 'I had had too much of making other people look as great as I was making them look', she began to make a concerted effort to acquire her own composing credits, turning down uncredited work. It was a brave move that resulted in 'a little, terribly frightening, dry period'.

Walker was respected for her dedicated approach to her work and acknowledged for her role within the industry. Crucially, she was also a mentor to younger composers trying to build their careers. Academy Award nominee Laura Karpman described her as 'the foremother' of composers in Hollywood. She recalls their first meeting at the Sundance Institute in 1987, which is significant in itself: 'I was the only woman there, as I was in all of these places. Shirley was there, but not as a mentor, but as the wife of Don, her husband who was doing the tech work. So you have to know – I'm going to say something that I've never said, but I'm in that kind of a mood – how little *regard* there was for her expertise. Publicly, of course. Privately, sure, but publicly, I mean why in God's name would she not be – I mean, she was there! – would she *not* be mentoring *everybody*, not just the girls.'

*

In 2014, the American Society of Composers, Authors and Publishers (ASCAP) launched the Shirley Walker Award to honour 'those whose achievements have contributed to the diversity of film and television music'. Winners of the award have included Pinar Toprak and Germaine Franco. There's still a long way to go in terms of gender parity in the world of film scoring but, without Shirley Walker, the gap in Hollywood would be even bigger.

To get a sense of just how pioneering Walker was, it's worth remembering once again that no woman had won a scoring Oscar until Rachel Portman in 1997 for *Emma*. Portman went on to earn subsequent nominations for *The Cider House Rules* (1999) and *Chocolat* (2000), and as of 2025, she remains the *only* woman to receive more than *one* Oscar nod in a scoring category. She was also the first female composer to win a Prime-time Emmy Award, for *Bessie* (2015) – a TV film about the blues singer Bessie Smith.

Portman studied music at Oxford University which, she tells me, 'was incredibly stuffy and dry', and found her calling as a film composer after scoring the student film *Privileged*, which was released in 1982 and starred a young Hugh Grant. This was the first time she had composed to picture, watching a VHS cassette over and over again, and she recruited the student orchestra to perform the score. 'I listen to it now,' she remembers, 'and the main theme was OK, but some of the bits that I wrote for the scary bits with Hugh Grant being attacked in a dark alley were really *really* dodgy! The kind of music you might have written to a horror film in the 1940s. I had no idea.'

In her twenties, Portman gained experience scoring TV films and radio plays, but says that it wasn't really until Jim Henson's *The StoryTeller* (1987–1989) and *Oranges Are Not the Only Fruit* (1990) that she began to think, 'Oh, this ball is rolling, now I'm fully employed.' She says: 'But I wasn't ever *not* going to be a composer. I was totally determined to be a film composer. I was doing odd jobs, you know, working as a cook or waitressing, but I was definitely a film composer in my own mind!'

In these crucial early years, during which she worked with

upcoming director Mike Leigh on his 1984 TV project *Four Days in July* and his 1987 short *The Short & Curlies*, Portman said yes to everything ('I think when you start out you have to be a Jack of all trades') and learned valuable lessons which cemented her ambition and drive. 'I knew that in order to get anywhere it was really important that I was someone who was collaborative. The music for a film is a craft; it's there to enhance the film, and not to enhance my career.'

Having won a BFI Anthony Asquith Award for her rich and colourful music for *The StoryTeller*, Portman went on to create an eerily atmospheric score for Herbert Wise's 1989 TV adaptation of *The Woman in Black*, and then to create a gorgeously memorable score for Mike Leigh's 1990 feature film *Life Is Sweet*. (One of the great joys of my life was sitting with Rachel at her piano in her home studio as she recalled playing *Life Is Sweet*'s lilting main theme to Leigh for the first time, and then discussing at length with the director whether the last notes of a descending phrase should go up or down.)

The fact that Portman has proved so adept across a range of genres, combined with her disarming ability to discuss music in a conversational style that allows for maximum creative interactivity, is a key element of her success. But whether working in down-to-earth drama, fantasy fable, tragedy or comedy, Portman's decades-spanning career has produced scores that can steal your heart with an apparent simplicity that belies the intricacies and depth of the melodies. Her scores for Lynne Ramsay's masterful coming-of-age feature debut *Ratcatcher* (1999), Robert Redford's folksy golf drama *The Legend of Bagger Vance* (2000), Michael Sucsy's cheesy true romance *The Vow* (2012), Shamim Sarif's flawed Cold War drama *Despite the Falling Snow* (2016) and the extremely likeable TV-foodie doc *Julia*

(2021) are all further proof of her versatility. While the genre and quality of the films may be wildly varied, Portman's music is never less than adroitly engaging.

*

When asked about her own musical influences, Portman has regularly cited two celebrated film composers: John Williams and Ennio Morricone. In 2019, a year before the Italian maestro's death at the age of ninety-one, Hans Zimmer described Morricone to me as being 'very disciplined in his work, and I think that's very important. He doesn't just phone it in.' The term 'prolific' could be used to describe many other film composers, but when you start to make your way through Morricone's extensively eclectic back catalogue, you realize that he really is in a league of his own.

There are more than *five hundred* film and TV scores credited to Morricone. Having spent a lot of time listening to them – our Scala show boasted a 'Weekly Ennio Morricone pick' – I took foolish pleasure in attempting to compartmentalize them into a range of playful subsets. First, there's his lushly orchestrated romantic and expansive music for the likes of *The Red Tent* (1969), *Love Affair* (1992), *The Best Offer* (2013) and the much-loved *Cinema Paradiso* (1988), one of his ten collaborations with director Giuseppe Tornatore, who made the 2021 documentary *Ennio – The Maestro*, which celebrates the composer's legacy. These scores wear their hearts on their sleeves, bordering on swooning, yet they are too textured to fall into pure schmaltz.

Next, a substantial number of Morricone scores could be filed under 'Epic Vocals', with either chorus or female soloists at the forefront. A trained trumpeter, Morricone enjoyed incorporating brass into his scores but seemed particularly to relish utilizing voices as instruments, often adding whistles or breathy whispers to create his own unique soundscapes. Fine examples include 'Exultate Deo' from *El Greco* (1966), the earworm-tastic 'Abolição' from *Burn!/Queimada* (1969), 'A Voice from the Inside' from *Fateless* (2005) and the outstanding 'On Earth as It Is in Heaven' from *The Mission* (1986) which, to my mind, eclipses the popular choice 'Gabriel's Oboe'.

Then there are Morricone's poppy-sounding scores that are very much of their time, like *Slalom* (1965), *Menage all'Italiana* (1965), *Come Play with Me/Grazie Zia* (1969) and *Collector's Item/La Gabbia* (1985). Dig a bit deeper down this particular Morricone rabbit hole and you'll encounter more groovy fare that I fondly categorize as 'Cinzano Time' tunes, for the images they conjure of brown leatherette sofas and cheese-and-pineapple sticks: scores like *Danger: Diabolik* (1968), *The Master Touch/Un Uomo da Rispettare* (1972) and *La Cage aux Folles* (1978).

There's also a significant portion of Morricone's scores that can simply be labelled 'Crazy-Go-Nuts': allow me to direct you to *When Women Had Tails* (1970), *Bluebeard* (1972) and even Pasolini's 1966 oddity *The Hawks and the Sparrows/Uccellacci e Uccellini*, one of the few soundtracks to feature a main title sequence in which the credits are *sung* with great gusto. And then, of course, there's *Exorcist II: The Heretic* (1977), arguably the worst film ever made, yet somehow boosted by Morricone's utterly bananas score which manages to slip between the lyrical beauty of 'Regan's Theme' – which was repurposed by Quentin Tarantino for his 2015 epic *The Hateful Eight* – and the demon-ically bonkers 'Magic and Ecstasy', which sounds as though the devil didn't go down to Georgia, but instead went to a New York nightclub where he got off his head on acid. William Friedkin described *Exorcist II* to me as 'the product of a demented mind', and no one knew how to orchestrate that madness better than Morricone.

Romantic, Epic, Pop, Groovy and Crazy-Go-Nuts – a whole world of film scores by the maestro to discover before you get to the genre for which he's best known: the Western, or rather, the Spaghetti Western, the term coined to describe the genre films made in Europe from the mid-sixties onwards. Lesser-known Morricone scores of note in this section include *A Pistol for Ringo* (1965), *Navajo Joe* (1966, on which he was credited as Leo Nichols), *Death Rides a Horse* (1967) and *The Big Gundown* (1967). All of these are worth a listen. But Morricone's signature soundtracks were of course for director Sergio Leone, starting with *A Fistful of Dollars* in 1964.

Morricone scored six films for Leone – his *Dollars* trilogy and his *Once Upon a Time* trilogy – and these soundtracks have achieved legendary status. *The Good, the Bad and the Ugly* (1966) stands out for boasting not one, but two iconic tracks: 'The Ecstasy of Gold', featuring knockout vocals by one of Morricone's regular collaborators, Edda Dell'Orso; and the Main Theme which featured an intriguing combination of wails, drumbeats and electric guitar. A cover version by Hugo Montenegro became a pop hit on both sides of the Atlantic, the perfect twangy evocation of the film's broiling desert setting.

Along with his Western scores, Morricone made a significant contribution to the world of horror films, lending a cutting musical edge to the *giallo* stylings of Dario Argento (who co-wrote Leone's *Once Upon a Time in the West*) with his scores for *The Bird with the Crystal Plumage* (1970), *The Cat o' Nine Tails* (1971) and *Four Flies on Grey Velvet* (1971). He also lent his eerie talents to Aldo Lado's genre classic *Short Night of Glass*

Dolls (1971) and Massimo Dallamano's controversial *What Have You Done to Solange?* (1972), both of which have become established cult favourites with collectable soundtracks.

While he was, and remains, a big influence on Hollywood, Morricone famously refused to move there and never learned to speak English, retaining an inherently European sound even as his worldwide popularity grew over the decades. All this perhaps made him more attractive to directors in the US like Brian De Palma, Terrence Malick and Quentin Tarantino, because when Morricone scored your film, you got the unique Morricone seal of approval – one of accessible quality, variety and confidence.

This was a dedicated composer who was ready to turn his hand to any genre or film. He was awarded an honorary Oscar at the 79th Academy Awards in 2007 – only the second composer to receive the accolade – 'in recognition of his magnificent and multifaceted contributions to the art of film music'. However, he didn't win a competitive statuette until 2016, when he finally triumphed with his work on Tarantino's *The Hateful Eight* – a score which, as we noted, uses a recycled cue from *Exorcist II: The Heretic.* And if that's not a case of the devil getting the last laugh, then I really don't know what is.

Morricone continued to compose and conduct film scores (his concerts were regular sell-outs) throughout his eighties. When news of his death broke in 2020, A. R. Rahman took to social media to declare his awe at what Morricone had achieved. 'Only a composer like Ennio Morricone could bring the beauty, culture and the lingering romance of Italy to your senses in the pre-virtual reality and pre-internet era,' he said. 'All we can do is celebrate the master's work and learn!' By the time he wrote this, Rahman had won two Oscars for his work on Danny Boyle's

Slumdog Millionaire and earned further nominations for re-teaming with Boyle on *127 Hours* (2010). He had also written the music for Andrew Lloyd Webber's Bollywood-themed stage show *Bombay Dreams* (2002) which transferred from London to Broadway, won praise for his score for Swedish director Lasse Hallström's cross-cultural dramedy *The Hundred-Foot Journey* (2014), worked with directors Jeff and Michael Zimbalist on their biopic of Brazilian football star *Pele* (2016), provided music for Iranian director Majid Majidi's seventh-century epic *Muhammad: The Messenger of God* (2017) and collaborated with British director Gurinder Chadha on the partition drama *Viceroy's House* (2017) and the Springsteen-inspired coming-of-age tale *Blinded by the Light* (2019). Yet even for a composer as prolific and versatile as Rahman, Morricone was always in a league of his own.

Despite his globetrotting success, Rahman has retained an affection for the Indian film industry in which he first flourished. 'When you're a composer in India,' he told me, 'they don't judge you, or what genre of stuff you do. They just want something *good*. You know, you can score like John Williams; you can score like Zimmer; you can score like yourself; and then you can write a song like Michael Jackson, or a folk song. And they don't judge you, they don't say "Oh, that guy can only do *that*." That is one of the biggest advantages of doing Indian movies. They just want something *great*. They just want an experience. Whereas, when you go to Hollywood, if they need a rap song, they go to a certain person; if they need a country song, they go to another person. So even though it's nice to stick to one, the fun which we have *here* is fantastic.'

In 2017, Rahman won his fourth World Soundtrack Award, scooping the Public Choice Award for his score for *Viceroy's*

House. At that same ceremony, Icelandic composer Jóhann Jóhannsson was named Film Composer of the Year for his work on Denis Villeneuve's melancholy sci-fi masterpiece *Arrival* (2016). The next year, Jóhannsson would share composer credit on Garth Davis's *Mary Magdalene* (2018) with Hildur Guðnadóttir, a trained cellist who had performed on several scores, including Jóhannsson's work with Villeneuve.

When Jóhannsson died in 2018, Guðnadóttir (who remains admirably modest about her extraordinary talent) seemed to be the natural heir to his crown, scoring *Sicario: Day of the Soldado*, the sequel to *Sicario* (2015) for which Jóhannsson had been Oscar nominated. Guðnadóttir quickly became in demand and won multiple awards for her 2019 score for *Joker*, but despite this she insists that 'I've always been very music-focused, I've never been very career-focused. I've never had a manager and I'm barely on social media. I don't really know how any of that works! I've always been in my little bubble. I've never lived in Hollywood and I have no intention to move there!'

When asked about her extraordinary career path, she demurs: 'I almost don't really know how any of this happened and I don't know how anyone found me in the first place.' Guðnadóttir certainly did not court Hollywood, and yet Hollywood continues to come to her. As with Morricone, when studios hire her to score a film, they know what her magic touch will provide: 'They're aware that I have a very strong resonance in a certain musical direction, so people will normally not expect me to try to be able to write like everyone else. I get hired mostly to be myself.'

For Guðnadóttir, the story is key. She recalls making the connection between storytelling and music when she was very young: 'I remember being two or three years old and listening to my dad practise. He's a clarinet player and he was playing the "Flight of the Bumblebee" [by Rimsky-Korsakov] and I remember the sense of feeling the bumblebee becoming an *actual* bumblebee through the music. I vividly remember how the music had the power to become something real just by putting together these notes, so I was like "Play it again, play it again!" '

Guðnadóttir's film scores never feel tacked on. Her seemingly simple plucked guitar motifs and sombre bowed strings become part of the very fabric of Sarah Polley's Oscar-winning adaptation of Miriam Toews's *Women Talking* (2022), like the intricately braided hair of the characters. The instrumentation is largely minimal (although it becomes more expansive in the film's later stages), evoking the sparse lives of the women within this tortured Mennonite community. Most significantly, the musical cues are restrained and deployed sparingly, with Guðnadóttir apparently encouraging Polley to hold back and let the film's silence speak for itself (as Mica Levi would do with Jonathan Glazer's *The Zone of Interest*). The result is a delicately deployed score that lends a yearning, melancholic strength to the proceedings, perfectly melding ancient and modern elements, quietly enhancing a tale that is at once timely and timeless.

Through her varied work on Todd Field's *Tár* (2022), Kenneth Branagh's *A Haunting in Venice* (2023) and more recently Todd Phillips's impressively divisive *Joker: Folie à Deux* (2024), Guðnadóttir is proving to be extremely influential, not least because she *isn't* particularly influenced by her film music forebears. This outlook, combined with the breadth of her work – which encompasses TV, film and video game soundtracks along with solo material – demonstrates how the path to becoming a screen composer is ever-changing and fluid.

Guðnadóttir provides a welcome breath of fresh air, acknowledging the evolution of film music without being restrained by what's gone before.

'I don't really think of it as any different when I'm composing for the screen as when I'm just composing,' she says, echoing Erich Korngold's words from a previous century that 'Music is music, whether it is for the stage, rostrum or cinema.' As Guðnadóttir explains, 'I didn't study film music in particular, so I'm not one of these people who have been living and breathing film music all my life! I didn't really even know that those people existed until a few years ago – you know, people that are completely *obsessed* about film music.'

Hearing these words, I am taken back to that birthday party with Ken Russell, and his love of Korngold's score for *The Sea Hawk*. Ken loved music, and he didn't care whether it was written for films, plays or concert halls. But he also loved movies, and somehow the combination of sublime music and transportative visual imagery struck a chord deep in his soul.

When he heard music, he saw pictures, and vice versa.

I think Ken would have loved Hildur Guðnadóttir.

I have no idea what she would have made of him.

Soundtrack Selection:
Drive My Car (2021)

At the 94th Academy Awards, Ryûsuke Hamaguchi's gently sprawling emotional drama *Drive My Car* (2021) became the first Japanese film to be nominated for Best Picture. It would go on to win the Oscar for Best International Feature, with two further nominations for Best Director and Best Adapted Screenplay, the latter recognizing Hamaguchi and co-writer Takamasa Oe's sinewy reimagining of Haruki Murakami's short story, published in the 2014 collection *Men Without Women*.

In that same year, the Oscar for Best Score went to Hans Zimmer for his grand-scale accompaniment to Denis Ville-neuve's science fiction epic *Dune*, with nominations for Nicholas Britell's *Don't Look Up*, Germaine Franco's *Encanto*, Alberto Iglesias's *Parallel Mothers* and Jonny Greenwood's *The Power of the Dog* (all 2021), the last of which earned a Best Director statuette for New Zealand film-maker Jane Campion. These are all worthy nominees – although in my opinion Green-wood's (*un*-nominated) score for Pablo Larraín's Princess Diana film *Spencer*, from the same year, was superior to them all, using the sounds of a baroque string quartet collapsing into skittery jazz to represent the breakdown of stringent royal decorum. (Greenwood had enlisted a classical string ensemble, and then one-by-one replaced each player with a free-form improviser, orchestrating an organic sonic slide from rigid order to unbound adventure. Genius!)

My favourite score of that year, however, was Eiko Ishibashi's music for *Drive My Car*, which barely registered on the Academy's radar. Not only did Ishibashi's deceptively seductive keyboard-led music provide the audience with an emotional entry into the sometimes alienating drama, but it also worked as a superb standalone album to which I have listened on hard rotation since first seeing the movie.

The plot of *Drive My Car*, which expands upon and departs from Murakami's source, is somewhat convoluted. Hidetoshi Nishijima plays theatre director Yūsuke Kafuku, whose intense relationship with his unfaithful wife Oto is brought to an abrupt end when she dies, about three-quarters of an hour into the movie. At which point, the action jumps forward two years (only then does the film's title card finally appear on screen), and we find Yūsuke in Hiroshima, where he has agreed to direct a multilingual production of Chekhov's *Uncle Vanya*. For contractual reasons, Yūsuke is not allowed to drive his own car and must be chauffeured by Misaki – a young woman who, we discover, is the same age as the child that Oto and Yūsuke lost many years ago. As the pair's low-key relationship grows, both reveal hidden guilts and griefs, many of which resonate with the key themes of the theatre production in which Yūsuke is now immersed.

As you can probably tell from this potted synopsis (which barely scratches the surface of Hamaguchi's strange film), *Drive My Car* is hardly straightforward emotional fare. Yet the film finds a direct route to the audience's psyche through the lyrical melancholia of Ishibashi's music, which mixes wine-bar chintz with something quietly profound in a manner that reminded me of Angelo Badalamenti's work on David Lynch's misunderstood 1992 masterpiece *Twin Peaks: Fire Walk with Me* (itself the subject of a Soundtrack Selection later in this book).

At times, Ishibashi's score seems to possess the soothing swoon of airport music – or, more accurately, of Brian Eno's hypnotically ambient *Music for Airports*. But as the key themes of the score cycle round and round in an entrancing spiral, shifting and mutating, we start to feel something deeper, as if the music is dragging us into the drama, with all its conflicting strains of love and despair. Brushed drums and brooding double bass accompany broad electronic moodscapes, with a gently played piano picking out top-line melodies that tiptoe through our consciousness, into our *sub*conscious.

Speaking to the trade paper *Variety* in March 2022, Hamaguchi explained that he had asked Ishibashi to create music that 'feels almost like the scenery – the landscape of where this story is taking place', adding: 'When the depiction emotionally became somewhat cool in the visual, we decided to expand emotionally on that musical palette.' As for Ishibashi, she remembers Hamaguchi telling her, 'I want the music to connect the audience to the film, because the images will be the ones that separate them,' proposing the inclusion of a hummable theme song similar to those created by Henry Mancini decades earlier.

The allusion to Mancini is intriguing, since it suggests that Hamaguchi – who had previously used music only very sparingly in his films – had found a way to pivot into a more constructive dialogue with film composers. He has since worked again with Ishibashi, and (like Greek director Yorgos Lanthimos and British composer Jerskin Fendrix) the pair appear to have found a common creative language that brings out the best in both of them. A shared love of the works of John Cassavetes, Douglas Sirk and Rainer Werner Fassbinder clearly connected the two imaginative spirits, but Ishibashi's music bears very little relationship to the sound of those directors' films, or to the sounds of her own favourite film composer, John Barry. Instead, she has managed to craft something unique – a score that seems on the surface to have a tranquil, background-music feel, but which actually packs a weighty emotional heft that builds cumulatively, rather than peaking in dramatic bursts.

'Half of the soundtrack was created after reading the script,' Ishibashi told me when I asked her about the process of writing the soundtrack. 'The other half was written after some of the images were created – after I'd seen parts of the movie.' She went on to explain that a hiatus due to the Covid-19 pandemic lockdown had interrupted production of the film in a manner that strangely mirrored its broken-backed structure. 'Shooting was stopped due to the coronavirus, so for a long time I was only able to see the footage up until the scene where Kafuku's wife died. But the script was so strong that it was not so difficult to make music.'

After viewing an assembly of the first forty-five minutes of the film (the section shot before the pandemic), Ishibashi prepared a series of motifs that she would demo and send to Hamaguchi, with suggestions as to where these motifs might sit within the film thus far. Hamaguchi would then respond with his own notes and suggestions, and Ishibashi began to orchestrate, using an ensemble palette that ranges from acoustic and electronic keyboards to vibraphone, pedal steel guitar, violin and viola, and electric and acoustic bass. According to the director, this process unlocked his own ability to communicate with the composer, enabling him to use visual cues (rather than abstract conversations) to express his intentions, while Ishibashi responded intuitively to the images she was sent.

'*Drive My Car* already had a great script and performances, surrounded by the sounds of cars, boats and cassette tapes,' Ishibashi told me. 'So I tried to find a music that would find the places where they met, both blending them and possibly highlighting the spaces *between* them.' Perhaps it's that emphasis on the *spaces* in the film (rather than the dramatic beats) that gives Ishibashi's score such resonance.

Driving from Exeter to Cornwall with the *Drive My Car* soundtrack album on the stereo, I had intended to focus my mind on the specifics of what made the score work, in preparation for writing this segment. Instead, I found myself transported back into the psycho-geography of the film, imagining that the beaten-up VW I was driving was actually the cherry-red Saab 900 turbo that glides through the movie.

Like all the best pieces of film music, Ishibashi's score defies clinical assessment, quietly inviting the listener to abandon logical inquiry and simply breathe in the landscape of the film. By the time I arrived in Cornwall, my mind was in Japan. Hamaguchi may be the director of *Drive My Car*, and Takamasa Oe its co-writer, but for me it will always be a film by Eiko Ishibashi, because here, more than ever, the music *is* the movie.

CHAPTER 5

The Long and Winding Road

From Composition to Orchestration (and Occasionally Rejection)

'I'm prepared to do whatever the film needs. The film talks to me. I don't talk to the film.' So said legendary composer Elmer Bernstein, who scored more than 150 films across five decades, including *The Magnificent Seven* (1960), *Thoroughly Modern Millie* (1967), *The Amazing Mr Blunden* (1972, one of my favourite films *of all time*), *The Age of Innocence* (1993) and John Landis comedies like *The Blues Brothers* (1980s) and the tongue-in-cheek-but-still-properly-scary *An American Werewolf in London* (1981). During an interview in the late 1990s about his working process, Bernstein restated his tried and tested belief in the need for total surrender to each individual project. 'I'll get hold of a film and look at it twenty times. I'll spend one week just looking at the film – once in the morning, once in the afternoon – until the film tells me what to do.'

The starting point for a composer can vary, by choice or circumstance. One thing is clear: there is no set formula for beginning work on a film score. Or, indeed, for ending it. Although each individual composer may have their own pre-ferred methods and rituals of composition and recording, the landscape of film music is littered with a dizzying array of techniques used to get the creative juices flowing, and then, ideally, to arrive at a version of the score that resembles the visions of both the composer and the director.

I remember having a conversation with a music student who was in the process of scoring their first short film, and they asked me what was the 'correct' or 'usual' way of going about the process. I asked them what instrument they were using to compose with – whether it was acoustic or electronic, rhythmic or melodic. They replied that they hadn't thought about that yet – they preferred to try and imagine the sounds of the film and then figure out how to make those sounds. I told them that this was as good an approach as any and reminded them that Chaplin (who, as we noted, won an Oscar for screen composition) could neither read nor notate music. To which they replied, 'Yes, but how did he *start*?'

Some composers prefer *not* to be guided by the film footage, but to find a way to access the core of the story at an earlier stage, usually through the script. 'Before I even get the film, I spend quite a bit of time in my studio by myself,' explains James Newton Howard. 'I'm just improvising, maybe on a piano, into my sequencer, which is essentially a digital recording device that every composer pretty much uses these days. One becomes better at recognizing when you've improvised something that's worth repeating, so if I do something, I'll go: "Whoa, what was that?" and I'll stop the sequencer and I'll go back and listen to it again. Then I'll usually take pencil and paper and write that out so then I can see it and I can play it over and over again.'

Improvisation allows the composer to tunnel their way into the heart of the score, although each composer has their own individual methods of allowing inspiration to flow. 'I sit and look at the picture at the same time while playing the piano,' Rachel Portman tells me when describing her typical working day. 'I might pause it for a second and work out a couple of bars here or there, and then I'll play it again. I know for lots of people, their recording *is* their playing, so they remember everything. But I still write everything down because I kind of know when something isn't working. What I often do is I record something, I take a break, then I listen to what I've just recorded, and I'll know what I didn't like or what needs to be made better.' A meticulous process of trial and error.

Howard Shore also prefers to see the notes on the page. 'I work things out on paper,' he tells me. 'I have a really traditional use of harmony and counterpoint. I was taught to write with a pencil by a teacher that I had of the clarinet many years ago, when I was about ten years old, and I've just continued with that. So pretty much all my scores are written in manuscript with pencil. And then I would orchestrate in ink. When computers became more accessible, I would orchestrate with a copyist, copying my orchestration into computer programs.'

For Isobel Waller-Bridge, the key to starting work on a film is to 'choose a scene that I know I want to score. It's not the beginning, it's not the end, it'll be something pivotal, and then I'll work back from that.' James Newton Howard opts for a similar approach, observing that 'oftentimes I'll do the biggest, nastiest cue first, like a five- or six-minute action sequence, because from that I can derive a lot of motifs and other ideas for other parts of the movie, once I've solved that.'

Approaches can vary depending on the type and genre of the film. Germaine Franco enjoys reading the script, 'just to see where it started, because you know it never ends up exactly the way it is on the page'. But in the case of the 2021 Disney/Pixar film *Encanto*, a script was not available. This is not unusual, because music production starts far earlier for animations, especially if there are set-pieces with songs, as these are required before the scenes can be created visually. 'Sometimes they just give you a still, and that's all I had on *Encanto* for months – just two or three stills!' exclaims Franco. 'It was a discussion. I didn't have a script, and then I got a list of Colombian pieces that the directors were moved by and I just listened to those all the time. Then I did my own research.' As animated films (unlike live-action movies) need to be constructed from the soundtrack up, it's not uncommon for composers working in this area to look elsewhere for inspiration – to 'do their own research' in an attempt to fill in the gaps.

If a film is an adaptation, Howard Shore immerses himself in both the script and the source text, extensively researching the period of the story's setting. He then begins to compose music based on 'the ideas of the film' rather than scene-specific cues. Only when enough music has been generated to form a 'body of work based on the ideas inherent in the film' does Shore start to shape the film score per se. 'It's kind of a multilayered process,' he says. 'It's not like I go directly to the film. First the music, the composition, the architecture of the score, the themes, the motifs, and then the scoring.'

It seems to be a matter of preference whether words or visuals are the main source of inspiration. Anne Dudley often receives the script in advance, but prefers to see footage of the film because 'I want to see the actors, I want to see the production design, I want to see the costumes, I want to see the *style* of it.' For Dudley, the script can only take her so far – it is the visual image that fires her imagination.

'I personally like to be guided – but not too much – by the

picture,' says Isobel Waller-Bridge, who appreciates having preparation time before watching any footage. 'What I would usually like to do is sketch from conversations that I've had with the director and then just be responding to the script. And then also any kind of stills, any kind of aesthetic references that I might be given. No scenes, no moving pictures yet, so that I can sketch away from it. Then by the time the picture arrives, I have things that I can just throw onto it, to see what works. I like to be able to experiment really freely and then see what is surprising about something that I put onto the picture afterwards.'

Hildur Guðnadóttir prefers to start work before shooting takes place. 'I like to have the time to set my own tempo with the story,' she explains, 'without being influenced in the beginning by the tempo and the scenario of the set and the cinematography and the acting. I really enjoy imagining the story completely from point minus ten. I think it's a bit different when you read things by yourself because you have this internal dialogue – you set this pace and you set the scenario.' From here, Guðnadóttir will discuss the work with the director, 'to see if what I'm feeling is in line with his or her ideas.' If they are in accord, she will begin the process of composition, writing music that (in an ideal world) can be played on set during the shooting of specific scenes.

This was famously the case with the 'Bathroom Dance' cue from her Oscar-winning score to *Joker*. As it was originally conceived and written, the scene was meant to feature Joaquin Phoenix's Arthur Fleck having a suicidal panic attack in the wake of a murder that he has just committed. His character was meant to enter the bathroom, hide his gun, wash off his clown make-up and then stare at himself in the mirror while asking, 'What have I done? What have I done?' According to director Todd Phillips, on the day of the shoot he and Phoenix decided that the scene didn't work – that it didn't mesh with the trajectory of Arthur's character, particularly when he was required to hold a gun to his head and pull the trigger, only to discover that he's run out of bullets. For an hour they discussed alternative possibilities while the rest of the crew waited outside. Then Phillips decided to play Phoenix a cue that he had received from Guðnadóttir, to which Phoenix started to dance . . .

'The acting and the scene is kind of born out of music,' says Guðnadóttir. 'Of course you can't do that with the whole film. But when you have these moments of allowing the music to set the tempo and the vibe, you can start to have the music as a part of the core DNA of the film. Then you can have a really interesting back and forth. For me, that's really the most interesting and fun way to work.'

*

Whether it's through conversations with the director, reading the script, looking at visuals, conducting personal research, watching footage, or all of the above, the composer's goal is to find musical inspiration from the essence of the film itself, and the story it wants to tell. Maurice Jarre achieved this with his Oscar-winning music for *Lawrence of Arabia* (1962) by extensively researching the film's enigmatic subject, T. E. Lawrence, and losing himself in the vast desert landscape of David Lean's breathtaking footage. It's hard to imagine the multi-award-winning epic film without his memorably bold and dramatic score. But Jarre wasn't the first choice to compose the music – far from it.

Long before Jarre came on board, several other composers had been attached to the project. Lean's initial choice had been

Malcolm Arnold, who'd scored his previous film, *The Bridge on the River Kwai* (1957), and received an Academy Award for his efforts. Producer Sam Spiegel was keen to commission William Walton in addition to Arnold, so the film could boast a score by two of Britain's finest composers. However, when they both watched a rough cut of the film after a long (and, some say, boozy) lunch, their feedback was none too positive (according to Walton, Arnold called it a 'bloody travelogue') and ties were severed.

An idea was mooted for one composer to score the scenes featuring British forces and another to focus on scoring the Middle Eastern setting, so Benjamin Britten and Aram Khachaturian were brought on board, with the comparatively little-known Maurice Jarre joining the team to fill in any potential gaps. This arrangement fell through because Khachaturian couldn't leave Russia (this was the summer of 1962 and the Cold War was heating up) and Britten requested more time due to other work commitments. Time, however, was in short supply since the premiere was only four months away.

Richard Rodgers (he of *South Pacific*, *Oklahoma!* and *The Sound of Music* fame) was the next composer on Spiegel's list, and the producer's plan was for Rodgers to write most of the score and for Jarre to orchestrate it and, again, fill in any gaps with his own original material. While Jarre was waiting for Rodgers to send over his themes from New York, he watched as much footage as he could get his hands on – around forty hours' worth. He started by watching visuals of the desert rather than scenes with the main actors, and music based on these images began to take shape. When Rodgers eventually sent over *his* musical suggestions, Lean wasn't impressed, not least because the headline composer had included a British military march which wasn't even an original tune. The frustrated film-maker then asked Jarre if he'd written anything; the composer played him his theme at the piano and got the main gig on the spot.

Jarre's challenge, one that's all too common for film composers to this day, was working to an incredibly tight deadline. He had six weeks to write and record two hours of music for around one hundred instruments – so he would work for four hours, have a ten-minute nap, and repeat.

There are countless stories of composers working under ridiculous time pressures, often due to replacing another composer at short notice. Max Steiner spoke candidly about having less than a month to compose a vast three hours and forty-five minutes of original music for the 1939 Oscar-winner *Gone with the Wind* as well as scoring another film and overseeing both of the recording sessions. 'I did it by getting exactly fifteen hours of sleep during those four weeks,' he remembered, 'and working steadily the rest of the time. You can't be a Beethoven under those conditions.'

The results of such a stressful process can end in tears. As Hans Zimmer once famously joked, 'You haven't made it as a film composer until you've had a film score rejected,' and it does seem to be a painful rite of passage for a composer to find themselves off a project, even after the score has been recorded and mixed into the soundtrack of the movie. Way back in 1932, Max Steiner was given just two weeks to replace W. Franke Harling's score for the jungle adventure *The Most Dangerous Game* after producer Merian C. Cooper deemed Harling's music to be too 'Broadway-light' for an action thriller.

Three decades later, we find Alex North (as we noted earlier) suffering the indignity of having the music he'd written for Kubrick's *2001: A Space Odyssey* being replaced by existing recordings of classical pieces. Then jump forward another three decades, to Vincent Ward's otherworldly drama *What Dreams May Come* (1998), originally boasting a score by Ennio Morricone which was ultimately ditched in favour of very different music by Michael Kamen when the producers started to panic in the editing room. Elmer Bernstein's score for Martin Scorsese's *Gangs of New York* (2002) was dropped at the behest of producer Harvey 'Scissorhands' Weinstein, and both Bernstein *and* Morricone worked on Roland Joffé's historical drama *The Scarlet Letter* (1995) before being superseded by John Barry, who took over at the suggestion of leading lady Demi Moore. In his excellent 2012 book, *Torn Music – Rejected Film Scores: A Selected History*, the late Gergely Hubai documents no fewer than 300 rejected or replaced scores, from the 1930s to the 2010s.

'It happens to everyone,' observes Natalie Holt. 'Sometimes that relationship doesn't work out. You're the last down the line to save a movie and if it's testing really badly, what can you change cheaply at the last minute? The score!'

But while having a score rejected is something of an occupational hazard for composers, Holt is one of the few people to have first-hand experience of an entire *movie* being dumped. She had written and recorded the score for the long-awaited *Batgirl* film when, in the summer of 2022, DC Films announced that – even though they'd reached the post-production stage – they were no longer planning to release it due to cost-cutting measures. On a trip to LA, Holt met up with Michael Giacchino, the Oscar-winning composer of Disney/Pixar's film *Up* (2009), who has suffered his own fair share of rejections. 'We had such a nice afternoon,' Holt recalls, adding that she also visited Danny Elfman, with whose theme from *Batman* (1989) she had been working when *Batgirl* got cancelled. 'It was just so nice to chat to these people that I really respect and get their thoughts. It was kind of like therapy: "OK, it happens, you just have to pick yourself up and move on."'

Having a score rejected can be a painful experience, but the composers who step in to fill the void can reap the benefits. James Newton Howard got his first Oscar nomination in 1992 for *The Prince of Tides*, a project he inherited after original composer John Barry didn't see eye-to-eye with director Barbra Streisand. And then a decade later, when Howard Shore left Peter Jackson's *King Kong*, he jumped in with just five weeks to go and earned a Golden Globe nomination and an International Film Music Critics Award for his trouble.

*

Having racked up his first feature composer credit back in 1985 on Ken Finkleman's black comedy *Head Office*, James Newton Howard is well placed to reflect on the technological advancements that have occurred over the years, and how these have changed composers' ways of working. 'Electronics have moved right into the forefront,' he says. 'Forty years ago, having a synthesizer on a score was a novelty, and slowly it just became part of the palette and part of the orchestra. That part has really gotten very strong, so it's pretty much routine on just about every score I do, even if it doesn't sound like it. A big action movie like *Jungle Cruise* [2021], the *Hunger Games* films [2012–], *Maleficent* [2014] – there are quite a few electronics that you don't hear specifically, but they're part of the texture of the music.'

Digital music software has allowed composers to create high-quality demos for comparatively small budgets. Mocking up cues using a digital orchestra or samples can be crucial for saving a composer's time and preventing them from spending too long going down the wrong musical rabbit hole. 'Nowadays, with the benefit of the computer programs that we've got,' says Anne Dudley, 'it would be very unusual for a composer to get too far down the line in writing too much stuff before the director's heard it. I think it's a good idea, once you've got some themes going, to make some pretty good demos of them, put them up against picture and start the dialogue early in the process.'

Digital demos not only ensure that the director and studio are on board with the composer's vision, they're also very helpful for the studio team and their preparations ahead of recording. These sessions provide a 'Finally!' moment when the score is truly experienced for the first time in all its glory. 'You can get so used to your demos and to the samples,' Amelia Warner tells me. 'You live with them for so long, and the director and the producers all live with it too. So then it's this really magical moment where you get to hear it played by *real* musicians with expression and nuance . . . I really love that bit because everyone's put all this faith in you and you keep saying "It'll sound much better, I promise!" And then you get to actually hear the real-life version and it can be a really exhilarating, lovely moment.'

Jonny Greenwood enjoys holding something back from the demos to add to that exhilaration, acknowledging: 'It's nice when the composer's imagination hasn't gone through a computer demo, and it's just paper, and then a piano version, sometimes, and then there's an orchestra playing it. That's one of the reasons why I'm always happy to crowbar in string effects and noises that *can't* be done as a demo. Because then you *have* to wait until the real thing, and everyone hears the real thing at the same time and gets excited about it.'

*

Depending on time, budget and the studio or composer's preferences, recording sessions can take place around the world, not necessarily in the country of the film's origin. One particular location embraced by both film and music lovers worldwide is the UK's Abbey Road. The legendary London studios began recording film scores in the early 1980s with *Lion of the Desert* (1981) by Maurice Jarre and *Eye of the Needle* (1981) by Miklós Rózsa.

The extensive list of the scores recorded within Abbey Road's hallowed walls includes – and this is just a handful! – *Raiders of the Lost Ark* (1981), *Return of the Jedi* (1983) and the three *Star Wars* prequels by John Williams, *First Blood/Rambo* (1982) by Jerry Goldsmith, *The Dark Crystal* (1982) and *Brassed Off* (1986) by Trevor Jones, *Brainstorm* (1983), *Aliens* (1986), *Apollo 13* (1995) and *Braveheart* (1995) by James Horner, *The Dead Zone* (1983) and *Brazil* (1985) by Michael Kamen, *Chocolat* (2000) by Rachel Portman, *The Hours* (2002) by Philip Glass, *Skyfall* (2012) and *1917* (2019) by Thomas Newman, *Gravity* (2013) by Steven Price, *The Hateful Eight* (2015) by Ennio Morricone, *The Shape of Water* (2017) by Alexandre Desplat, *American Animals* (2018) by Anne Nikitin, *Knives Out* (2019) by Nathan Johnson, *Emma.* (2020) by Isobel Waller-Bridge and David Schweitzer, *The Banshees of Inisherin* (2022) by Carter Burwell, *A Haunting in Venice* (2023) by Hildur Guðnadóttir, a selection of Aardman releases, various Wes Anderson films and *The Lord of the Rings* and *The Hobbit* trilogies by Howard Shore. Whatever your taste in movies, there's a pretty good chance that the music for some of your favourite films was recorded at Abbey Road.

Over the years, I've visited Abbey Road a few times – once to rehearse a piece that I was going to perform at the Royal Festival Hall (see my last book, *How Does it Feel?*, for all the grisly details), once to drop in on Jonny Greenwood who was working on the score for *Inherent Vice* (2014) with conductor Robert Ziegler, and a couple of times on behalf of Scala Radio. It's impossible to overstate just how much the history of Abbey Road seeps into every nook and cranny of the building – whether it's Studio 2, where the likes of The Beatles, Pink Floyd and Kate Bush recorded in the sixties, seventies and eighties, or the canteen where I bumped into an engineer holding a microphone which he merrily announced to be 'Ringo's bass drum mic'. (I asked if I could touch it, and he told me I could, as long as I was 'careful'. So I touched it. And it felt like a bass drum mic. Obviously.)

Studio engineer John Barrett joined Abbey Road in 2005 and has worked on an impressive number of film scores there, including a variety by Alexandre Desplat (such as *The King's Speech*, 2010; *Harry Potter and the Deathly Hallows Part 1* and *Part 2*, 2010/11; and *Florence Foster Jenkins*, 2016), Jonny Greenwood (including *Norwegian Wood*, 2010; *The Master*, 2012; and *Spencer*, 2021) and Carter Burwell (*The Twilight Saga – Breaking Dawn Part 2*, 2012; and *The Ballad of Buster Scruggs*, 2018). Barrett tells me how he prepares ahead of recording sessions: 'I correspond with composers and we discuss specifics about the set-ups and plans. Is there anything unique about the sound world they want to create or is there something they want to try specifically?' Armed with this information, he contacts the orchestral contractors who book the musicians to arrange the line-up of the orchestra for the session. He also speaks to the orchestrator to find out if there are any solos or featured parts that he needs to know about from a technical point of view. 'I need to make sure I've got the right coverage in terms of microphones and sounds,' he says, 'and also in terms of laying out the orchestra.' While there is a standardized orchestral layout, film scores can be wildly inventive and recording them may involve rearranging the line-up and positioning of musicians to get the best results. 'The great thing about film scores is that you can do pretty much whatever you want! It's one of the few genres where, if you want to do something with twelve clarinets, you can do it! It's open-ended in terms of creativity.'

The biggest challenge during recording sessions is working within the studio's and orchestra's time constraints. The composer needs to ensure that everything runs as smoothly and effectively as possible. When asked how he prepares, Academy Award nominee Daniel Pemberton – who's recorded over twenty scores at Abbey Road, including *The Trial of the Chicago 7* (2020), *See How They Run* (2022) and both *Spider-Man: Into the Spider-Verse* and *Across the Spider-Verse* (2018, 2023) – says, 'I'll spend ages going over the scores and really working out a game plan of how I'm going to approach it, which is in my head but not in anyone else's. And that can change. You might have, let's say, twenty pieces of music to record in four hours, and you might be like, "OK, these ones are going to be easy; this one is going to be tricky, it's going to eat up a lot of time; this one'll probably be tricky but I don't care about it, I'll just do it; and this one's got to be *amazing*, it's got to be the best moment in the entire film, so I'll spend loads of time on that." The whole thing is like a game of 3D chess.'

On the day of the recording session, engineer Barrett will have selected and positioned the microphones, and set the recording levels. Getting the sound balance right is crucial, but so too is the process of ensuring that each musician is able to hear whatever they need for their performance, including 'certain things like metronomes or backing tracks so they can play in time and in tune'. Barrett can also find himself serving as the engineer in the control room, becoming 'more involved in score production as well – asking for more takes or shaping the performances'. This of course varies depending on the composer, each of whom will decide how much input and support they do or don't need (or want) from him. It's a fine balancing act that requires a level of both musical and *social* dexterity. As Barrett says, 'You've just got to gauge that on the day.'

Barrett's earlier role was 'recordist' – one of several generally unsung heroes behind large-scale orchestral film scores. The arrival of digital editing software Pro Tools to Abbey Road in the early 2000s meant that the engineer no longer needed to fret that the tape might run out during a take, and also introduced the capability to record sections with specific parts of the orchestra separately, known as 'stems'. This gives the team more control to experiment with the volume levels of individual musical elements during the mix.

Ahead of the session, the recordist, or Pro Tools operator, builds a recording template with lots of input tracks assigned for specific sections of the orchestra, and they'll do much on-the-spot editing during the session because, as Barrett explains, 'you might end up recording lots of layers of things. Their preparation and being on top of what's going on is very important in the process because if it's not prepared well, you can lose lots of time and things can get very confusing.'

Composer Lorne Balfe, whose CV ranges from big-budget

action fare like the *Mission: Impossible* franchise (to which we'll return in Chapter 7, 'Play Through the Action') to animations like Aardman's most recent Wallace & Gromit outing, *Vengeance Most Fowl* (2024), is keen to sing the recordists' praises, 'because you're not playing pieces of music in one straight performance, you're playing sometimes individual bars and there's a lot of punching into the music, and speed is of great importance. It costs a lot of money to record with all these musicians and a recording studio, so time is of the essence.'

Balfe likes his orchestrator to be present during his recording sessions because 'they're the ones that have actually taken the notes that you've written and put them onto the manuscript paper for the musicians to play'. Orchestrators are also a lifeline for Amelia Warner, who doesn't have a traditional musical training, and who finds that recording sessions can be 'completely foreign territory'. For her, it's really important to have an orchestrator whom she trusts and engages with because 'I can't speak to the orchestra, I don't have that language. I literally sit there and say "I need it to go *'sings melody'*" and my orchestrator will go "OK" and they'll translate.'

Another key figure during a recording session is the music editor, who serves as a bridge between the film and the score. 'They don't get mentioned enough in the film music process,' says Balfe. 'They're essential! I always look at it as they know where the bodies are buried when it comes to the music because the composer will write it, and then the picture will continuously be being changed, and they're the ones that will make sure the music's always updated. Sometimes when you're scoring, you're already out of date because you're recording a month before the finish line.' As Abbey Road's John Barrett explains, the music editor 'has an understanding of where all of these new edits in the picture have happened, and then ultimately their job will be to take whatever we record and edit that together so that it works with the new picture.'

Reflecting on over forty years working in the film music industry, James Newton Howard sees the arrival of digital film editing software like Avid as presenting the greatest challenge for modern composers, since it allows the edit of a film to be in constant flux right up until the moment of release. In the past, a film editor would have to cut and splice footage manually, a time-consuming procedure that effectively prevented last-minute changes from being possible. But in the age of digital editing, the cut of a film can remain terrifyingly fluid almost until the release date. 'Now, it's not unusual to get three or four new cuts a week,' says Balfe. 'Every time they send me a new cut, I have to redo the music and that can go on for months – even to the point that a new cut can arrive *while* I'm recording. It's pretty hair-raising.'

An early – and extreme – example of this ever-changing-edit syndrome is Peter Jackson's big-budget blockbuster series *The Lord of the Rings* trilogy. Howard Shore's vivid, detailed and epic score is an enduring hit with film fans, but it was beset with challenges for many reasons, including multiple re-edits. For the first film, *The Fellowship of the Ring* (2001), Jackson cut scenes in New Zealand for which Howard Shore would compose music to be recorded at Abbey Road. The engineers would then mix the recordings onto a digital eight-track recorder, and then onto Pro Tools, before sending it to the final dubbing session in New Zealand – a lengthy task in itself because digital file-sharing was still in its infancy. By the time the sound file arrived in New Zealand, Jackson would have recut that scene, and the process would start all over again. Eventually the studio had to intervene by setting a completion date that ensured an end to the alterations.

Another significant player at recording sessions is – of course – the conductor, who has a number of responsibilities. Not only are they 'someone who stands out in front of the musicians and helps keep them in time and, on a very basic level, tries to get a performance out of them,' says John Barrett, but they're also 'a fantastic way for the control room to communicate with the musicians. It's an amazing way of being able to reduce that barrier created by being behind the glass. You've got that focal point who you can talk to, [and] it feels more personal for the musicians.'

London orchestras are renowned worldwide for their high pedigree of performance, and (equally importantly) for their ability to sight-read scores perfectly. If you think the film music you love the most was rehearsed to perfection before recording, think again. Maxine Kwok is a first violin in the London Symphony Orchestra and has been performing on film scores for decades. 'You go in, sit down, have a minute at the most to look at the music, and you may just start recording straight away because there's a limited window of time,' she says. 'Mostly, you probably rock up a bit early, go into the studio, have a quick look through, especially if you're a principal because you might find you've got some big solos. And you just start!' Nor are scores traditionally recorded in order, from the opening credits to the closing themes. Instead, the musicians can be thrown into a cue from the middle of the film and just be expected to keep up. 'Once the red light's on,' says Kwok, 'you've got to play flat out.'

Other recording session personnel might include the musicians' contractor, the composer's assistant, the runner and assistant to the engineering team, the copyist who prints out the music and checks it all beforehand (yes, studios like Abbey Road still use paper transcripts) and the technical engineers who set everything up for the recording rig. Plus, the director, producer, music supervisor and random studio executives may all be in the control room, alongside the odd actor or two who might turn up to experience the creation of such a significant part of the film.

It can become quite busy and, as Isobel Waller-Bridge puts it, 'really high pressured' because 'you've got lots of people in the room who are involved, and who also might have an opinion on things'. As Howard Shore observes, 'A lot of people don't understand the creation of music or the process, so it can generate misunderstanding that can develop into anxiety, and then the result is not good. You don't want anxiety when you're working on a film. I've never felt that with Cronenberg or Scorsese – those recordings were done with such good energy. But once you get into the worrying, or the anxiety of it, that kills the creativity, and that can destroy your work.' Jonny Greenwood refers to a friend who's worked as a conductor on a lot of scores, 'and he describes these situations of producers who have to sign off every single cue. And there are five producers and you need to get five ticks on every single thing before anything can even be recorded. And then they change their mind. And then you've got twelve hours to rewrite everything.'

'You've got a lot of cooks in the kitchen nowadays,' says soundtrack album producer, mixer, editor, film historian and preservationist Mike Matessino. 'You've got a *lot* of opinions. There's a feeling that back in the Golden Age, it would be left to the composer: "I know what I'm doing. I'll give you the score. I'll sit down with the director, and we'll map it out, and the score is done." You didn't have all these other people getting involved.'

Daniel Pemberton likens a typical recording session to frantically spinning plates, because 'you're trying to read the score, listen to the score, watch the picture, think about what you're meant to be doing in three cues' time, looking at your clock . . . it's probably the most intense brain activity I've ever had in my life. It's so intense and exhausting, but it's really thrilling when it goes right. When it goes wrong, *not* so thrilling.'

*

Depending on the project or preference, the composer may either be in the studio or behind the glass in the control room. 'Sometimes the composer might be the conductor,' explains John Barrett, 'or they could be the orchestrator as well. It varies.' Some composers prefer to be in the control room because they want to hear the music as it sounds on the recording, rather than in the performance room. Others want to be out there among the musicians, shaping the performance by talking directly to the orchestra. For example, if there is a flute solo, the composer may wish to have a specific dialogue with the flautist to ensure that the piece is played with certain nuances that are crucial to their vision of the score.

Barrett worked with Ludwig Göransson on his score for *Black Panther* (2018), for which the composer would win his first Oscar. 'The choir were dancing away,' he recalls. 'They were having a great time! I remember Ludwig was there, singing some of the stuff down the talkback to change the performances and get the rhythms how he wanted them. It was interesting because there was a lot more of him jumping on the talkback mic and just singing the ideas than would normally happen on other sessions. A lot of the time people are a bit more embarrassed or a bit shy, whereas I think because Ludwig had come from a pop background, he was straight on the talkback. Sing it down there, job done!'

While the composer tends to lead the recording session, it's clearly a group effort when it comes to getting the best results within the vital time and budgetary constraints. Daniel Pemberton credits the in-house team at Abbey Road with changing the way he creates scores by allowing for more flexibility during recordings. 'All the staff who work there are so good at getting things done quickly, being able to jump on changes and ideas,' he says. 'What that gave me as a composer was the realization that going into a recording session didn't need to be the end of the writing process. I could take the creativity that I'd had and the nimbleness of a home studio and take that into a massive environment.'

Depending on the project, Lorne Balfe will either conduct the orchestra himself or, if the director is in attendance, he'll be in the control room to respond to feedback and new ideas. 'When you've got your director with you,' he observes, 'you'll find this is now the next stage of the film-making process and the director will be inspired by it and say, "What happens if we try this?" or, "What does it sound like if they play really quietly?" So then the next level of experimentation begins.' As the London Symphony Orchestra's Maxine Kwok notes, 'The film director might be there and say, "I'm not sure if that works, I want to hear more of *this*." So changes happen on the spot. Things need to be done quickly, so when you're on, you need to be *on*.'

Pemberton recalls a particular cue from Danny Boyle's 2015 biopic *Steve Jobs* as an example of adjusting a score during a session. And by 'adjusting' I mean 'rewriting'. 'Everything was going great except for this one cue,' he says, 'which is the one everyone likes, called "Revenge". And that was an absolute headfuck of a process.' Pemberton remembers that he was reworking the piece over and over again as the studio clock was ticking. Yet despite time running out, he just couldn't get it to a place with which Boyle and his editor were happy. Finally, at the eleventh hour, Pemberton arrived at a version which he felt would work, and promptly told his orchestrator, Andrew Skeet, to go ' "hide in a pub because as soon as this is signed off, you're going to have to orchestrate this!" Then they hear it, they love it – thumbs up!'

Skeet worked overnight on the orchestration, and the next morning the whole orchestra played the new version for the first time. 'It's so huge,' Pemberton recalls. 'It's the biggest thing you've ever heard. My agent's there and he goes, "This is amazing!" But Danny says, "No, this is *not* what I want, this is *way* too big."' After which Pemberton had to start pulling the piece apart *again*.

'It was *insanely* stressful, but everyone's helping you. And I want to help Danny achieve what he wants because he's a brilliant film-maker and he has a vision. So you have to really work very quickly – "OK, what if we take this bit out, record this separately." That piece, for me, always reminds me of this incredibly stressful time, with this huge orchestra, trying to get it to how Danny wanted it. But we got there!'

Attending a recording session at Abbey Road is a fascinating experience, not least because watching an orchestra play *note-perfect* a piece they are reading for the first time always seems like an extraordinary magic trick. Even more intriguing is the effect that the studio space has upon the music and its recording. Studio 1 is vast and famously has a lot of reverb. John Barrett says he loves the way the studio responds to the dynamics of a performance, 'so if it's quiet, it can actually sound quite contained and a bit dry, and when it gets louder it becomes more reverberant.' Barrett cites Alexandre Desplat's Oscar-winning score for *The Shape of Water*, which involves a lot of strings being played very softly, as a perfect example of the studio's versatility. While Studio 1 can create a 'big and massive' sound for the action-packed strains of a Marvel score (the physical size of the studio allows for a large number of players), it also proved perfect for the more low-key feel of Desplat's score, providing a sonic environment that is surprisingly intimate when considering the sheer space of the room.

According to Barrett, Studio 2 (The Beatles' favourite recording space) 'feels a lot more contained, a lot more controllable, and you can make things a lot more intimate there . . . Typically in Studio 2, you would do much smaller-size ensembles, and you would be more likely to record things separately. So you would record the strings and woodwinds maybe, as a separate session, and then the brass as a separate session, and then you'd do percussion. So you're layering things up. Whereas in Studio 1, the great thing about that room is that you can almost do everything together. You can finish a cue in half an hour – it's done.'

It all adds up to a lot of work, a huge amount of invention, and a healthy dose of trial and error – chaotic perhaps, yet ultimately creative and inspiring. But considering how much effort it takes to mount a studio recording, and bearing in mind the quality of modern composers' digital demos and how close they can now get to the 'real' thing, are we in any danger of AI-assisted technology making orchestras obsolete? Why go to the bother and cost of recording an orchestral score if technology can give you a decent imitation at a fraction of the price? What do we gain from live musicians that can't be captured in the digitally sampled demos that have been approved in advance by the studio and the director?

'Weirdly, the way I've always looked at it is that what you capture are the mistakes and the imperfections,' says Lorne Balfe, whose score for the Marvel film *Black Widow* (which wrapped in 2019, but didn't release until 2021) featured the biggest orchestra ever seen at Abbey Road, with a total of 116 musicians. It also happened to be the last film score session at the studio before the Covid lockdown came into force in 2020 – hence the delayed release.

'The thing is, the samples are *perfect*, and that's the point of them. They're perfect, they're clean, and they also have one singular voice, in one respect, to the performance. And really that's where technology suffers. Every studio you record in has got a different tone, every orchestra has got a different performance, and that's fundamentally what I look for. What we want when we're doing large orchestras, or *any* orchestra recording, is to have that recording that is *not* perfect. It sounds strange because obviously you want a "perfect" recording. But it's because of eighty musicians all having individual voices that brings this unique tone to it.'

'It's that human quality,' says John Barrett. 'It's just that extra 20 per cent or something – you just get that shape, that emotion, that *feeling*. You can have a cue that can be really simple and it won't work with samples. Then you play it with the orchestra and it just magically comes together. It could just be a sustained chord that crescendos and gets slightly more out of tune and then goes back in again, and you can't do that with samples.'

*

Clearly, even in the modern digital age, the fusion of live performance with a range of players and instrumentation brings something special to a film score. But German-born British composer Max Richter surely holds the award for the most unusual instrument ever to grace a soundtrack – whether acoustic *or* electronic. A polymath who works across a range of genres (his CV includes composing, arranging and performing music for theatre, opera, ballet and screen, collaborating with performance, installation and media artists), Richter achieved record-breaking success when his 2015 album *Sleep* – an eight-hour concept album designed around the neuroscience of sleep – became the most-streamed classical album of all time. In cinema, he won a European Film Award for Best Composer for his hauntingly inventive score for Ari Folman's animated documentary *Waltz with Bashir* (2007), and he provided a bracing orchestral accompaniment to Josie Rourke's period drama *Mary Queen of Scots* (2018), which channelled the spirit of Handel's 'Zadok the Priest'. Richter also composed a hugely atmospheric score (augmented by some 'additional music' from Lorne Balfe) for James Gray's compromised but still occasionally arresting moody space epic *Ad Astra* (2019).

Most famously, Richter composed and performed 'On the Nature of Daylight', a piece that first appeared on his 2004 album *The Blue Notebooks*, and which has subsequently reappeared in a dizzying number of film and television projects, from Martin Scorsese's psychodrama potboiler *Shutter Island* (2010) to Denis Villeneuve's breathtaking 2016 sci-fi pic *Arrival* (on which it serves as both opener and closer, eclipsing Jóhann Jóhannsson's score), to the first season of the groundbreaking HBO video game adaptation *The Last of Us* (2023).

One of Richter's lesser-known scores, however, includes his most intriguing instrumentation. The end credits of Scott Cooper's revisionist Western *Hostiles* (2017) list all the players involved in recording Richter's score, including a credit for an instrument called the Yaybahar. Having never heard of a 'Yay-bahar' before, I googled it, and discovered – after much trial and error – that it is a Turkish instrument invented (and played) by musician Görkem Şen. It looks like a tricycle crossed with a bedstead and involves a baffling assortment of springs, wires and vibrating membranes that can be variously hit, bowed and bent. The sound it produces is ethereal and oddly earthy, like the strange growly orchestral washes that a Moog synthesizer can create. But the Yaybahar (and at that point, there was only *one* of them in existence, so it really was *the* Yaybahar) is an entirely acoustic instrument, generating only organic sounds, without need for electronic wizardry.

'I wanted the landscape of the film to have a voice of its own,' Richter told me when I asked him about his use of this extraor-dinary instrument in the recordings of the *Hostiles* score. 'This voice should not be recognizable as an acoustic instrument,' he continued, before adding, 'I also wanted to avoid anything electronic. I was looking for something that felt abstract, alien and other.'

Richter started searching around for something that would fit the bill and came across a video of Şen's Yaybahar in Istanbul. So he headed out there to record it. 'As far as I know,' he tells me, 'it's not been recorded before or since. Most of the drones and sustained textures in the film are made by a combination of the Yaybahar and avant-garde orchestral techniques. The orchestra acts as a kind of resonating chamber for the Yaybahar and vice versa.'

The result is both subtle and affecting, as if the landscape of the film were speaking directly to the characters and to the audi-ence. Moreover, the fact that Richter recorded the Yaybahar in Istanbul and the rest of the score at Air Studios' grand Lyndhurst

Hall in London (one of the world's largest recording rooms) offers an insight into the ways in which various forms of music creation can be brought together to make a single coherent soundscape.

Richter's score for *Hostiles* is a richly complex work, issued on the Deutsche Grammophon label, which has a reputation for bringing the very best orchestral works to the most discerning listeners. Yet Richter's adoption of the Yaybahar somehow allows that score (which features the renowned London Voices choral ensemble alongside the orchestra) to break the confines of even that vast studio, reaching out across the world to some strange and wondrous places, while remaining firmly rooted in the landscape of virtuoso live performance.

As for the wider body of film music, the studio recording session – be it at Abbey Road, Air, or elsewhere – remains the culmination of the composer's hard work, where their vision is made real, and it can produce a thrilling alchemy in which everything gels and the film is conjured more fully into existence. As Lorne Balfe says, 'The stressful thing is the initial beginning of the process: writing. Being able to record with the best musicians in the world should be pleasurable.'

Last word to Anne Dudley, who describes the orchestral recording experience as 'the culmination of months and months of work, when you finally get into the studio with however many musicians and a whole new thing happens. Because no matter how good your demos are, they're not going to be as good as having world-class musicians play your notes. It's always a thrill.'

Soundtrack Selection:
Brazil (1985)

A cold, cold winter was struggling to turn into a supposedly uplifting spring when I first saw Terry Gilliam's dystopian master-piece *Brazil* at the Odeon Oxford Road in Manchester in early 1985. I remember everything about that screening as if it were yesterday – the slightly fading grandeur of the cinema; the astonishing visual impact of Gilliam's future-retro world (think 'Steampunk George Orwell meets Borowczyk's *Goto, Island of Love*'); the weird Christmas setting which turned Santa Claus into a murderous dictator; and the ultimate triumph of the imagination over the hideous pain of the 'real' world.

At the end of the movie, Jonathan Pryce's romantic-dreamer-turned-accidental-rebel Sam Lowry is strapped into a torture chair that combines the horrors of past inquisitions with the nightmare of future regimes, about to be hideously assaulted by a man wearing a baby-mask – the collision of the childish face and the pointed object held in his captor's hand merely ampli-fying the anguish. To make matters worse, the man behind the mask is Jack Lint (Michael Palin), a 'friend' who now blames Sam for putting them both in this terrible position.

And then, just as the torture is set to begin, Sam's imagination intervenes and dramatic liberation falls from the sky . . .

'He's got away from us, Jack,' declares Peter Vaughan's Mr Helpmann, despite the fact that Sam is still right there in front of him, bound and incapable. Yet Sam has indeed made his escape, signalled by his humming of Ary Barroso's popular 1939 tune 'Aquarela do Brasil' (literally, 'Watercolour of Brazil'). As the camera pulls back and the credits start to roll, we hear the carnivalesque sounds of Michael Kamen's 'Bachianos Brazil Samba' and feel the spirit of Sam flying away beyond the confines of this prison – free at last, even if only in his mind.

It's a devastating ending and, as the lights went up, my friend Duncan Cooper and I made our way in silence to the darkened stairwell to exit the cinema. After a while, I turned to Duncan and said simply, 'My God, that was . . . amazing.' To which Duncan replied, 'What? It was terrible. *Terrible*. Absolute rubbish.' I was shocked! We had both sat there in the same cinema, watching the same film, hearing the same music, and (surely) having the *same* experience. But no – apparently we'd seen completely different movies, one of which was life-changing, the other of which was an utter waste of time.

Over the years I've come to treasure that memory, not least because it perfectly embodies the duality at the centre of *Brazil* – the eternal battle between the worlds of the past and future, the internal and the external, the real and the imagined, the triumphant and the tragic. To this day, if things get really difficult, I find myself involuntarily humming 'Brazil' (as 'Aquarela do Brasil' is more commonly known in the English-speaking world), and remembering the look of serene absence on Jonathan Pryce's face as the world around him descends into madness which can no longer touch him.

Many years after that first viewing, when I was working at Radio 1, my great colleague and now much-missed friend Bob McCabe went to a launch at the Roundhouse in Camden for the newly issued soundtrack CD of *Brazil* – a launch which gave me an excuse to run a feature on the score, and then to play tracks from it every week on my film show. Indeed, I loved that CD so much that we adopted the cue 'Central Services: The Office' as the bed for our regular news update section, the sound of percussive typewriters providing an urgently satirical backdrop to all the latest movie gossip.

Gilliam's battles with studio head Sid Sheinberg, who *hated* the director's cut of *Brazil*, are well rehearsed, with Sheinberg desperate to give the film a 'happy' ending before allowing anyone to see it. During those struggles, the score by Michael Kamen – one of the most important elements of the film – nearly hit the floor, as Universal attempted to turn a dark vision of the future into an upbeat entertainment that would leave audiences smiling.

'Just before Christmas I heard they were tossing the score and shopping for a new composer,' Kamen remembered. 'My friends said that would put me in the ranks with the greats, but I was totally desolate. I was working on another film, but I couldn't think – I was calling Terry constantly and saying, "Say it isn't so!" and he'd say, "Don't worry!"'

The fact that Gilliam held firm and remained true to his vision turned *Brazil* into one of the most written-about science fiction movies of the modern era, spawning Jack Matthews' must-read book *The Battle of Brazil: Terry Gilliam vs Universal Pictures in the Fight to the Final Cut*. Perhaps more importantly, it reminded filmgoers and film critics alike of the symbiotic relationship between movies and their music – a relationship in which, at best, each feeds off the other in inseparable fashion.

Gilliam's inspiration for *Brazil* famously occurred in Port Talbot, Wales, where he was scouting locations. The area was bleak, particularly the beach, which was overcast and doom-laden. Yet on that beach was a man with a transistor radio, listening to music that conjured up a faraway paradise entirely removed from this downbeat, depressing reality. That image gave birth to the film, which Gilliam promptly insisted would be called *Brazil*, despite the objections of almost everyone to whom he pitched the idea. (The movie had been developed under the title *1984½*, a name which cheekily combined the legacy of George Orwell with a hint of Fellini, whom Gilliam regularly cited as one of his key directorial influences.)

When Kamen came on board as composer, Gilliam asked him to build his music around the themes of Barroso's 'Brazil', variously reinterpreting it through melodies and leitmotifs that could embody the warring ideas of the movie: the crushing bureaucracy of the near future; the overcrowded bustle of an oppressive totalitarian world in which posters declare, 'Don't Suspect a Friend – Report Them!'; and the rich internal fantasy life in which Sam grows wings, falls in love and battles monsters, both real and imagined.

'After a while, Terry had talked me into thinking I had *written* "Brazil"', Kamen said in 1986 of the tune which sparked the director's imagination. 'I assimilated that piece until it was coming out of my ears. In fact, it's *still* coming out of my ears.'

'Imagine someone saying "Can you base your entire score on this please?"' says Mirek Stiles, head of audio products at Abbey Road studios where Kamen's *Brazil* score was recorded. 'Michael Kamen was so concerned about the publishing rights that he hired specialists to listen to all the cues he'd written to try and work it out and see who was owed what. I think he was pleasantly surprised that they said, "We can't really see a huge amount of resemblance." But he still managed to capture the essence of it.'

Kamen's score was the first to be recorded at Abbey Road following the installation of a new state-of-the-art control room, replacing its sideways-on predecessor which had provided a restricted view of the performers in the studio, about which artists were starting to complain. 'Back then we were still finding our feet,' says Stiles. 'Michael Kamen was the first session with that brand-new control room. He was here for about thirteen weeks doing that score and he used pretty much every studio here.' By comparison, *Return of the Jedi* was recorded at Abbey Road in a mere ten days. 'I think in total, Kamen worked on the score for six months with [music coordinator] Ray Cooper,' says Stiles, who stresses the extraordinary level of experimentation involved in creating the *Brazil* soundtrack. 'He was using all sorts of instruments – kazoos, typewriters as percussion – just really creative scoring.'

The results speak for themselves. Drop into any track from Kamen's OST (Original Soundtrack) and you will immediately be transported to the world of Gilliam's fertile imagination; a world in which dreams really can come true, but only if we abandon 'reality' and let our musical thoughts take flight. Nestled amid that OST are some hidden gems, such as a recording of Kate Bush evocatively performing the title song, prefaced by the sublimely agitated sounds of Ian Holm demanding: 'Ah, has anybody seen Lowry? Has *anybody seen SAM LOWRY?*'

But of course, Sam is nowhere to be found – having disappeared into his dreams, lifted above the clouds by Kamen's stirring orchestration, which promises to take the listener to equally dizzying heights, time and time again.

CHAPTER 6

Switched-On Electronica

Among the most exciting and affecting film scores of the twenty-first century is Scottish composer Anna Meredith's startling electronic accompaniment to Bo Burnham's sublime 2018 coming-of-age tale *Eighth Grade*. Burnham's brilliantly empathetic first feature has been described by its writer/director as 'an attempt to represent the kids who live their lives online'; youngsters who have been 'mischaracterised as self-obsessed, narcissistic, shallow', but who are actually 'self-conscious'. At the centre of the movie is rising star Elsie Fisher, who is astonishingly natural as Kayla, a socially anxious thirteen-year-old approaching the end of middle school. Crushingly voted 'most quiet' in class, Kayla struggles to connect with her peers in person, passing in silence through the corridors of her school. Yet Kayla has a second life online, where she posts cute selfies and self-help videos on 'Being Yourself' and 'Putting Yourself Out There'. Undeterred by the fact that no one is watching, this engaging soul seems to be using her vlog channel to talk to herself, like the time-capsule video message she buried a few years ago as 'a gift to a future you'.

While Fisher may be the star of the film, Anna Meredith's

soundtrack to *Eighth Grade* is every bit as crucial to its success as the actor's beguiling central performance. Meredith's score interweaves music written specifically for the movie with a sprinkling of existing pieces from her previous electronic repertoire. One such is 'Nautilus', a track Meredith first unveiled on her 2012 EP *Black Prince Fury*, and which *GQ* magazine hailed in 2019 as the 'Go-To Song for Personal Hell' after it resurfaced in the soundtrack to Netflix's 'existential dramedy' *Living with Yourself*. Describing Meredith's work as a 'trance-inducing barrage of sound . . . pure maximalist mayhem', *GQ* called her 'the most exciting composer to break out since Mica Levi and Nicholas Britell' – an assessment that is entirely justified.

A former composer-in-residence with the BBC Scottish Symphony Orchestra, Meredith emerged from the classical music scene, first gaining widespread acclaim with a composition she created for the 2008 Last Night of the Proms, which was broadcast by the BBC to an audience of over forty million people. In 2009, Meredith was the classical music nominee for the Times Breakthrough Award, and the next year she won one of the Paul Hamlyn Foundation Awards for Composers. But it was her move into electronic composition that proved a crucial career development, leading to her 2016 album *Varmints*, on which 'Nautilus' serves as an arresting curtain-raiser, winning the Scottish Album of the Year Award.

Asked what first drew her to film composition, Meredith tells me, 'I remember seeing *Jaws* when I was quite young. I saw it with a friend who said, "You'll *know* the shark's coming because of the *music!*" I remember latching onto that, and hiding under my seat whenever the music kicked in. In a way that was the dropping of the veil of childhood. I remember realizing there and then that not everything was designed to make you feel good, or feel secure.'

As a student composer Meredith first experimented with combining her music with visual material, working with up-and-coming animators and visual artists on short experimental pieces, but had yet to work on anything narrative. *Eighth Grade* was her first feature film score, although some early original scoring work made its way onto *Emilia Pérez*-director Jacques Audiard's earlier work *Dheepan* (2015). Meredith was asked to compose some original cues of which one was used in the film, but on the whole the energy wasn't exactly what the director was after: 'He wrote me this lovely email, being so kind about the strength and confidence in the music I'd written but that it wasn't quite the right fit.' By this stage, however, she'd caught the film-scoring bug. The growing interest in Meredith's work in film circles brought her to the attention of Greek director Yorgos Lanthimos, the offbeat auteur behind films like *Dog-tooth* (2009), *The Lobster* (2015) and *The Killing of a Sacred Deer* (2017). Although, as we have noted, he has recently struck up a fruitful relationship with British composer Jerskin Fendrix, Lanthimos had not yet worked with a composer when he came to make his Oscar-courting international hit *The Favourite* (2018). As Lanthimos told me in 2023, 'I am always searching, really *searching* – listening to music. And when I was preparing *The Favourite* I thought it might be good to try and work with Anna.'

Meredith wrote some original electronic pieces for the film but the director was after more acoustic instrumentation, so he ended up using some of her existing tracks which he'd already selected for the temp. 'The problem wasn't that the new music wasn't good,' Lanthimos clarifies, he just preferred the 'exact tone' of the pieces with which he was already working. These came from Meredith's 2005 composition *Songs for the M8*, performed by the Renoir Quartet, an ensemble formed in 1995 who won the Ministry of Culture Prize at the Bordeaux International Competition in 2023. *Songs for the M8* is an acoustic work featuring violins, viola and cello rather than the synth sounds with which Meredith was now working. Since *The Favourite* was a period piece, set in the reign of Queen Anne, the quartet's strings felt more appropriate to Lanthimos's vision, despite the anachronistic modernity of his film.

Things were very different when Meredith came to work with Bo Burnham on *Eighth Grade*. This time, Meredith's credentials as a leading electronics composer with a background in more traditional orchestration made her a perfect fit for a tale of age-old anxieties in a very modern world. 'The way that Bo found me for *Eighth Grade* was the result of a very specific shopping list,' Meredith tells me. 'He wanted a classically trained composer who had moved into electronics; he wanted someone who had "warmth" at the core of their sound; and ideally he wanted a woman. That was the list he had – and honestly that list didn't include a huge amount of people!'

Meredith explains that Burnham had very strong aspirations for the role of music in the film and was happy to follow her lead at times. He had initially intended for the opening cue to be another composer's pre-existing track but Anna was keen to create something herself to keep it in her voice, 'and in the end, very sweetly, he had to re-edit the scene to work musically around the time signatures and musical cycles that I wrote. He said later on that he was glad he did – which was encouraging.' Meredith's skills were put to the test when the film was being completed to a tight turnaround in time for the Sundance festival: 'I remember it was Christmas Eve and I was back at my parents' house in Edinburgh. And the film company got in touch and said, "Look, we've tried all this other music and it's now just *so* much in your voice – can you write something for the end credits? The only thing is, we need it *tomorrow*." '

The fact that Meredith was able to compose and record such a significant piece of music for *Eighth Grade* at such short notice, with no access to other musicians, says much about the way that electronica has changed – and perhaps *democratized* – film music. In her fascinating 2020 documentary, *Sisters with Transistors*, film-maker Lisa Rovner makes a compelling case for the radical potential of synthesized sounds to break down barriers in music production – specifically gender barriers. From the experimental music pioneer Clara Rockmore, who achieved international celebrity as the world's premier thereminist, to British composer Delia Derbyshire, who conjured the sounds of *Doctor Who* under the banner of the BBC Radiophonic Workshop, and 'diva of the diode' Suzanne Ciani, who has been hailed as the first solo female composer to score a major Hollywood feature, Rovner's documentary maps the rise of women composers alongside the evolution of electronica, suggesting compellingly that the two stories are inextricably intertwined.

The paths that lead each of Rovner's subjects into the field of electronica are varied and diverse. Daphne Oram, a British trailblazer of *musique concrète* (an experimental compositional form that uses recorded sounds as its raw materials), was one of the first women to set up a personal electronic music studio. In 1942 she turned down a place at the Royal College of Music to become a BBC studio engineer, a move that led her into tape experimentation and soundtrack design. (The groundbreaking work of Oram's contemporary, Scottish electro-pioneer Janet

Beat, would later provide archival inspiration for the brilliant 2024 low-budget synth-based horror *Dead Mail*.) Clara Rockmore, conversely, was a prodigiously talented violinist who, at the age of four in 1915, became the youngest ever student at the St Petersburg Conservatory. Later, she attended the Curtis Institute of Music in America, where her violin skills continued to astonish. But the onset of tendinitis caused problems with her bowing arm, restricting her playing. For a while it seemed that her physical ailment might have blighted her musical career, but through a friendship with fellow Soviet émigré Leon Theremin, a cellist and scientist, Rockmore (née Reisenberg) discovered an electronic instrument that utilized her prodigious fingering skills without making the physical demands upon her arms and hands that the violin required. Rockmore and Theremin became good friends (he reportedly proposed to her more than once) and she worked closely with him, refining the instrument to which he gave his name.

*

The theremin became a defining element in the evolution of electronic film soundtracks, as explored in Steven M. Martin's Sundance Award-winning documentary *Theremin: An Electronic Odyssey* (1993). Tracing Leon's life story from his time in a Soviet gulag to international tours showcasing his invention, Martin's lively doc details the numerous films for which the theremin provided a signature sound. The Oscar-winning Hungarian composer Miklós Rózsa, for example, famously featured a theremin in three of his film scores; for Hitchcock's psychological thriller *Spellbound* and Billy Wilder's drunken film noir *The Lost Weekend*, both in 1945; and then again in Delmer Daves's less celebrated 1947 thriller *The Red House*. For Rózsa, the theremin provided a window into the variously unhinged psyches of the characters for whom he was writing – whether it was Gregory Peck's dissociative amnesia in *Spellbound*, gloriously manifested in Salvador Dalí's nightmarish dreamscapes, or the existential despair of Ray Milland's bedraggled alcoholic in *The Lost Weekend*, struggling his way through the eerie fog of addiction. A decade later, Elmer Bernstein would use a theremin to accompany a ghostly appearance of the Angel of Death in Cecil B. DeMille's 1956 revisiting of *The Ten Commandments*, to striking effect.

While Rózsa's work with the theremin brilliantly exploited its ability to dramatize off-kilter psychological states, it was Bernard Herrmann who would cement the theremin's reputation as the instrument of choice for science fiction films. Adapted from Harry Bates's 1940 short story 'Farewell to the Master', Robert Wise's *The Day the Earth Stood Still* was a bold release for 20th Century Fox in 1951 – a sombre black-and-white interstellar adventure that played out entirely on Earth, containing a dire warning for mankind in the age of nuclear weapons and potential space travel. The enigmatically tall and slender Michael Rennie played Klaatu, a visitor from outer space who arrives in a sleek flying saucer that lands in Washington DC. Lock Martin, towering over the 6'4" Rennie (Lock was over seven foot), portrayed Gort – the silvery robot who is Klaatu's minder, and from whose faceless visage comes a vaporizing ray that initially terrorizes the humans. But Klaatu and Gort have come in peace, to tell mankind that unless we adjust our aggressive ways, members of other planets who have been watching us may decide to step in and 'eliminate' Earth. 'Your choice is simple,' Klaatu declares. 'Join us and live in peace, or pursue your present course and face obliteration.'

Although *The Day the Earth Stood Still* is comparatively sparse on spectacular visual effects, its reputation as a groundbreaking science fiction picture was earned in no small part thanks to Herrmann's score. Having recently moved from New York to Hollywood, Herrmann – who had already earned three Oscar nominations (for *Citizen Kane*, 1941; the statuette-winning *The Devil and Daniel Webster*, 1941; and *Anna and the King of Siam*, 1946) – decided to mix electronic and acoustic instruments to conjure a futuristic accompaniment to the 'present day' drama. Along with electric violins and cellos and a selection of electronic keyboard organs, Herrmann employed not one but *two* thereminists to create the film's duelling theme. Outtakes of Samuel J. Hoffman and Paul Shure recording the harmonized theremin parts (one higher, one lower) confirm just how complicated it was for this notoriously sensitive instrument to be doubled-up on a single track. As any thereminist knows, theremins react to very small changes in heat and moisture in a manner that makes pitching them particularly difficult. Yet through a process of live recordings and tape reversals, Herrmann built a science fiction score that would be imitated for years to come, with the ghostly sound of the theremin wedded forever to outer space.

Herrmann's out-of-this-world work with theremins was not without precedent. In 1947, Samuel J. Hoffman had played the theremin on *Music Out of the Moon: Music Unusual Featuring the Theremin – Themes by Harry Revel*, a cassette tape of which Neil Armstrong took with him on the Apollo 11 spacecraft in 1969. That compilation included 'Lunar Rhapsody', a theremin melody that later featured heavily in Damien Chazelle's space travel biopic *First Man* (2018), inspiring composer Justin Hurwitz to learn the instrument himself and play it as part of that film's score. Meanwhile, Danny Elfman, who cites Herrmann's score for *The Day the Earth Stood Still* as a formative influence in his own journey to becoming a film composer, turned to the theremin (and its soundalike stand-in, the ondes Martenot) for Tim Burton's spoofy space pastiche *Mars Attacks!* (1996), echoing its use by Howard Shore in Burton's earlier work *Ed Wood* (1994), an affectionate account of the film-maker behind 'the worst movie ever made', 1959's *Plan 9 from Outer Space*.

Herrmann's 1951 score clearly had a huge influence on the science fiction genre, but in terms of the development of electronic film scores, *The Day the Earth Stood Still* laid the groundwork for a far more adventurous work that would follow five years later – a film that would provoke both amazement and outrage for its total rejection of traditional musical sounds in favour of something altogether more experimental.

*

Shot in CinemaScope and Eastmancolor, and marketed with the single-word tagline 'Amazing!', *Forbidden Planet* was one of MGM's flagship releases in 1956, an ambitious science fiction fantasy that took inspiration from Shakespeare's *The Tempest* and promised to transport viewers to strange new worlds where they would encounter new life and ancient civilizations. The film's iconically eye-catching poster featured the supine form of Anne Francis's Altaira in the giant mechanical arms of Robby the Robot – a creature that cost so much to build he would subsequently be rolled out in a string of inferior film and TV projects, earning the sardonic nickname 'the hardest working robot in showbusiness'.

Forbidden Planet was an ambitious attempt to create something serious and meaningful within a genre that had often been derided as little more than a camp curiosity. Sure, the history of much modern cinema was built upon the sturdy foundations of Fritz Lang's silent 1927 German masterpiece *Metropolis*, and films like Alexander Korda's 1936 British production *Things to Come* had brought H. G. Wells's vision of the future to the screen in what cultural historian Christopher Frayling would call 'a landmark in cinematic design'. But years of *Flash Gordon* serials had lent a sheen of disreputability to science fiction on screen, a stigma that MGM were determined to dispel once and for all with *Forbidden Planet*.

Budgeted at close to $2 million (an extremely high figure for a 'genre picture' in those days), director Fred M. Wilcox's movie scored a number of significant firsts, including being the first major feature film to depict mankind travelling faster than the speed of light in a spaceship, allowing the action to play out in a distant solar system. More significantly, it would also become the first studio feature film in *any* genre to boast an entirely electronic score, breaking the decades-long mould of orchestral accompaniments that had flourished in the wake of the invention of synchronized sound.

Throughout the thirties and forties, Hollywood film studios had increasingly relied upon their in-house orchestras to lend a key element of drama, comedy, romance and mystery to their big-screen productions, with sought-after classical composers often finding themselves in back-to-back employment creating music for the movies. A production such as *Forbidden Planet*, with its sweeping planetary vistas and action-adventure-romance narrative seemed ideal for the full-scale orchestral treatment, with the music emphasizing the scope and grandeur of the production. Traditional composer David Rose was initially enlisted to write and record a score, while experimental music pioneer Harry Partch, whose work involved microtonal tunings beyond the scope of the standard twelve-tone Western octave, was approached to come up with more futuristic elements. Both were ultimately superseded, however, by Bebe and Louis Barron, who had collaborated with the likes of Ian Hugo and Anaïs Nin (and, later, Maya Deren) on experimental short films, and who now made their first (and only) foray into scoring a full-length feature film.

Brought onto *Forbidden Planet* by MGM executive producer Dore Schary, the Barrons created seventy minutes of soundtrack material in their bespoke New York studio after stubbornly refusing MGM's attempts to relocate them to Hollywood. In hindsight, this was to prove a key creative move, establishing a form of independence that would flourish within the electronic film score world. The fact that MGM agreed to the Barrons' insistence that they make their music in *their* studio indicates just how invested they had become in the couple's creative endeavours, even if few understood the processes involved in that creation. As it was, *Forbidden Planet* would become the first MGM feature film to have its score entirely produced outside of the confines of the studio lot.

Explaining their working methods on the sleeve notes for the long-delayed *Forbidden Planet* soundtrack album, Bebe and Louis describe how they built circuits which they viewed as 'cybernetic organisms', using 'individual cybernetic circuits for particular themes and leitmotifs, rather than using standard sound generators'. These circuits were contained within vacuum tubes in which they would live and die – slowly burning out as they produced electronic vibrations that could be amplified and recorded, creating a library of sounds from which to compose music. Bebe would later describe the activation of the circuits to composer Jane Brockman as 'a burst of the most glorious kind of energy', after which they would fall silent, never to be revived.

From the outset, the Barrons were determined not to reproduce familiar sounds, but instead set out to create a brand-new sonic world to accompany the film's unique vision, discarding anything that sounded like an instrument. Nevertheless, the couple's screen credit of 'Electronic Tonalities by' (rather than 'Music by') was more the result of a contractual wrangle than of any artistic manifesto. The Barrons did not belong to the Musicians Union, and a contract lawyer from the American Federation of Musicians ensured that MGM did not credit their contribution as 'music'. Despite awestruck responses from critics and audiences alike, the Barrons thus missed out on Oscar eligibility, with only 'special effects' being nominated. As for a soundtrack album, that didn't materialize until 1976, a full twenty years after the film's initial release. (David Rose's ditched theme from *Forbidden Planet* became available on record years before the Barrons' 'tonalities' were published on disc.) Nevertheless, Bebe and Louis Barron would take their place in the history books as co-creators of the silver screen's first all-electronic feature score, inspiring subsequent generations of electronic composers to strike out in their own individual manner, beyond the confines of traditional studio scoring.

*

While the fifties saw the advent of electronic scores, it wasn't until the end of the seventies that the genre achieved the respectability of an Oscar win. Alan Parker's *Midnight Express* (1978), adapted from Billy Hayes's memoir of the same name, told the gruelling story of Hayes's imprisonment in – and eventual escape from – a Turkish prison, after being convicted of hashish possession. Despite being marketed with the tagline 'It couldn't happen, but it *did*', the film (which was scripted by Oliver Stone) took several liberties with its true-story source, fictionalizing both Hayes's time in captivity and his escape, and presenting a distinctly colonial Western worldview that was widely criticized as being 'anti-Turkish'. Nevertheless, the film remains a powerful viewing experience, greatly enhanced by a pulsing electronic score from Italian composer/producer Giorgio Moroder, who (along with Stone) became one of the film's two Oscar winners.

Known within pop-music circles as the 'Father of Disco', Moroder had founded the Musicland Studios in Munich in the early seventies, where his experimentations with Moog synthesizers had produced several hit singles. In 1977, alongside releasing his own synth-driven album and single 'From Here to Eternity', Moroder effectively kick-started Hi-NRG disco with Donna Summer's genre-defining 'I Feel Love'. An earworm classic in which the entire backing track seems to throb to the rhythm of the song, 'I Feel Love' transformed the sound of seventies dancehall pop, spawning a generation of imitators who would take Moroder's backing track as a blueprint for future hits. Indeed, when Parker approached Moroder to score *Midnight Express*, he reportedly asked him to create a cue that would have the same urgent energy as 'I Feel Love'. The resulting song, 'Chase', became an instrumental disco hit in its own right, with Harold Faltermeyer's arrangements turning the track (which featured an insistent Minimoog bassline and skipping Roland SH-2000 top-line melody) into a key Hi-NRG cut. As *Pitchfork* magazine noted in 2006: 'It's impossible to state, let alone list, the amount of composers and films who've ripped off "Chase" – it's responsible for a *lot* of deeply uncool '80s kitsch music (much of it produced by Moroder himself) but also for a lot of undeniably transcendent moments.'

When I interviewed Alan Parker for a BBC radio documentary in the nineties, he told me that what had attracted him to Moroder was the speed and efficiency with which he was able to work. Budgeted at a very moderate $2.3 million (it would go on to take over $35 million worldwide, making it both one of the most successful movies of the year and the *cheapest* Best Picture contender at the 51st Oscars), Parker's sophomore cinematic feature was a tight production. 'I remember being impressed that [Moroder] could just conjure this music pretty much all by himself,' Parker told me. 'We'd talk about the music, and what we felt each scene required, and he'd just go off and make it happen – right there in his studio. It was oddly liberating – these compact machines, but these very *big* possibilities.'

Moroder would go on to become one of the foremost electronic film composers, collaborating with writer/director Paul Schrader on *Cat People* (1982) and *American Gigolo* (1985), and earning two further Oscars for his Original Song compositions on *Flashdance* (1983) and *Top Gun* (1986). Yet, decades after its release, Moroder would continue to cite *Midnight Express* as his most rewarding screen experience, capped off by that history-making Academy Award win, which seemed to signal a sea change in the film industry's approach to electronic music.

For all its groundbreaking qualities, however, *Midnight Express* did not arrive ex nihilo – rather, it arrived in the immediate wake of a number of influential electronic scores, including one for a film that had flopped a year earlier, in 1977, but whose synth soundtrack would later be recognized as a milestone of the genre.

*

American director William Friedkin first saw German synth pioneers Tangerine Dream playing live in 1974, in their best-known line-up consisting of Peter Baumann, Christopher Franke and founder Edgar Froese. As he told me, 'They were playing in the middle of the night in this church in the middle of the Black Forest [in Germany]. I remember we drove for hours to get there, and when we arrived there were no lights on in the venue. All you could see was the lights on the keyboards – these little pinpricks of light on stage. And when they started play-ing, it wasn't distinguishable songs. There were just these great swathes of musical noise, coming over you like waves. It was very atmospheric, very ambient, and I loved it.'

Having scored a huge international hit with *The Exorcist* (1973), on which the search for the right music had proven to be an extremely fraught process (which we'll come to in Chapter 9, 'A Frightful Noise'), Friedkin opted to do something completely different by mounting a modern-day adaptation of Georges Arnaud's 1950 novel *Le Salaire de la Peur* (*The Wages of Fear*), which had previously been adapted for the screen with nail-biting results by French director Henri-Georges Clouzot. Friedkin's production, titled *Sorcerer*, on which Universal and Paramount shared a budget that spiralled to a then-whopping $22 million, is now regarded as one of the great gritty master-pieces of late twentieth-century cinema – an existential tale of four disparate men with nothing left to lose, attempting to transport an unstable cargo of nitroglycerine across hellishly inhospitable terrain, with deadly results. But, at the time of its opening in 1977, *Sorcerer's* desolate worldview proved out of step with audiences flocking to the upbeat spectacle of George Lucas's *Star Wars*. A financial disaster (it took less than $10 million worldwide), *Sorcerer* effectively sank without trace, before being reclaimed and rediscovered in the twenty-first century. Yet somehow the score survived the film's rejection, becoming the one element of the movie that actually found an audience on initial release.

'The music of Tangerine Dream was an early and major inspiration for the film of *Sorcerer*,' Friedkin wrote in his effusive sleeve notes for the film's soundtrack LP. 'I first heard the music of Tangerine Dream while in Munich for the opening of *The Exorcist* . . . Had I heard them sooner, I would have asked them to score that film.'

The idea of *The Exorcist* being scored by German synth-merchants may sound ludicrous now (the film is famous for its use of Mike Oldfield's 'Tubular Bells' theme, alongside tracks by Krzysztof Penderecki and George Crumb), but Friedkin always had a keen ear for cutting-edge composers, and Tangerine Dream were certainly that. A year after seeing them in Germany, Friedkin met the band in Paris. 'I told them the story of [*Sorcerer*] and gave them a script. It took more than two years to make *Sorcerer*. One day, in the middle of a Primeval forest in the Dominican Republic, about six months into shooting, a tape arrived from The Dream containing ninety minutes of musical impressions. It is from this tape that the film has been scored though the musicians had not then, nor even now as this is written, seen any of the footage. Yet somehow they were able to capture and enhance every nuance of each moment where their music is heard. The film and the score are inseparable.'

Friedkin's description sounds hyperbolic, yet it is strangely accurate – Tangerine Dream's music *did* become inseparable from the film for which it was composed, despite the fact that Friedkin made comparatively sparse use of the musical material he had been given. Large sections of *Sorcerer* have no musical accompaniment at all, yet Tangerine Dream's prowling cue 'Betrayal' (also known as the 'Sorcerer Theme') captured the quietly threatening tone of Friedkin's bleakest work, raising the movie's profile when it was released internationally as a single. A creeping half-tone synth bassline underpins a keyboard top-line full of swooshing otherworldly mystery – an element that perhaps added to the popular misconception that *Sorcerer* would be a supernatural thriller with a touch of horror. In fact, the film's title (it was originally pitched as the altogether less poetic 'Ballbreaker') refers to a word painted on the side of one of the trucks used to transport the nitroglycerine. Aside from a very briefly seen demonic face (resembling that of the Pazuzu statue from *The Exorcist*) carved into the rock face past which the trucks drive, *Sorcerer*'s narrative contains no 'magical' elements, although for Friedkin the title worked because 'The Sorcerer is an evil wizard and in this case the evil wizard is fate.'

In the UK, Tangerine Dream's *Sorcerer* soundtrack spent seven weeks in the album charts in 1977, peaking at Number 25 – the third-highest chart position for a band whose following was, at best, esoteric. Meanwhile, in the US, Paramount instructed exhibitors to play a pre-film overture of Tangerine Dream's music, setting the scene for the drama – an instruction that they insisted be followed, or the film would be pulled. When *Sorcerer* bombed at the box office (it opened to poor reviews and worse audiences) the album continued to sell, becoming that rarest of things – a hit soundtrack to a flop film. You can hear echoes of its key themes not only in Moroder's work on *Midnight Express* but also in John Carpenter's signature two-fingered synth sounds for *Halloween* (discussed in greater detail in Chapter 9, 'A Frightful Noise') – two of the defining electro scores of the late seventies.

While *Sorcerer* may have been a career-threatening catastrophe for Friedkin, it proved a career-boosting success for Tangerine Dream, establishing them as respected soundtrackers whose film work would flourish in the eighties. During that decade they scored Michael Mann's *Thief* (1981) and *The Keep* (1983), the Tom Cruise hit *Risky Business* (1983) and the neo-noir Western/vampire hybrid *Near Dark* (1987), the first solo feature from director Kathryn Bigelow, who would go on to become the first woman to win the Oscar for Best Director with *The Hurt Locker* (2008). Indeed, so popular were the band's soundtracks that in 1985 they were enlisted by Universal to re-score Ridley Scott's *Legend* for the American market, after the US distributors decided that Jerry Goldsmith's original orchestral score was one of the reasons the film was failing to connect with the all-important youth audience. In short, having survived the box-office wreckage of *Sorcerer*, Tangerine Dream became the go-to purveyors of saleable film music – a key element of the sound of populist eighties cinema.

*

Looking back on the band's evolution in a 2020 interview with *Music Radar*, Peter Baumann remembered the formative influences that had shaped Tangerine Dream's sound. 'All of us were listening to what you might call classical electronic music,' he told music writer Danny Scott. 'People like Stockhausen and Morton Subotnick. And some of the other hybrid bands, like Kraftwerk, Can, Agitation Free. Then, of course, Roxy Music, Pink Floyd and Bowie. But there were not too many "electronic" acts at that time. The ones that we listened to most were Ligeti, Conrad Schnitzler, and Walter/Wendy Carlos.'

The last of these is of course the composer to whom all modern electronic music – and, more importantly here, electronic *film music* – owes a debt. Born in Rhode Island in 1939, Carlos learned to play piano as a child, using a keyboard which her father had drawn on a piece of card so she could practise between lessons (the Carlos family couldn't afford a piano of their own). At the age of fourteen, she won a science competition after fashioning an elementary computer, and as a teenager she became an avid fan of making and listening to electronic music. Her inspiration? Experimental sound pioneers Louis and Bebe Barron.

As a music and physics graduate, Carlos met Robert Moog in New York in 1964 and worked with him on the development of his synthesizers, which would become the default instruments for so much early electronica. In 1968, working with producer Rachel Elkind, Carlos released *Switched-On Bach*, a compilation of classical pieces reinterpreted for Moog, performed by Carlos with assistance from her friend at the Columbia–Princeton Electronic Music Center, Benjamin Folkman. The album hit a popular nerve, winning Grammy Awards for Best Classical Album, Best Classical Performance and Best Engineered Classical Recording. It also topped the Billboard classical albums chart, remaining a bestseller for three years, selling a million copies by 1974. By 1986, *Switched-on Bach* had become only the second classical album to be certified platinum.

Carlos's first foray into film music was a false start; she was invited to provide a Moog score for John Sturges's 1969 space epic *Marooned*, but the invitation was withdrawn when the film-makers concluded that no composer was needed to depict the airless abyss of space. In the meantime, Carlos and Elkind had been experimenting with a 'spectrum follower' (an early iteration of what we now know as a vocoder) in an attempt to create 'the first electronic "vocal" piece', working from the choral movement of Beethoven's Ninth Symphony. Carlos also began work on what would become 'Timesteps', described by the composer as an 'autonomous composition with an uncanny affinity for *A Clockwork Orange*', since she was reading Anthony Burgess's novel when she was writing the music. When news arrived that Stanley Kubrick was adapting Burgess's story for the screen, Carlos and Elkind sent him a sample of their audio experiments, leading to a meeting with the director, who then asked Carlos to work with him on the film.

The resulting soundtrack offers an extraordinary blend of the past and the future, opening to the distinctive strains of Henry Purcell's *Music for the Funeral of Queen Mary*, stunningly re-imagined by Carlos as a sinister synth dirge, full of ominous threat and playful pomp. Elsewhere, excerpts from 'Timesteps' rub shoulders with 'Suicide Scherzo' (a fragment of Carlos's take on Beethoven's Ninth Symphony), conjuring a world in which futuristic ultra-violence meshes seamlessly with classical themes, encapsulating the dichotomy of *A Clockwork Orange*'s young narrator, Alex, who is as erudite as he is appalling.

Carlos's relationship with Kubrick was not without discussions and disagreements, and various versions of the soundtrack to *A Clockwork Orange* were issued on vinyl and later on CD, representing the cues that were featured in the finished film, and music that Carlos had *intended* for use in the movie that was ultimately dropped by the director. Several years later, Carlos and Elkind would again collaborate with Kubrick on his 1980 Stephen King adaptation *The Shining*, producing large amounts of music, very little of which featured in the finished film, with Kubrick turning instead to existing cues by Penderecki, Bartók and Ligeti. Indeed, one of Carlos's most memorable cues for *The Shining*, prominently featured in the famous 'bloody elevators' teaser trailer, was notable by its absence from the film, and remained unavailable until it resurfaced years later in Carlos's 'Rediscovering Lost Scores' series, the liner notes for which declare that: 'Some of [the] music will be familiar to those who know the film, and some will not, in these richly orchestrated selections. Other tracks hint at a lost world of possibilities for the film left unexplored on its release.'

Carlos's other major film commission (other than being hired and then dropped from the sub-*Alien* nineties Brit-pic stinker *Split Second* – a bullet dodged!) was for Disney's family-friendly 1982 sci-fi romp *TRON*, which promised to take the viewer into a virtual electronic world. Carlos was a perfect fit and composed a score using both analogue Moog keyboards and Crumar's GDS digital synthesizers. She also wrote sections of music to be performed by the London Philharmonic Orchestra, which would be blended with her electronic work. The writing and recording of the score proved extremely difficult, with the orchestra reportedly struggling to get note-perfect takes of Carlos's compositions ('My music is simply difficult to perform,' she told Robert Moog for *Keyboard* magazine.) For years, the soundtrack to *TRON* remained unavailable on CD, reportedly due to a dispute between Carlos and CBS Records. Later, Carlos revisited her original master tapes, which had deteriorated over time but were saved using a technique called 'tape baking' – literally baking the tapes in an oven to 'harden the glue'!

The year before *TRON*'s release, Suzanne Ciani had similarly blended electronica with traditional orchestration for Joel Schumacher's *The Incredible Shrinking Woman*. 'We recorded in Rome at the Forum studio because there was a strike in Hollywood at that time,' Ciani tells me. 'I did bring a lot of electronic gear from my studio, including a Synclavier. I blended electronics into the score, sometimes featuring it more or less. The entire score, every sound in the film, was something that I designed and composed . . . so all the source music, and all the sound design as well was mine.'

Fast-forward to the twenty-first century, and Anna Meredith explains that her own move from orchestration to electronica was driven by her wish to be more fully in control of her own music – to able to work independently, from start to finish. 'It all came out of that desire to be more autonomous,' she says decisively. 'What happens as a composer is that you write a piece of music and then you hand it over to an orchestra and you're not at all involved in the performance. And a lot of these pieces are just played once and never again – they're not recorded or broadcast. And often they're played to a slightly nonplussed audience who just wish they'd hurry up and get to the Elgar! I wanted to take some control back – to write stuff that would have some longevity. So my relationship with electronics started because it was a way of me being able to do the whole thing on my laptop. I didn't really know what I was doing – it wasn't anything I had been trained in and I was just feeling my way with the software. But I really enjoyed how much I could control everything from start to finish.'

*

While electronics provided a relief from the constraints of orchestral work for Meredith, the opposite was true for composer Benjamin John Power, who rose to popularity with his band Fuck Buttons, and who now scores movies and television series under the name Blanck Mass. Power's credits include Tony Stone's 2021 psychodrama *Ted K*, which traced the internal struggles of 'Unabomber' Theodore Kaczynski, powerfully played by Sharlto Copley; and the award-winning 2023 sports documentary series *Gazza* about the footballer Paul Gascoigne. Film fans may also recognize a thunderous piece by Power entitled 'Chernobyl' which was used by Ben Wheatley in his 2013 film *A Field in England* and then resurfaced during the surreal climax of Prano Bailey-Bond's brilliantly inventive 'video nasty' fantasy *Censor* (2021). But it was Power's Ivor Novello Award-winning score for the intense 2019 Brit-pic *Calm with Horses* that really put him on the movie map.

Power's score for *Calm with Horses* was a key part of Bafta-nominee Nick Rowland's feature debut, an immersive tale of tortured masculinity and divided loyalties that pulls the viewer right into the raging-bull mindset of its haunted protagonist. Set in rural Ireland, and boasting something of the 'West Country Western' flavour of Sam Peckinpah's Cornish epic *Straw Dogs* (1971), *Calm with Horses* is a dark fable of failed fathers and false families, unflinching in its depiction of grim realities but laced with a redemptive transcendence. Power's music gets right under the skin of the drama, lending an edge of frayed distortion to melancholy melodies, capturing the film's blend of roughness and innocence. Like Daniel Lopatin's pulsing electronic accompaniment to the Safdie Brothers' *Uncut Gems* (2019), the score for *Calm with Horses* seems to inject itself into the bloodstream of the film's central characters, helping us to see the world through their eyes, and share their often fractured experiences.

Power appears to be a quintessential modern electronic composer – working alone in his studio, guided only by his own instincts, surrounded by machines. But when I speak to him, he confesses that he has always wanted to work with an orchestra.

'I've been making music in one way or another since I was twelve years old,' he tells me, 'and my formative years were spent in punk bands and heavy-metal bands. When I started out I was living in a flat in Dalston and I was absolutely broke. I had about one-sixteenth of the amount of machines I have now – it was mainly just stuff I would use with Fuck Buttons. But in my head, I really wanted the first Blanck Mass record to be an *orchestral* record. But I just didn't have the finance and the connections or anything like that to go ahead and make that happen. So I had to use what I had electronically to hand to try and recreate how I heard a symphony in my head.'

Power's interest in film music dates back to an early encounter with the work of one of the great movie composers of the twentieth century. 'For me, it all comes back to Morricone. I remember hearing the theme from *The Good, the Bad and the Ugly* and thinking, "This is incredible and I'd love to do something like this – but this isn't somebody's *job*, surely."' He found himself gravitating towards instrumental music with a strong sense of narrative, and in 2015 he was commissioned by the East End Film Festival to curate an alternative score to the neo-*giallo* film *The Strange Colour of Your Body's Tears* (2013). Although that project introduced him to the world of film, Power recognized that he was 'on a two-year cycle with music: spend a year writing a new record, and then spend the next year touring it after that', so scoring a feature didn't seem like a feasible possibility.

Nevertheless, he managed to carve seven weeks out of his schedule to create the music for *Calm with Horses*, working alone in his studio without the need for multiple players – in much the same way that the Barrons, Wendy Carlos and Giorgio Moroder had made *their* scores before him. Power's key collaborator was the film's director – something which continued in his subsequent film work. 'I need an over-saturation of adjectives,' he tells me. 'That's the main focus. When I'm looking at a cue, or I'm in a spotting session, the very first question I'll ask is, "Whose perspective is this from? Is this from the perspective of the protagonist or the antagonist, outside looking in, or inside looking out? How might this person or entity experience their surroundings? Or is it from an observer's point of view?"' Many of his projects to date have homed in on the central character's experience, so these descriptions are vital for him in order to get under their skin.

Of his particularly distinctive sound, which uses a lot of analogue-style distortion, Power acknowledges that 'historically I have certainly gravitated towards the more extreme side of things, but without losing any sense of beauty within. I do feel that as Blanck Mass I've got to a stage where there's some kind of thread between the nastiness and the delicateness. I don't shy away from the extremely tender now, whereas before everything was very abrasive.'

Remembering the formative influence of Morricone, and

his original desire to work with orchestral compositions, I ask Power whether he considers himself to be part of the tradition of electronic film music – from Carlos to Tangerine Dream, to Moroder and beyond. 'Of course all of that stuff is massively interesting to me, even coming a little closer to where we are now with the likes of John Carpenter and such . . . When you start to notice that more and more electronic scores are being used in films, that's when it starts to become a possibility for you.' He sees it as a fruitful time to be an electronic musician scoring for the screen and cites OneOhTrix Point Never (Daniel Lopatin's occasional alias), Mica Levi, and Geoff Barrow and Ben Salisbury (frequent collaborators with writer/director Alex Garland on films including *Ex Machina*, 2014; *Annihilation*, 2018; and *Men*, 2020) as standout talents.

When I ask Anna Meredith to name the contemporary film composers with whom she feels an affinity, she too mentions OneOhTrix Point Never and Mica Levi, alongside Colin Stetson (whose scores include *Hereditary*, 2018; *Color Out of Space*, 2020; and *The Menu*, 2022) and Jonny Greenwood, emphasizing her own straddling of classical and electronic music. She also stresses that she doesn't listen to other music when she's composing, but has a very particular way of visualizing her own film scores.

'I have these maps that I do for all my music, to help me through the pacing,' she says. 'That's very important to me. I draw these very graphic sketches for everything. And those maps are like a horizontal line with shapes that follow the dramatic contours. So that helps me plot out the track – where certain elements should come in, where cross-rhythms should happen. It's a pacing chart. I still do that for the film music – I map it out, and also map out what's happening visually so I know what the music has to hit.'

Meredith's composition method is a complex blend of classical skills and electronic innovation, reflecting her discovery that 'I was actually better using the skills I already had rather than getting into the nuts and bolts of how other people write electronic music.' As for Power, he describes his own process as 'highly explorative', built upon an 'organic' relationship with machines that 'often lead the way for me to get to where I feel like it's a good place to land'.

It's clear that the rise of electronic instruments and composition techniques have revolutionized the way in which film scores are created. Yet when I ask Power what his ambitions are for the future, his answer takes us right back to the beginning of our conversation – and to the beginning of film music itself. 'I do feel like I have a fully orchestral score in me,' he laughs. 'At least one. No electronics whatsoever, just a fully orchestral score. And I can't see any reason why it *couldn't* happen. So that's where my head's at right now – waiting for it all to come full circle.'

Soundtrack Selection:
Blade Runner (1982)

'He will sit and watch every frame, and cue off a frame, cue off the expression of an actor. He doesn't just lay on score and say, "Well, that works." He goes through *everything*. He thinks himself *into* the film.'

That was how director Ridley Scott described to me the work of Greek composer Vangelis in my 2000 documentary *On the Edge of Blade Runner*. As for Rutger Hauer, the Dutch actor who breathed such sparkly life into replicant (or artificial human) Roy Batty, he said simply: 'I remember when the first notes hit me, I was like . . . WOW!'

It's hard to overstate the significance of Vangelis's score for *Blade Runner* (1982), Scott's science fiction epic that flopped on first release but went on to become one of the most influential genre pictures of all time. The opening titles of the film tell us that the music was 'composed, arranged, produced and performed by Vangelis', which may sound like a composer building up his part, but in fact serves to remind us that one of the most influential science fiction soundtracks of all time is the singular creation of one man.

And a *lot* of synths.

Impressive for both its simplicity and its experimentation, the soundtrack to *Blade Runner* feels futuristic, nostalgic and time-less all in one. Yet, despite now being recognized as a milestone film soundtrack, it was unavailable as an OST for over a decade after the film's initial faltering release, only finally coming onto the market in an official form long after an under-the-radar pressing on the 'Off World Music, Ltd' label had given diehard fans what they wanted – or at least *some* of it.

The electronic pop artist born Evangelos Odysseas Papa-thanassiou was awarded the Oscar for Best Original Score for *Chariots of Fire* on 29 March 1982. One month later, he submit-ted his compositions for *Blade Runner*, an adaptation of Philip K. Dick's novel *Do Androids Dream of Electric Sheep?*, set in a dystopian future (specifically Los Angeles, 2019) where repli-cants have turned against their creators and are being hunted by the authorities to be 'retired'.

The opening glissando of the 'Main Title' plays out over a jaw-dropping cityscape, the keyboard sounds intermingling with the swooping whoosh of a vehicle that flies high over a darkened night-time vista, broken by bursts of flame from high-stacked towers (as Hauer said: 'WOW'). It's an impres-sively non-melodic scene-setter, with Vangelis more intent upon generating a mood than giving the audience a hummable theme tune. As he said in a 2007 interview marking the film's twenty-fifth anniversary, 'What interested me the most for this movie was the atmosphere and the general feeling, rather than the distinct themes'.

Vangelis came to *Blade Runner* through a number of connec-tions. Ridley Scott, who famously started out making adverts, had used music from Vangelis's 1979 *China* album to sell Chanel

No. 5, and *Blade Runner*'s editor, Terry Rawlings, had cut *Chariots of Fire*. Vangelis worked on the score for *Blade Runner* in his Nemo Studios, a disused school in London's Marble Arch. Preferring to be led by images rather than script, Vangelis worked in the moment. He watched scenes, surrounded by his trusty synths – his favourite being the Yamaha CS-80 – and allowed his initial reactions to dictate the music: 'When I compose, I perform the music at the same time, so everything is live. Nothing is pre-programmed. I don't do demos. Improvising isn't quite the word for it, but I do use the first idea and impression that comes into my head.'

The tools employed by Vangelis to create this unique soundscape and score include the VP-330 Vocoder Plus, the ProMars, the Jupiter-4, an E-mu Emulator sampler and the CR-500 drum machine, along with traditional instruments like the gamelan, glockenspiel and tubular bells. The handheld video game Bambino UFO Master Blaster Station from the early seventies provided additional bleeps, while a sense of foreboding was created by putting a bass drum noise through a MasterRoom spring reverb unit. The sound of ersatz nostalgia – crucial to a film about the fabrication and manipulation of memory – was brought to life by filtering a Steinway grand piano through an Electro-Harmonix Electric Mistress guitar flanger pedal.

This pre-fab nostalgia toys with our own preconceptions of how emotions 'should' sound, none more evident than in the plastic sheen of the saxophone played by Dick Morrissey in the 'Love Theme'. The woozy sax suggests a veneer of romance, one that seems deliberately unconvincing, and this proves to be a suitable match for the decidedly unromantic encounter between Deckard and Rachael in which he physically prevents her from leaving his apartment and forces her to say she wants him.

The soundtrack's feeling of timelessness is heightened by the inclusion of songs that appear to be rooted in the past, providing an old-school film-noir-inflected counterbalance to the modernity of Vangelis's science fiction synths and electronic wizardry. 'One More Kiss, Dear', which plays in the background when Deckard orders a drink after killing the replicant Zhora (and which can be heard very faintly during his subsequent conversation with the inscrutable Bryant) sounds like a Music Hall standard. Yet, as with so much in the world of *Blade Runner*, this song which *seems* like a memory is in fact a modern construction – a faux imitation of the past, created in (and of) the future.

The intended vocalist on 'One More Kiss, Dear', for which Peter Skellern provided the lyrics, had been Vangelis's regular collaborator Demis Roussos, with the composer keen to bring Middle Eastern elements into the cultural melting pot of the soundtrack to mirror that of the film itself. But when artist manager Don Percival sang the temp track demo, Vangelis was so taken with his singing style and the era it conjured that he kept it in. Roussos in turn can be heard on the haunting track 'Tales of the Future', and snippets of his searing vocals appear on several occasions in the film, most notably when Deckard goes in search of Zhora. Roussos sings as though his life depends on it, expressing an otherworldly pain. Yet while the lyrics may sound similar to Arabic words, Vangelis was keen to remove any discernible meaning, concentrating instead on the *sounds* of the singing.

Despite an end-credits announcement that an original soundtrack album for *Blade Runner* would be available on Polydor Records, no such album was forthcoming. The box-office failure of Scott's movie, which cost $28 million to make and recouped

only $17 million on first release in 1982, seems to have con-
vinced everyone that there was simply no market for authentic
tie-in merchandise. Instead, fans were fobbed off with an ear-
scrapingly cheesy recording by the New American Orchestra
under the direction of Jack Elliott, which takes a swathe of
Vangelis's shimmering electronic themes and turns them into
hokey chicken-in-a-basket knock-offs that wouldn't sound out
of place on a seventies lunchtime TV show.

It wasn't until a decade later, when Scott's 1992 'Director's Cut'
of *Blade Runner* (which removed both the droning explanatory
voice-over and the tacked-on happy ending) led to a wholescale
re-evaluation of the film, that plans started to be made for
a Vangelis soundtrack release. By this point, fan remixes and
cobbled-together reconstructions of Vangelis's original score
had become the stuff of legend – a subject I wrote about in a
1994 issue of *Sight and Sound* magazine, when the first proper
OST CD of *Blade Runner* was finally issued.

Released in the wake of Tarantino's hugely popular *Reservoir
Dogs* soundtrack, which (like its successor, *Pulp Fiction*) helped
to repopularize the use of dialogue clips on OST discs, the 1994
Blade Runner album was littered with choice snippets from the
film, such as Deckard using the 'Esper' to scan photos ('enhance
57–19; track 45 left; stop') in dour neo-noir detective fashion
over the 'Main Titles'. Several other cues contain speech lifted
from key scenes, most notably the final track, 'Tears in Rain',
in which Rutger Hauer recites the now iconic speech that he
scribbled on a piece of paper on the night of the shoot ('I've
seen things you people wouldn't believe . . .'). An exercise in
understated restraint, the wistful synths of Vangelis's score add
a childlike wonder to the replicant Roy Batty's final words on
Earth.

It's the perfect conclusion to the album, one that creates far more of a gut punch than the actual 'End Titles'. This closing cue is propulsive, comparatively energetic, and also arguably the most dated-sounding track, although Vangelis explained why he chose to pick up the pace: 'I was just feeling we shouldn't end melancholically – we should end in a more dynamic way.'

In 2007, the *Blade Runner Trilogy* offered a three-CD set featuring the 1994 album, previously unreleased music from the movie and newly composed pieces by Vangelis inspired by it. More than forty years after its all but catastrophic first release, *Blade Runner* has become one of those movies that can be endlessly repackaged and resold to a still-growing army of fans who are captivated by its blurring of the lines between human and android, and the still-burning question of whether Deckard himself *is* a replicant. (I did an onstage interview in 2017 with Scott and *Blade Runner 2049* director Denis Villeneuve in which the two nearly came to blows over the issue.)

For some, that blurred line ('more human than human') is represented musically by the mix of electronic and acoustic instruments that Vangelis employs, although the composer doesn't share that view, saying: 'I have never felt there is a distinction between electronic or acoustic instruments. For me, any object producing sound is important and will always have its place.'

For many, this soundtrack *is* the sound of science fiction films. If you want to consider its influence, look no further than fellow synth-fan Hans Zimmer and his music on the *Dune* films. (Coincidentally, Ridley Scott originally turned down directing *Blade Runner* because he was meant to be making *Dune* for Dino de Laurentiis, a project that sadly didn't come to fruition.) Zimmer had played with the *Blade Runner* train set when co-composing the *Blade Runner 2049* score with Benjamin Wallfisch, and perhaps this built his 'synth confidence' to more epic proportions. The dust on Arrakis may be a million miles away from the 'futuristic' 2019 Los Angeles in *Blade Runner*, but Vangelis's vision is as far-reaching as Philip K. Dick's vast imagination.

CHAPTER 7

Play Through the Action

'I would hate to be stuck in the action picture thing. One car chase after the other. Because I think there are basically two car chases you can write, and that's it.'

These were the words, somewhat surprisingly, of Hans Zimmer, in an interview he gave back in the early nineties. Zimmer presumably had a change of heart in the decades that followed because, while he's by no means 'stuck' in the action genre, he's certainly contributed heavily to it, scoring more than his fair share of frenetic scenes in *The Dark Knight* trilogy (2005–12), *Mission: Impossible 2* (2000), *Inception* (2010), *Rush* (2013), *No Time to Die* (2021), *Top Gun: Maverick* (2022) and more. Indeed, you could argue that his thunderous 'braaams' have made an indelible impact on the overall sound of action movies, influencing countless other composers simply to throw everything they've got at the screen when scoring for the genre.

And yet, Zimmer has a point.

There's a strong argument to be made that action scores *can* limit a composer in terms of creativity. They're weighted with expectation. There's a sense of knowing what a chase sequence 'should' sound like, and composers may feel restricted in delivering what the director, producers and audience want. They must lean into the tropes – but not so *far* in as to sound hackneyed. It certainly seems harder to find a distinctive voice as a composer when scoring for this particular genre.

James Newton Howard has composed plenty of action and action-adventure films over the decades, including *The Fugitive* (1993), *I Am Legend* (2007), *Salt* (2010), *The Bourne Legacy* (2012) and the ongoing *Hunger Games* series, as well as co-composing *Batman Begins* (2005) and *The Dark Knight* (2008) with Zimmer. Shedding some light on how he approaches this broad genre compared to other projects, he explains: 'A good action score is a very different beast. It's loud, you're making a lot of noise, you're writing a lot of notes. It's not the same [as other genres], you can't just write strings and piano. You're writing all-hell-breaking-loose with lots of brass and lots of pre-recorded synthy stuff and percussion and every kind of imaginable thing. I think that is very exhausting. I find it very tiring, but I think I'm good at it, dare I say it – I think I'm a *good* action writer. And I am excited by it. I get so adrenalined – my adrenalin just runs so high when I'm working on a really great action sequence. But I'm also really scared because it's really *hard* to write a great action sequence!'

Five-time Emmy Award-winner Laura Karpman has scored the big-screen Marvel Studios projects *The Marvels* (2023) and *Captain America: Brave New World* (2025), along with associated TV series *What If . . . ?* (2021) and *Ms Marvel* (2022). When asked if the action genre can be restrictive for a composer, she asserts that 'Everybody's experience is different. In terms of the experience that I've had, you want to write a hummable theme. And that theme needs to have a single phrase nugget, and then a longer exploration of what that is. The first thing that the studio wants is a suite: basically, you take a theme or themes through the various paces that they'll have to go through. If you have a hero theme, you want it for the heroic moments, you want it for the tense moments, you want it for the action-y moments, you want it for the sad moments. You have to have a theme that can survive all those treatments. I don't find that restrictive, I find that interesting . . . that there's more room for dissonance and modernism and really playing with different musical ideas in these films than just about anything else.'

Still, there's the challenge of acknowledging the additional sound effects that tend to feature in action films – screeching car gears, gunshots, whirring helicopter blades, skidding tyres, trains hurtling on the tracks, beeps and horns from surrounding traffic – and somehow working around them or (at best) incorporating them into the themes of the score.

'I think sound effects take you a certain way,' says David Arnold, the longest-serving James Bond composer after John Barry (he has scored five outings for 007, from 1997's *Tomorrow Never Dies* up to 2008's *Quantum of Solace*), whose action movie CV also includes Roland Emmerich's *Independence Day* (1996) and *Godzilla* (1998), and John Singleton's street-racer sequel *2 Fast 2 Furious* (2003). 'But it's a *visceral* response that you get with sound effects. Whereas music gives you an *emotional* response. Sometimes hearing an explosion or *another* bullet or *another* helicopter isn't going to make you any more excited or feel any more threatened. Whereas music will do *all* of that.'

Arnold's observation chimes neatly with Golden Age composer Miklós Rózsa's claim that 'the function of music is not to illustrate but to complete the psychological effect'. In action movies, this means that the composer's greatest challenge is to ramp up the high-octane adrenalin-pumping drama while *simultaneously* providing signals about the characters and their motivations. In effect, the ideal action score needs to tread a fine line between accompanying the action and offering additional depths.

For Karpman, there's no point in getting bogged down with expectations, because 'the truth is that it comes down to whether you can write a good tune. And can that tune get you through an entire series or a two-hour movie? If you look at the other Marvel people like Alan Silvestri [whose Marvel Cinematic Universe – or MCU – scores include *The Avengers*, 2012, and *Avengers Endgame*, 2019] and Michael Giacchino [*Doctor Strange*, 2016; *Spider-Man: Homecoming*, 2017], they write great *tunes*! I think it's less about *action* music than you might think it is.'

*

'Action cinema' is of course as old as film-making itself. Edwin S. Porter's 1903 film *The Great Train Robbery* proved a huge hit with turn-of-the-century audiences, in part because of its dynamic and violent action, boosted by Porter's groundbreaking use of parallel editing to depict several tense sequences playing out at the same time – a technique that has since become the standard grammar of the genre. By the 1920s, the term 'action-adventure' was making its way into movie PR, being used as a descriptive term for films like *The Gaucho* (1927), a romping silent tale of a bandit-turned-hero played with derring-do panache by Douglas Fairbanks, who also produced and wrote the picture.

As cinema transitioned from silent movies to talkies, the rise of synchronized film music allowed composers to hit specific onscreen moments with musical stabs and cues. After watching *The Jazz Singer* (1927), Walt Disney committed himself to making one of the first sound cartoons. The result was the 1928 animated short *Steamboat Willie*, which boasted synchronized sound with music by Wilfred Jackson and Bert Lewis. The film was a success, but it also gave rise to the cautionary musical term 'Mickey Mousing', a phrase still used to this day to describe music that is *too* literal in its synchronized representation of the onscreen action.

In *Steamboat Willie*, every movement has an accompanying musical note or sound effect, and while this may have felt immersive to audiences at the time, it soon started to wear thin. Max Steiner, who laid the bedrock for film scoring as we know it today, was no stranger to Mickey Mousing. He even admitted that he overdid it at times when asked about 'hitting' (rather than 'playing through') the action. Yet Steiner's ability to use music both to create a spectacle *and* to portray a character's true feelings were game-changers at the time.

To today's ears, Steiner's scores for hits including *The Informer* (1935), *Gone with the Wind* (1939), *Now, Voyager* (1941) and *Casablanca* (1942) may sound overly dramatic. But his ambition was always to respond emotionally to the story, just as a member of the audience would. And if that meant creating music that exactly matched the hero or heroine dashing across the screen, so be it. A retrospective of Steiner's work by Paul Cote on the International Film Music Critics Association (IFMCA) website states that 'Mickey Mousing for Steiner isn't simply an act of mimicry; it's an act of emotional interpretation.'

Steiner had no greater success at showcasing action and emotion in his music than with *King Kong* (1933), still considered one of the finest examples of how music can connect with audiences on a visceral and emotional level. Steven C. Smith, author of biographies of Steiner and Bernard Herrmann, told *Variety* in 2020 that it's 'the most influential music score of all time', setting the blueprint so that composers 'still look at [it] and say, "Oh, *that's* how you score a film."'

For all the orchestrated drama of *King Kong*, Steiner knew when to let the music do the talking, and when to provide a moment's pause. When Kong escapes after being chained up and exhibited to a packed theatre audience in New York, there isn't any music as the press photographers approach and the flashing cameras terrify the great ape. But the moment the first chain breaks open, there's an orchestrated crash, after which chaos ensues. Later, the famous scene at the top of the Empire State Building starts with the unaccompanied sound of planes circling and shooting at Kong. Only when Kong leans down towards Fay Wray's Ann does the music – the emotional centre of the film – enter the scene. The score here is certainly dramatic, but it's tinged with sorrow, foreshadowing Kong's eventual fall, and the famous declaration that 'It was Beauty killed the Beast'.

For a composer like Steiner, whose scores incorporated character leitmotifs while also hitting the action, every project was an immersive and potentially draining experience. Steven C. Smith notes that Steiner grew fearful of films full of action sequences due to the physical strain they would inflict, not least on his eyesight. These were the days when composers had to write every single note out on paper, so Steiner would declare, 'I will be blind by the end of this film.'

By the late 1950s, German-Austrian composer Hanns Eisler could be heard bemoaning 'this awful Wagnerian illustration technique' that, in his opinion, beset contemporary cinema, although as Paul Cote observes of Steiner's scores: 'the overall effect might not have been subtle, but then, neither were the pictures.'

*

In 1959, William Wyler's action-packed religious epic *Ben-Hur* (a remake of Fred Niblo's 1925 silent film) earned its place in the history books as having the largest production budget of any movie up till that point. It would go on to win eleven Academy Awards – a feat only matched since by James Cameron's *Titanic* (1997) and Peter Jackson's *The Lord of the Rings: The Return of the King* (2003). For his *Ben-Hur* score, Miklós Rózsa composed three hours' worth of music, of which around two and a half hours feature in the final film. Recorded by the hundred-strong MGM Symphony Orchestra through twelve recording sessions totalling seventy-two hours, the score was the longest ever composed for a motion picture at the time, and to this day remains one of the longest scores for a single film.

At the centre of *Ben-Hur* is the legendary chariot race, a breathtaking nine-minute sequence that is still considered one of the greatest action set-pieces of all time. It's prefixed by 'Parade of the Charioteers', a grand march full of brassy fanfare, signalling the start of the event. Yet the race itself is one of the few parts of the movie that is presented unscored, *without* music. Instead, Wyler relies upon the cheers of the crowd, the galloping of the horses, the cracking of the whips and the crashing of the chariots to keep the audience gripped.

'Nothing is as loud in films as silence,' noted Bronisław Kaper, the composer of stirring scores for films such as Lewis Milestone's historical drama *Mutiny on the Bounty* (1962). It's a sentiment shared by accomplished soundtrack album producer and editor Mike Matessino: 'Music can't say anything unless it's absent,' he states firmly. 'The first thing that I tell a young person when they say they want to get into film music is, "Learn the art of spotting, learn when to be silent."' For Matessino, the difference between great film scores and, for example, the muzak of shopping malls is that while the latter is designed to be a comforting, forgettable drone, the former exists to create an *impact* – and 'a large part of that impact is because of when it chooses to be silent. Then when the music comes in, something in your subconscious perks up, and realizes that "OK, the stakes have just gotten higher for some reason, or a character has had a revelation."'

In short, if the music of a film simply continues uninterrupted, it becomes mere background noise, signifying nothing.

Look at Alfred Hitchcock's magnificently entertaining spy thriller *North by Northwest* (1959), for which Bernard Herrmann provided a memorably arresting score – one which goes notably silent during the film's most famous scene. Cary Grant's advertising executive Roger Thornhill travels to a remote bus stop in Indiana to meet the mysterious George Kaplan, a US government agent for whom he had been mistaken at the opening of the film. Apart from the road, there's nothing but cornfields as far as the eye can see – and then we hear the whirring of a crop-duster plane which proceeds to target Thornhill, in terrifying fashion. As the action continues, Herrmann's score remains mute, with just the sound of the plane bearing down on Grant, and then flying higher to prepare for another attack. The scene feels eerie, claustrophobic and strangely 'loud' in exactly the manner that Kaper describes. Only when the plane flies into the side of an oil tanker, effectively *ending* the chase, does Herrmann's music kick back in to walloping effect, its first chords coinciding with the tanker exploding in flames. According to *Variety*, this is the scene in which 'the seed of all modern action cinema was planted'. Ian Fleming was so impressed that he was keen for Hitchcock to direct the first film about his fictional spy, James Bond.

Laura Karpman credits Herrmann's music for *North by Northwest* as being one of the finest action scores of all time because it 'rides this thin line between something that can be dramatic and scary and something that can be funny'. She also highlights the significance of the crop-duster scene as 'the seminal collaboration between music and sound [in which] the film-maker is making a very effective choice, where music doesn't come in until you absolutely feel like you cannot live another moment without it'.

Sometimes, music can help in the editing of an action scene without featuring in the finished film. In 1971, William Friedkin's definitive New York actioner *The French Connection* lived up to producer Phil D'Antoni's promise to create a car chase to top his previous thriller hit *Bullitt* (1968). In *The French Connection*'s most famous sequence, Gene Hackman's detective 'Popeye' Doyle pursues Pierre 'Frog Two' Nicoli into a metro station, where the hitman/enforcer evades him on a departing train. Flagging down a passing car, Doyle attempts to chase the train which is travelling on the elevated section of the railway, speeding through heavy traffic as the train rattles overhead.

Sections of that sequence were shot on unguarded roads, with the car weaving dangerously through real-life traffic and (in one instance) creasing the side of a city bus. 'It was insane,' Friedkin told me. 'I said to Bill Hickman, who was driving the car, "You haven't shown me anything." And he said: "You wanna see some driving?" I said, "Yeah," and he said "OK, if you've got the balls to get in the car with me . . ." ' So Friedkin sat in the back of the car, with Hickman in the driver's seat, and New York cop Randy Jurgensen crouched down in the well of the passenger seat, his badge in hand – and off they went. According to Friedkin, Hickman ran twenty blocks, at speeds of up to seventy miles per hour, dodging cars and stop lights, leaving the director to conclude that 'It was a miracle no one got hurt.'

When editor Gerald Greenberg came to assemble the footage, he realized immediately that he had the material to make something genuinely nail-biting and dynamic. Unlike the chase scene in *Bullitt*, *The French Connection*'s pursuit played out on crowded streets, cranking up the levels of danger. As Greenberg cut the scene, he looked for musical inspiration and found it in Santana's recording of 'Black Magic Woman', with the propulsive guitar solo seeming to provide the perfect rhythmic template for the action.

In the finished film, however, the temp track that proved so helpful in the editing is entirely absent. Instead, Friedkin opts for the sounds of the city – frantic car horns, trains zipping over the tracks, vehicles skidding over the road. Amid the cacophony of New York, we see Doyle shouting from behind the wheel but, disconcertingly, we can't hear him as the urban soundscape becomes all-pervasive.

As with *North by Northwest*, the score for *The French Connection* (by Don Ellis) only reappears when the chase is effectively over. As 'Frog Two' attempts to pull open the doors of the now-stopped runaway train, we hear a low drumbeat alongside the remaining street sounds, developing into deep staccato stabs that end abruptly when Doyle shoots Nicoli in the back – a scene that would provide the controversial poster image for the film. *The French Connection* would go on to earn eight Oscar nominations, including Best Sound and Best Editing, with five wins including Best Film and Best Director.

*

One of the longest-spanning action series of modern screen entertainment is the *Mission: Impossible* franchise, which started life as a sixties TV show that lasted into the seventies, was briefly revived in the eighties, and then got a big-screen reboot in the nineties that is still thriving in the 2020s. Argentine composer Lalo Schifrin (who scored *Bullitt*) created the catchy 5/4 theme tune for the TV show, while on the big screen Danny Elfman scored the first film (Brian De Palma's *Mission: Impossible*, 1996), followed by Hans Zimmer (for John Woo's *Mission: Impossible 2*, 2000), Michael Giacchino (who worked on both *Mission: Impossible III*, 2006, and *Ghost Protocol*, 2011) and then Joe Kraemer on *Rogue Nation* (2015).

Scottish composer Lorne Balfe picked up the *Mission: Impossible* baton for 2018's nail-biting *Fallout*, and followed up with *Dead Reckoning Part One* (2023). Balfe, as we have seen, is a seasoned screen composer who has won acclaim for his video game, TV and film music. In the action movie genre, he has scored the likes of *Terminator Genisys* (2015), *Pacific Rim Uprising* (2018), *Black Widow* (2021), *Black Adam* (2022) and the recent belated *Bad Boys* outings *Bad Boys for Life* (2020) and *Bad Boys: Ride or Die* (2023). He's also scored a couple of Michael Bay movies and provided a lively accompaniment to the surprisingly rip-roaring adventure *Dungeons and Dragons: Honour Among Thieves* (2023).

'I try to not necessarily look at "action" as a genre,' says Balfe. 'Film music has evolved for the viewer, and what we used to

221

listen to as horror music forty years ago would sound like a parody now. So it's a difficult thing to try to categorize the genre.'

For his work on the *Mission: Impossible* films, Balfe inherited Schifrin's much-loved TV show theme, which had been variously reworked throughout the feature film series. When asked if he felt any pressure working with this musical legacy and incorporating the instantly recognizable motif into his scores, Balfe says, 'There's no burden. The first thing you do is remove any nostalgia to do with it and treat it as if it was a brand-new theme, written the day before. That's how I look at it. It's a blessing that you get given the DNA of something that the whole world knows. The hard work is done, in one respect.'

Nonetheless, Balfe remains aware of the perils of incorporating music that may be identified with a different era when working on a 'modern' movie. 'You've just got to make it connect to this generation,' he states. 'My aim has always been to try to take things and be honest; to honour the past but bring it to the present, so the audience don't feel you're being tricked into some nostalgia trip.'

Balfe was Hans Zimmer's assistant for around a decade, starting with additional writing on *Batman Begins* (2005). He credits Zimmer with providing the best steer for taking on the mantle of Schifrin's theme – that it's crucial to have fun. 'And I think that's the key to it, because you're invited into this family,' he says.

Balfe trained as a percussionist and as such has 'always regarded action music as percussive', but appreciates the need to provide additional depths. 'I think that action music is difficult to write,' he observes, 'because you've got to also have emotion in it, somehow, so the audience can feel connected.'

The composer cites as formative influences such Jerry Bruckheimer and Don Simpson co-productions as *Beverly Hills Cop*

(1984) and *Top Gun* (1986), both of which series he contributed to, musically speaking, when they returned to our screens decades later as *Top Gun: Maverick* (2022) and *Beverly Hills Cop: Axel F* (2024). Looking back at eighties and nineties action sequences and their accompanying scores, Balfe notes that 'the key-change was the classic trick that a composer would use to push and create extra anxiety in an action scene. Now, a key-change is a slightly cheap cop-out. You grin when that happens.'

For Balfe, the evolution of the audience's expectations is vital to understanding the development of film music: 'What they emotionally connect to is far more advanced than it was before.'

One of the great action movie composers – and, significantly, one of the greatest film composers to avoid being pigeonholed, simply because he excelled and innovated in *all* genres – is Jerry Goldsmith. He once said that his role was to score the emotion, not the visuals. His wife Carol recalled lectures Goldsmith used to give in which he would tell film students that 'if they were scoring a scene for a man on a horse galloping away, you don't score the gallop but you score the fear of the rider'.

Goldsmith experimented throughout his career, from the atonal squonks of his brilliant *Planet of the Apes* score to the fusion of intricate orchestral performances with electronic effects deployed for Paul Verhoeven's sci-fi actioner *Total Recall* (1990), for which the composer was said to have impressed even himself with the dizzying pace of the notation. For James Newton Howard, Jerry Goldsmith was 'my biggest, first hero and was very supportive of me in my early days'. While Howard has 'had to find my own way, my own voice' in the world of action films, Goldsmith's scores helped him on this journey.

When Howard was working on his first big-budget action

score, the Harrison Ford starrer *The Fugitive* (1993), he admits, 'I was terrified. I didn't have a long time to write it, like six weeks or something, and it was way out of my comfort zone.' In fact, despite being best known for his work on films like *Pretty Woman* and *Flatliners* (both 1990), Howard *had* already written an action score for *Fugitive* helmer Andrew Davis's little-seen 1989 offering *The Package*. Davis was keen to work with him again, despite the composer's anxieties. 'So I took a Jerry Goldsmith cue from *Total Recall*. There's a huge sequence in *The Fugitive* where Harrison Ford steals an ambulance and there's a helicopter chase. It's such a great sequence, and I put one of Jerry's cues up. And it was just so great that I wanted to shoot myself!' The experience was humbling but also inspiring, driving Howard to create his own propulsive score for *The Fugitive* which influential *New York Times* critic Janet Maslin would hail as being 'hugely effective'.

*

Laura Karpman started writing music at the age of seven and received training and mentorship from the illustrious teacher and composer Nadia Boulanger (whose students included Quincy Jones and Philip Glass). She had had a rich and acclaimed career scoring for the screen decades before she was invited into the MCU family, and she is keen to provide context.

'There were simply not the opportunities for women or any other recognized groups to play in those sandboxes,' she states firmly. 'It just didn't happen until very, very recently. I mean, I went to Juilliard, I got a doctorate in musical composition. I had been prepared to write large-scale orchestral scores for thirty years before I got the opportunity to do so. It's not like it just happened. It happened as a result of my and other people's efforts to really open up the field and make diversity something that was sought after rather than some kind of punishment.'

Karpman, who is one of a still relatively small number of women to receive an Oscar nomination for scoring, for *American Fiction* (2023), co-founded the Alliance for Women Film Composers (AWFC) in 2014 with fellow composers Miriam Cutler and Lolita Ritmanis, and film music PR specialist Chandler Poling. The AWFC website states that it was formed 'out of a need and desire to raise visibility and create opportunity for female composers'. Karpman reflected on its achievements in the run-up to its tenth anniversary: 'My goal was for it to be bigger than you can imagine in five years, and *gone* in ten. And it's *not* gone, although I think we've made progress. I think now there's opportunity where there was none.'

The fact that the group still exists, and is still *needed*, is telling. 'The only reason why the Alliance started was because we had numbers – we had researchers who were including us in their stuff and we could say, "Hey, we're only 2 per cent of the top 250 box-office films." But what I encourage you to do is look at who's scoring the top 250 box-office films and go take a look at who's in the running for the Oscars this year, and come to your own conclusions ... Are we close to parity now? No. We're still at, like, 12 to 16 per cent. What is it going to take to get us there? A *lot*!'

When discussing her work in the usually male-dominated field of big-budget action films, Karpman says, 'I have been very ready for this for a *very* long time and I am very appreciative of it. Being able to record with an orchestra has been absolutely amazing, and in many ways a fulfilment of something that I've always wanted to do. I remember when we heard *The Marvels* on the dubbing stage for the first time. My wife Nora [Kroll-Rosenbaum, also a composer] was there with me and we just looked at each other and it was like, "Oh my God, *finally*, a big movie!"'

The list of women composers who have top billing for scoring large-scale action films is indeed dismayingly short. Pinar Toprak became the first woman to score a major superhero movie with *Captain Marvel*, and Natalie Holt wrote music we may never hear for the axed *Batgirl* film. Why is there such reticence from the big studios to hire women for action movies?

Karpman is quick to praise Kevin Feige, the president of Marvel Studios: 'He keeps hiring me over and over and over again, and he trusts me.' Yet she also provides much-needed (and generally depressing) insight into life as a woman composer in Hollywood. 'You have to understand the profound – and I mean *profound* – belief that was said out loud to me many times, by famous composers, that women *can't* write action scores. It was said to my students, in 2020.' On what grounds? 'I've been told multiple times that my music is not masculine enough, muscular enough, every conceivable pejorative.'

For Karpman, Marvel has proved to be the exception, because 'people are thinking more about what they want for a particular set of characters, just like on any project, whether it be superhero or documentary, it's the same.'

The idea that action music *needs* to be 'masculine' or 'muscular' often means simply that it leans heavily into more percussive elements, with the music effectively replicating the onscreen sounds of a chase, or a fight. We've all seen plenty of forgettable action films in which it becomes impossible to distinguish between the sounds of drumbeats and gunfire, or in which the score strives to accentuate every body blow, simply doubling up on already crunchy sound effects. The challenge is to find a balance between these elements, for the composer to work *with* the soundscape rather than attempting to enter into a battle of volume.

Laura Karpman praises the Oscar-winning sound mixer Lora Hirschfeld, with whom she has collaborated on Marvel projects, for helping her to find that all-important sweet spot. 'There's so much editing and so much trying and retrying,' she says. 'Everybody puts *everything* in and then things are refined later. On *The Marvels*, it was a very long post-production process so we had a longer opportunity to really get into that. There were certain things, like the planet of Aladna, that had very specific needs, so I collaborated very, very closely with Sound on that. Other times you're just going forth and hoping for the best at the end, and hoping that you have a good sound mixer and film-makers who understand when is right for sound effects and when is right for music.'

For Karpman, the key question is always: 'How can we have a presence of music in a sequence where there's a tremendous amount of sound? What part of the aural spectrum is available?' As David Arnold recalls, 'In the early days, it was very much the war of the twenty-seven Pro Tools systems in the dub, twenty-*six* of which had sound effects and dialogue on them, versus *one* with the music on it!' For Arnold, close collaboration with the sound designers is crucial, enabling the different elements to work together, although 'sometimes you just have to wait for the moment for the music to take over and hope that the sound guys are on the same page'.

*

Sound supervisor and designer Richard King has won five Academy Awards for his work, three of them for Christopher Nolan films: *The Dark Knight, Inception* and 2017's *Dunkirk* – all masterclasses in fusing sound and music to intense effect. King has worked with the director on each of his films since *The Prestige* (2006) and, in 2017, he described his role as building a world for the *characters* to live in, whereas the composers create the sounds for the *audience* to hear.

When Ludwig Göransson was a guest on my *Kermode on Film* podcast to mark the release of *Tenet* (2020), he marvelled at Nolan's acute awareness of the audience's sonic experience, and how this impacts the film as a whole: 'He's figured out a completely new way of mixing music and working with the speakers,' Göransson explained. 'Something that's interesting with cinema is that the screen hasn't really changed in the last fifty years. You go into the theatre and you're sitting down and you see a huge screen in front of you. But something that keeps changing every five to ten years is the speakers and the sound. We can get to new frequencies and we can find new ways of giving the audience a crazier experience and, in terms of music, that was something that Chris was really into.'

One of Nolan's most high-profile sonic experiments has been his use of the so-called 'Shepard tone', an auditory illusion named after American cognitive scientist Roger Shepard. First adopted by Nolan on *The Prestige*, the Shepard tone is essentially a superimposition of octave-divided sine-waves, which, as Nolan explains, creates 'this illusion of a continuing rise in pitch that never goes out of range'. It might be easier to visualize it as the musical equivalent of a barber's pole on which the red spiral appears to move forward while actually remaining stationary.

The Shepard tone has featured within various Hans Zimmer scores for Nolan films and has also been used as part of the sound design. For example, it helped create the sonic motif for the Batpod (the motorbike version of the Batmobile) in *The*

Dark Knight. Zimmer is keen to hint, however, that the Shepard tone is just the *start* of the experimentation, telling me in 2019 that 'Chris [Nolan] and I swore to each other, and we've stuck to this, that everybody gets the rising note, that's fine, but there's an equally important element which we will *not* tell you. There's a secret ingredient, and the secret ingredient nearly killed all of us. You know how that is – it seems like such a good idea at the time, nobody's done it, and then you find out why nobody's done it, because it will kill you!'

Nolan seems to have incorporated the structure of the Shepard tone into the very fabric of *Dunkirk*, his gripping war drama told from the land, sea and air, the three elements woven together with heightening intensity. Ingeniously, these separate strands play out over three different time periods: one week, one day and one hour, respectively. As the stories interlace, with boats, boots and planes converging at Dunkirk, so time itself is variously compressed and elongated in *Inception*-like loops, conjuring shifts and reversals as complex – yet still crucially clear – as those of Nolan's 2000 psychological thriller *Memento*. For all its visual splendour, *Dunkirk* is a masterclass in dextrous temporal elasticity, a recurrent theme for Nolan.

Appropriately for a film in which time plays such a crucial role, the score and sound design of *Dunkirk* make astute use of a ticking clock to propel the tension. Sound effects are as vital to the storytelling as the dialogue; it's no coincidence that the script was about half as long as Nolan's previous films. As the director reflected ahead of the film's release, 'In the editing, we were layering in the sound effects and these tracks according to this rhythm, as we were cutting picture, so in that way, for better or for worse, we've been able to achieve a fusion of music, effects and picture in *Dunkirk* that we've never really been able to achieve before'.

Beneath it all is Zimmer's devastating score: a blend of regret, tension and expectation that rises like the tide, moving from metronomic staccato stabs through growling bass beats to ethereal elegiac suspensions that bizarrely bridge the gap between Elgar and Angelo Badalamenti. Even the most nail-biting sequences have a mournful quality (Nolan cites the 1930 film *All Quiet on the Western Front* as a tonal inspiration) with which Zimmer is perfectly in tune. It was clearly a labour of love: 'I can't tell you what a miracle it is that we managed to finish that score . . .' says Zimmer. 'Us getting really nerdy and really out of control and, yep, paying the price.'

Nolan's next film, 2020's *Tenet*, may seem to be more 'typical' action fare (it has car chases and heist sequences aplenty), yet, as with *Inception*, these saleable elements are just window-dressing for an altogether more complex tale in which time is bent, manipulated and reversed.

Unsurprisingly, Ludwig Göransson tells me he was grateful to have the luxury of time for his first collaboration with Nolan. 'Chris and I worked together on this for about one and a half years, on *just* the music,' he explains. 'We had about six months to experiment before they actually started to shoot, which is really important because that's when Chris has some time to spare. So I would write music every day and present that to him every other week. I would go to his office and we would listen to it together, dissect every little sound, every little theme, every little melody. We'd go over what we liked about it, what we didn't like about it, and we did that for four months together. So when he took off to shoot, he had about two hours of music and sounds that we'd been collecting and building together in his headphones.'

Having the music with him on set allowed Nolan to give very specific feedback to his composer while shooting the film. 'He would send me emails like "Hey, I'm listening to this, we're shooting a scene now. About three minutes into this cue that you wrote, I'm envisioning the terrorists coming in – can you add more distortion to the synths here?" That's a great note, but I was like, "OK, what's he *seeing* here?"'

If Göransson felt as if he was writing blind, he put his faith in Nolan's exacting vision. When the director returned from the shoot and started editing, he invited the composer to his studio to watch the opening scene. Göransson recalls: 'He had taken the five-minute cue that we'd been working on, the one that he sent me notes on from Estonia. He'd taken that music snippet and just put it into the scene. It was crazy, it was like an out-of-body experience for me because I'm seeing this and I'm hearing my music, almost like I've scored it for the film but it's the *reverse*. Chris listened to it while he was shooting and shot it to the music, almost.' Oddly appropriate for a palindromic movie in which the action plays backwards and forwards in head-scrambling fashion.

*

Lorne Balfe notes that contemporary action scores tend to feature 'irregular rhythms, interesting and strange time signatures, something that would never happen thirty years ago. Now, the audience aren't shocked by it any longer, they welcome it.' *Tenet* is a great example of pushing such boundaries, and Göransson explains that 'the main rhythm of *Tenet* is what opens up the whole movie. That rhythm is four bars of 3/4 and one bar of 4/4.' That final bar feels like a wake-up jolt because it's not where you think it's going to be, keeping the viewer on their toes. You might not be conscious of it happening, but you're aware that *something* odd and out of place is occurring.

Laura Karpman enjoys the freedom provided by action scores for playing with time signatures, believing that 'Having a distinct or a recognizable rhythmic profile, even outside of what's going on note-wise and harmonically, is really important.' She also admires composers who can take a step back with their scores and offer the audience a broader overview.

'Something that I like and admire about Hans Zimmer's work', she observes, 'is that sometimes he'll create these long lines that are really neat and that play over action as opposed to addressing it specifically. I've thought a lot about that, where it's not really tight but you're doing a larger emotional arc over a sequence.'

In other words, playing *through* the action.

However, Karpman adds, 'if there's one major criticism I have of modern action films, it's that film-makers really need to focus on what they want sound to do at any given moment, and that is really, really important.'

It's a concern that's echoed by David Arnold, who warns against the practice of simply turning everything up to eleven (music, sound effects, whatever) to give a scene greater impact. Instead, Arnold tries to show directors and producers how – as well as *where* – the music he's recorded will go in a scene, manually operating the levels. 'I always have the dialogue and effects on one fader and the music on another, and then I just duck and dive; music up when it really drives it, and down when the effects should be doing the work. You do a little live mix of it, to sell the idea of how it's working in the movie.'

For Arnold, balance is everything. 'When the music is loud,' he says, 'a lot of the effects and the bits and pieces are redundant in a way. Sometimes I've seen films that I've done where I thought the music was too loud. And there's certainly a couple where I felt like it was *so* exciting when we heard this in the studio, and the producers and the director got *so* excited because it was really working well – and then you find out that it's been buried under an avalanche of usually helicopters or explosions or bullets.'

These experiences shape how Arnold approaches action scores now. 'You learn not to write so much underneath that stuff, because you know that if you're *seeing* things like explosions on screen, then you're definitely *hearing* them.' (He adds: 'The worst thing is when you hear *off*-screen stuff that you didn't even know was there . . .!')

Whether it's fighting for space with sound effects or avoiding falling into stereotype, Lorne Balfe is mindful of the challenges unique to composing action films, as it's a musical world in which he spends a lot of time. He observes, 'Every project you do as a composer, you're trying to have a new approach, you're trying to bring a new voice. And if you keep doing the same genre continuously, it's very difficult to bring something new to the table.'

For James Newton Howard, that task of bringing something new to the table drives him to question every note he writes, and self-critically to ask whether it could be better. 'I'm constantly trying to avoid clichés,' he says with disarming candour, 'yet I'm constantly writing things that *are* clichés and going, "James, *why* did you write that, it's so *lame*, you gotta go back . . ." I have to rein myself in constantly, but that's a process of self-improvement. I'd like to think that with every score I do, my intention is to make it the best score I've ever written. I think if I don't do that, I should quit.'

Soundtrack Selection:
Crash (1996)

Very few movies could be described as 'perfect', but every once in a while, one comes pretty close. My own personal list of (near) perfect films would include Maya Deren's *Meshes of the Afternoon* (1943), Powell and Pressburger's *A Matter of Life and Death* (1946), Céline Sciamma's *Petite Maman* (2021) and David Cronenberg's *Crash*, the last of which benefits immeasurably from the shattered shards of Howard Shore's score – my favourite score of 1996.

I was working as film critic for the UK pop station BBC Radio 1 when Cronenberg's adaptation of J. G. Ballard's 1973 novel became a scandalous *cause célèbre* that made international headlines. When the film premiered at Cannes, it was denied a deserved Palme d'Or win thanks largely to the disdain of jury president Francis Ford Coppola, who seems to have detested the movie. Instead, *Crash* earned a 'special jury prize', which Cronenberg called 'the jury's attempt to get around the Coppola negativity'. Speaking in 2021, on the eve of a 4K restoration of *Crash*, Cronenberg noted sardonically: 'I've run into [Coppola] several times at various festivals. Always the first thing he says is: "Remember, we gave you this award." In fact, during the final closing night ceremony he wouldn't hand me the award. He had someone else hand it to me. He wouldn't do it himself.'

Lambasted by the *Evening Standard* ('beyond the bounds of depravity'), boycotted by the *Daily Mail* and banned from cinemas in Westminster (really), *Crash* proved to be a brilliant screen translation of a text whose author had variously called his source a 'psychopathic hymn', a 'cautionary' tale and 'the first pornographic novel based on technology'. Focusing on individuals seeking 'a new sexuality born from perverse technology', both book and film explore the fetishized eroticism of car crashes in a manner that is at once deeply existential and darkly comedic.

As I said: near perfect.

Shore's crystalline score exactly captures both the alienation and the fascination at the core of *Crash*, using brittle-edged electric guitars to evoke the glimmer of shiny metallic surfaces and spiralling shattered windshields. It's an unsettling listen, to be sure, but (as with the film) there is a strange beauty behind the horror – a sense of sadness underpinning the elements of shock.

At the Edinburgh International Film Festival, I hosted an onstage event with Shore in which he brought along a then-futuristic laptop computer from which he played some early stems of his work on *Crash*. Those stems were more agitated than the sparse notation of the finished score, and I vividly remember Shore explaining the process of filtering out the noise of his first stabs at the theme, likening the process to picking through a million shards of broken glass to find the few pieces that were the key to the mosaic of the music.

'I don't recall saying that!' laughs Shore today. 'But it's an interesting approach. In actual fact, the score to *Crash* came out of the score to *M. Butterfly* [1993], which was an earlier film that I did with David. In the orchestration of *M. Butterfly*, I used two orchestral harps, and I positioned them to the left and right of the podium. These were live recordings, and I was interested in that two-harp counterpoint. And then I wanted to extend that – to write a piece for *three* harps. But after I finished work on *M. Butterfly*, I didn't have a place for it.'

When Cronenberg and Shore began to discuss the director's next project, however, the seeds of a sound had already been implanted in the composer's head. 'I had started to sketch out these counterpoints and harmonies for a three-part harp piece,' he says. 'And once I had that, I then thought I would apply that to *Crash*. So then I adapted the harp music for three electric guitars – times two. It was two guitars on each part, which became six. So the music from *Crash* really grew out of an earlier piece.'

What's most remarkable about this process is that, despite one project growing organically from another, the scores for *M. Butterfly* and *Crash* could not be more different. The former, written for Cronenberg's screen adaptation of David Henry Hwang's stage play (which was itself inspired by real events), boasts lush orchestration and a tender sense of romance, tinged with loss and melancholia. The dual harp lines amplify the emotional core of the film; this is a score that, almost literally, plucks at our heartstrings.

Crash, on the other hand, is jagged and abrasive, an edgy collection of spiky guitar riffs that don't so much intertwine as do violent battle with each other. There's no comfort or warmth here, nothing designed to lure us into an unfolding love triangle. Instead, the music suggests a void-like feeling of emptiness – an extraordinary sense of alienation and alarm, wrapped around a sinewy air of threat and intrigue.

Two scores almost diametrically opposed in design and execution.

And yet one gave birth to the other in a manner that Shore finds entirely unsurprising.

'My music has been very linear,' the composer explains. 'It's really like I've been writing one very long piece, and I've been applying that music to various projects in different ways.'

Similarly, he tells me that his arrestingly dramatic music for *The Fly* – Cronenberg's radically visceral 1986 remake of a fifties creature-feature, based on George Langelaan's short story – was inspired by his regular visits to the Metropolitan Opera in New York. 'I had a seat at the Metropolitan Opera for twenty-five or thirty years,' he recalls. 'I was going to the opera all the time. And *The Fly* is heavily influenced by watching Puccini and Verdi performed there. That score was written with the passion of a great tragic opera, which later on, I did turn into an opera that played in Paris and in Los Angeles.'

As for *Crash*, my bold declaration on Radio 1 that it featured 'the best film score of the year' was promptly stickered onto CD releases of the soundtrack in the UK. I always wondered whether anyone bought that soundtrack on what appeared to be the recommendation of the nation's leading pop-music station. If so, what on earth would they have made of the disorientatingly glacial and occasionally jarring sounds that make up that brilliantly worrying score? It's hardly a poptastic celluloid-jukebox choice, although I did play several tracks from it on my Radio 1 film show, until I was politely asked to stop doing so by the management, who found it 'a little harsh on the ears'.

Nearly three decades later, it still sounds pretty much perfect to me.

CHAPTER 8

Pop Goes the Movies

There is a theory that the marriage between pop music and cinema began in 1955, when director Richard Brooks slapped a Bill Haley B-side onto the opening credits of his hard-hitting social drama *Blackboard Jungle*, and unwittingly changed the world. The American musician and author Marshall Crenshaw lends great weight to this theory in his hugely readable 1994 book *Hollywood Rock: A Guide to Rock'n'Roll in the Movies*, and I pretty much repeated it in a chapter that I wrote for the British Film Institute's book *Celluloid Jukebox: Popular Music and the Movies Since the 50s*, published in 1995 to celebrate 'Forty years of popular music and the movies'. The theory goes something like this:

In May 1954, Bill Haley & His Comets released 'Thirteen Women (And Only One Man in Town)' on the Decca label, a single which achieved at best moderate success. On the flip-side of the disc was an upbeat Max C. Freedman and James E. Meyers (aka Jimmy De Knight) composition, recorded in haste at the end of the same session which had produced the A-side. According to legend, Sammy Davis Jr was in the lobby, waiting for *his* turn at the microphone, so Haley had to wrap things up fast.

At around the same time, film-maker Richard Brooks was working on his screen adaptation of Evan Hunter's novel *The Blackboard Jungle*, a streetwise tale of racially diverse kids at an inner-city school, many of whom engage in what was politely called 'anti-social behaviour'. Brooks's film starred Glenn Ford as new teacher Richard Dadier, who attempts to quell and harness the anger in these pupils. The cast also includes Sidney Poitier in a breakout role as the talented but rebellious student Gregory W. Miller. The subject matter was clearly controversial ('It's Real . . . It's Timely! A Shock Story of Today's High School Hoodlums!'), and Brooks was keen to give his movie a sharp contemporary edge. So he went looking for an up-to-the-minute tune to evoke the youth milieu central to the picture.

Exactly what happened next is a matter of debate, and several versions of the story are in widespread circulation. The most popular of these has Brooks rifling through Ford's son Peter's record collection and chancing upon Haley's 'Thirteen Women', which he promptly flipped over . . . and flipped out. MGM duly licensed the B-side track from Decca, who reissued it when *Blackboard Jungle* became the movie of the moment. 'Rock Around the Clock' subsequently spent eight weeks at the top of the Billboard pop chart, and went on to become the first rock 'n' roll record to hit the Number 1 spot in both the US and the UK.

The genius of this epochal cinematic needle-drop is that Haley's previously obscure recording somehow lent Brooks's movie a sparkling air of 'now-ness' that was then miraculously reflected back onto the record itself. The tune helped the movie become a sensation – but it was the movie that turned the record into a smash hit. Moreover, despite the fact that there is no other rock 'n' roll in the film, *Blackboard Jungle* somehow became the 'first rock 'n' roll movie', attracting audiences who wanted to hear 'Rock Around the Clock' blaring out through movie-theatre speakers far more powerful than those of the jukeboxes in coffee bars. Reports started flooding in of kids dancing in the aisles and slashing cinema seats, overwhelmed by the heady mix of pop music and moving images. As contributing writer David Rubel says in *Hollywood Rock*: 'Watching *Blackboard Jungle*, you get the feeling that when the schlockmeisters in Hollywood saw this film for the first time, they shot right up out of their seats and shouted, "Yes! That's it!"'

Brooks's movie did indeed kick off a string of films that married pop music and movies to lucrative effect, thereby ensuring its place in the history books. But look closer and you'll discover that the genetic connection between these two art forms can be traced back much further – right back to the 1920s, when the arrival of 'sound cinema' first promised to dazzle audiences with high-fidelity sound and vision.

*

On Saturday 29 June 1929, the Baltimore newspaper *The Afro American* ran a page-eight piece headlined ' "St. Louis Blues" to be new picture'. According to the story, 'Plans have been completed and work begun on an all-talking, all-singing photoplay version of W. C. Handy's world-famous song by that name, by the R.C.A. Photophone company'. The article went on to explain that in the two-reel short feature 'Bessie Smith will be the star "blues" singer . . . and will be supported by a chorus of 35 voices selected from the best musical organisations in this city'. The setting of the movie, according to *The Afro American*, would be 'a Memphis tenement house and dance hall', with promised appearances from bassist Freddie Washington, cornetist Johnny Dunn and Jimmy Johnson on the piano.

Directly beneath that article was an advertisement for a local picture house ('If it is good, see it at the Dunbar'), emblazoned with the legend 'The Talkies are Coming!' and an announcement of George Bias's new recording of 'Tell the South!' on Columbia's 'Race Record Catalog'. Meanwhile, across the page, the Regent theatre boasted of the 'All Talking Fox Movietone Feature *In Old Arizona*', which was apparently playing to packed houses.

Filmed in the Astoria district of Queens, New York, director Dudley Murphy's sixteen-minute *St Louis Blues* (1929) is credited on screen as an 'Alfred N. Sack' presentation made 'by special arrangement with W. C. Handy'. The film opens with a group of men shooting dice at the bottom of the stairs in an apartment building (or 'rooming house'). A broom-wielding janitor interrupts their game, insisting that 'White man is paying me to keep this here place clean!' But a couple of bucks sends the janitor away happy, with the promise that the fun can continue as long as he gets his cut ('Don't come round *too* regular'). Enter Jimmy Mordecai's sharp-dressed rogue, who gambles, wins, and then retires to a room with Isabelle Washington's fancy girl, who assures him: 'Stick with me and you'll always have money.'

Thus far, it's good-natured if rather risqué fare. But when Bessie Smith bursts in on the couple who are using her room as a knocking shop, things take an altogether more sinister turn. At first, Bessie has the upper hand, slapping the young floozie around the head before chasing her out of the door. When the janitor returns, complaining about the hullabaloo, she smacks him too. But when Bessie plaintively begs the despicable Jimmy not to leave her, he places his hand squarely over her face and pushes her violently to the ground, where she remains for the rest of the scene. Packing his bag and buttoning up his suit (a suit that *she* bought him), Jimmy steps over Bessie's prone body, giving her a kick before slamming the door.

No matter how many times you watch *St Louis Blues*, the brutality of this scene remains shocking. Mordecai's performance may contain a hint of comedic pantomime villainy, suggesting that the film is winking at its target audience, and yet the material remains tough. A century later, the mistreatment of women would still be one of the most headline-grabbing elements of rock, pop and rap videos, with debates raging about whether they depict, deconstruct, or simply glorify such violence. Although it's clear that *St Louis Blues* sees the world through the eyes of Smith's battered heroine – her song providing the narration – it's worth remembering that the issues which still surround modern pop videos can be traced back to the very earliest talking pictures.

As Jimmy leaves the apartment, Bessie slumps against the wall, reaching for a bottle. Pouring herself a shot, she begins to sing: 'My man, my man . . .' We move to a close-up on her face and shoulder, as Smith downs her drink and wails: 'My man's got a heart like a rock cast in the sea . . .' The picture fades to black, and then cross-cuts to a speakeasy, where we find Bessie propping up the bar, still singing a capella. Behind her, the barkeep tends the glasses, a cigarette clamped coolly between his lips. And now cinematographer Walter Strenge's camera, which has previously been all but static, begins to move, tracking slowly through an array of patrons, across the front of a band (James P. Johnson on piano, Thomas Morris and Joe Smith on cornet, Bernard Addison on guitar and banjo) and back to the customers, who join in with choral accompaniment. We cut to a wide-shot as more patrons arrive. The Hall Johnson Choir ('arrangements by W. C. Handy and Rosamond Johnson') swells in mighty fashion, accompanied by Fletcher Henderson's orchestra, with Smith still belting out the lead from a bar stool. After a couple of verses, the tempo picks up and the band switch to a ragtime beat. We see couples dancing and waiters spinning trays, while Bessie still forlornly nurses a beer.

Then, Jimmy enters the club and starts to hoof energetically in the middle of the floor. A remarkable shot finds him with his head tilted down towards the camera, the top of his hat almost immobile in the middle of the screen, as crazy arms and legs fly out at every angle. Seeing Smith at the bar, he calls over to her: 'Bessie! Bessie!' She throws her arms around him, and they dance together, as a cornet reprises the key theme from *St Louis Blues*. But as they smooch, Jimmy's hand strays down Bessie's back, to pull some folded dollars from her garter, where she's presumably put them for safekeeping. Pushing Bessie away violently, as the crowd look on, he holds up the money, tips his hat, and swaggers to the door, the cornet sarcastically picking out a lick from Gershwin's 'Rhapsody in Blue'. As the chorus surges, Bessie is back at the bar – dejected, drunken, desolate.

The End.

Using a fairly advanced recording system, which allowed for post-production over-dubbings, *St Louis Blues* followed in the footsteps of other short features which had similarly tapped into the market for audio-visual blues. In June 1929, Columbia Pictures had released *Jailhouse Blues*, in which Mamie Smith sings for the release of her 'jailhouse rat' man who 'loves the jail so well he stays there all the time'. Dressed in a tartan hat and feathery top, Mamie sings while supporting players provide inmate accompaniment from behind bars. Two months later, King Vidor's 'all-Black' musical *Hallelujah* (1929) played to sell-out crowds in Harlem. As film historian and blues musician (not to mention fellow Dodge Brother) Dr Mike Hammond notes: 'It seems that with the coming of film sound, there was a genuine move to record blues or blues/jazz music through this new format. This tied in with the Harlem renaissance [the development of the neighbourhood as a Black cultural mecca in the early twentieth century and the resultant social and artistic explosion that followed] and the increasing influence of African American idioms on Tin Pan Alley songwriting.'

In short, the birth of sound cinema was linked from the outset to a surge in the reach and influence of African American blues. By extension, rock 'n' roll itself owed its very existence to the movies.

Although the chance to see and hear Bessie Smith sing was the primary selling point of *St Louis Blues* (the film is, as far as we know, her only screen appearance), what makes this short so timelessly compelling is the sheer level of artistry with which it is constructed. More than just a prototype pop video, *St Louis Blues* is an adventurously expressive film in its own right, a motion picture that takes full advantage of the changing landscape of cinema technology. In an article in *The Film Daily* on Sunday 15 September 1929, headlined 'Sound Makes Possible More Novelty in Shorts', production supervisor Richard 'Dick' Currier hailed the arrival of sound as being of the utmost significance to the development of short-form films, even more so than feature films. 'The old groove of the short subject, the program-filler groove, is outmoded,' Currier declared proudly. 'Here at Gramercy studios, we have been experimenting with the new sound phase and the short subject, and we feel that we have evolved a medium which is at once motion picture and dramatic talking action.'

Currier went on to explain: 'I also find that the boundless possibilities of the camera, with its numerous angles and changes of setting, lend to the talking short feature an opportunity for coherent blending of picture and sound. We have attempted to do this, as for example in "St Louis Blues" . . . in which the mood of the pictures is not only created by the talk and music, but by the pictorial action which has been harmonized with the sound.'

In these early days of the talkies, the Vitaphone sound-on-disc system became a popular way of providing synchronized film sound via the use of 16-inch phonograph records which would be played on a turntable mechanically connected to the rotation of the projector. This was the system that helped make *The Jazz Singer* a sensation in 1927: a series of records playing along to a silent picture in which Al Jolson proudly told cinema-goers: 'You ain't heard nuthin' yet!' This was also the system that made a star of Roy Smeck, whose virtuosity on a range of stringed instruments earned him the title 'Wizard of the Strings'. In 1926, Smeck starred in the Vitaphone short *His Pastimes*, in which he's seen playing a lap guitar, ukulele and banjo while seated on a small wooden bench, surrounded by flowers and foliage. During one song, he appears to swallow a small harmonica, before playing it (without hands) clamped between his teeth! The entire film consists of a single seven-minute shot, with unsteady camera wobble being the only movement. Smeck doesn't speak a word, but then neither did John Barrymore in *Don Juan* (1926), the feature film for which *His Pastimes* provided warm-up support, and onto which Warner Brothers had retrofitted a Vitaphone soundtrack featuring music and sound effects.

Smeck had already appeared on screen in the 1923 short *Stringed Harmony*, which used an early optical sound-on-film system developed by Lee de Forest and Theodore Case. But *His Pastimes* was Roy's passport to the stars, a sensation which brought his twanging antics to a previously unimaginable audience. In many ways, Roy Smeck was cinema's first true pop star, a pioneering musician who found international fame through film, and who went on to appear in a string of shorts such as 1932's *Club-House Party* and 1933's *That Goes Double*, the latter of which saw him playing lap steel guitar, banjo, ukulele and Spanish guitar simultaneously thanks to a then-mind-blowing four-way split-screen effect. The same year, Smeck played at Franklin D. Roosevelt's inaugural ball. Four years later, he performed for the coronation of King George VI. Pop stars really didn't come any bigger than Roy – thanks to the movies.

As the popularity of short musical films increased in the early thirties, Warner Bros launched the 'Spooney Melodies' series – short films (later renamed the 'Song'nata' series) that combined music with live action and simple animation. In 1930, for example, *Cryin' for the Carolines* featured 'The Singing Organist' Milton Charles and was hailed by *Photoplay* magazine as a 'beautiful' work that offered 'a distinct relief from the monotony of many sound shorts'. And in that same year, Paul Whiteman got his very own full-colour feature film, the lavishly mounted *King of Jazz* (1930), which bombed in spite of some surreal and spectacular visuals and an early appearance by Bing Crosby as one of the harmonizing 'Rhythm Boys'.

By the time the forties rolled around, the fusion of popular music and movies was well established, offering a route into

Hollywood, which was otherwise often denied to Black performers. The line-up of 1943's *Stormy Weather*, for example, included Cab Calloway (who would go on to steal John Landis's 1980s extravaganza *The Blues Brothers*) alongside Lena Horne and Bill 'Bojangles' Robinson. In the film's most celebrated scene, the Nicholas Brothers dance to Cab Calloway's 'Jumpin' Jive' – a sequence that takes the breath away with its grace, dexterity and athleticism. Fred Astaire called it the greatest movie musical number he had ever seen, with the Brothers leaping nimbly between the instruments of the orchestra, and doing flying splits up and down a giant staircase, as if suspended from above by invisible bands of elastic. It really is astonishing!

But it wasn't only song-and-dance pioneers who made their way onto the big screen. Overdub-recording innovator and inventor of the electric guitar Les Paul made *his* first feature-film appearance in 1944, popping up in *Sensations of 1945*, a musical comedy which picked up an Oscar nomination for Best Musical Scoring. A few years later, in 1947, Paul cameoed in *Sarge Goes to College*, playing one of his many home-made instruments in a jazzy jam session workout with Wingy Manone, Jess Stacy, Jerry Wald, Joe Venuti and Abe Lyman. The band's performance is a treat, spiced up by the sight of laid-back drummer Lyman reading the paper while playing, putting down his sticks to turn the pages, a fuming cigar chomped firmly between his teeth. According to the plot, the group are holed up in a single room in San Juan, en route to Hollywood where they're meant to be 'making a picture' – something which, by then, had become well established as the natural 'next step' for all upcoming musos.

*

All this and more had been playing out on screens around the world long before Richard Brooks gave us the 'first rock 'n' roll movie' in 1955. But while *Blackboard Jungle* may have followed in the footsteps of decades of films that had previously exploited the marriage of popular music and movies, it definitely opened the floodgates of a new pop-movie boom. From the prototype jukebox musical *Rock, Rock, Rock* (1956), in which 'King of Rock 'n' Roll' Alan Freed wrangles the likes of Chuck Berry, LaVern Baker and Frankie Lymon, to *High School Confidential* (1958), in which Jerry Lee Lewis famously performed the title track on the back of a flatbed truck, pop movies became a saleable sensation. Best of the bunch was Frank Tashlin's *The Girl Can't Help It* (1956), an audacious romp featuring onscreen musical offerings from the likes of Gene Vincent and the Blue Caps, Eddie Cochran, Julie London, Fats Domino and (most notably) Little Richard, all served up in CinemaScope and DeLuxe colour. Meanwhile, Fred F. Sears directed the incongruously aged and weirdly kiss-curled Bill Haley in both *Rock Around the Clock* (1956; 'It's the Whole Story of Rock and Roll!') and *Don't Knock the Rock* (1956), while *Shake, Rattle and Rock!* (1956) promised 'Rock 'n' Roll vs the "Squares"', with Fats Domino keeping things thrilling.

It was also 1956 that saw the release of a peculiar Western that gave third billing to an upcoming performer whose role in the movie would usher in a whole new era of saleable pop-star vehicles. That April, Elvis Presley topped the Billboard charts with 'Heartbreak Hotel' – becoming a media sensation through live performances, newspaper interviews, radio airplay and TV shows. But in November of that same year, the Western–musical hybrid *Love Me Tender* brought Elvis into the movie theatres, opening up an arena into which the star (whose lascivious hip-swinging initially scandalized audiences) would soon disappear.

Love Me Tender was the only time in Elvis's screen career that he did not receive top billing, his name appearing on posters beneath those of more established stars Richard Egan and Debra Paget. But by the time *Loving You* opened in 1957, Presley was the main attraction, his name dominating the publicity for *Jailhouse Rock* (1957) and *King Creole* (1958), the latter of which was grittily directed by *Casablanca*-helmer Michael Curtiz, from a novel by Harold Robbins.

These early vehicles, made before Elvis's stint in the army, were as powerful and profitable as any tour that the star could undertake. Shot relatively quickly, they served to promote his image and brand abroad, a substitute for the live appearances which Elvis notably failed to make outside the United States. More importantly, they also stand as evidence that Elvis, who idolized Marlon Brando, really could act as well as sing, suggesting that a career in 'serious' movies possibly lay ahead. Yet by the time Elvis finished military service, his wheeler-dealer manager Colonel Tom Parker (who was neither a real colonel, nor indeed a 'Tom Parker') had locked him into lucrative film contracts that saw him churning out cheap and often trashy movies, earning him a million a picture but effectively keeping him trapped exactly where Parker wanted him – in Hollywood.

While the big screen was suddenly awash with pop stars, the small screen was also getting in on the game with the emergence of the 'music video'. Some pop historians have credited Tony Bennett with creating the first-ever music video in 1956 – a short film of him wandering through London's picturesque Hyde Park, made to promote his hit 'Stranger in Paradise'. As for the term 'music video', this is generally believed to have been coined by

Jiles Perry Richardson Jr., aka The Big Bopper, in an interview with the editor of *Rockin' 50s* magazine. Speaking shortly before his death in February 1959 (he went down in the same plane crash that killed Richie Valens and Buddy Holly), Richardson described shooting three short promotional films for 'Chantilly Lace', 'The Big Bopper's Wedding' and 'Little Red Riding Hood', all on the same day in 1958, and he called them 'music videos'.

The twin strands of pop movies and music videos were given an anarchic boost in July 1964 by The Beatles' first big-screen feature, *A Hard Day's Night*. In stark contrast to the old-school vibe of Presley's 1964 offering *Viva Las Vegas*, which had been directed by George Sidney (who made *Annie Get Your Gun*, 1950, and *Show Boat*, 1951), *A Hard Day's Night* was shot in *cinema verité*-style black and white, and owed more to the French New Wave than to any Hollywood musical tradition. Directed by Richard Lester, who had greatly impressed the Fab Four with his Peter Sellers short *The Running, Jumping & Standing Still Film* (1959), *A Hard Day's Night* soon became the benchmark for adventurous pop movies. While *Viva Las Vegas* is a standard star vehicle rooted in the brightly lit big-screen productions of the forties and fifties, *A Hard Day's Night* is filled with non-linear jump-cuts and boldly comedic edits, helicopter shots crashing up against handheld-camera sequences, sped-up and slowed-down in manically carefree fashion.

What *A Hard Day's Night* amply demonstrated was that pop music is a chameleonic art form that reflects, mimics and occasionally shapes the zeitgeist, and if movies were to capitalize upon its appeal, then they needed to share some of that rock 'n' roll spirit in their own construction. Take Michelangelo Antonioni's swinging sixties classic *Blow-Up* (1966), a self-deconstructing tale of voyeurism and detection in which a photographer finds himself at the centre of a murder mystery that simply falls apart – much like the movie itself. Among the film's most celebrated set-pieces is a sequence in which David Hemmings's Thomas, a photographer, walks into a club where The Yardbirds are performing 'Stroll On/Train Kept a Rollin''. The sequence is historically important because it offers rare footage of both Jeff Beck and Jimmy Page on stage together, climaxing in them smashing up their instruments in the manner of The Who – the band Antonioni had originally wanted for the scene.

More importantly, that club sequence lent an air of up-to-the-minute cool to a movie that otherwise might have been overlooked as an arthouse indulgence, making it essential viewing for hip young audiences everywhere. Antonioni would repeat this trick with his 1970 film *Zabriskie Point*, in which the likes of (The) Pink Floyd, The Kaleidoscope, The Youngbloods and The Grateful Dead clash in a historic soundtrack whose original sleeve notes proclaim: 'It is more than just a case of a film of today demanding the music of today. Contemporary music doesn't merely tell a story or set a mood. It *is* the story, and *is* the mood.'

That description also perfectly fits Dennis Hopper's *Easy Rider* (1969), which cemented the arrival of the so-called 'New Hollywood' to the strains of Steppenwolf's 'Born to Be Wild'. The quintessential 'breakthrough' picture, *Easy Rider* was made for less than half a million dollars, and wound up taking in $60 million at the box office, its success driven in no small part by a hip rock soundtrack that brilliantly melded the counterculture sounds of the sixties – Hendrix, The Byrds, The Holy Modal Rounders – into an evocative document of a dying decade.

Throughout the late sixties and early seventies, every

fashionable film-maker in town was learning to plunder the jukebox in order to cement their cutting-edge reputations, while every 'serious' pop star seemed eager to get their music on screen for much the same reason. The results may have been variable (ranging from the adventurous to the purely exploitational), but the principle of a profitable bond between cinema and rock music seemed to have been set in stone. Alongside the seminal appearance of 'Come in Number 51, Your Time Is Up' on the soundtrack of *Zabriskie Point*, Pink Floyd's music would feature prominently in films by Iranian-born auteur Barbet Schroeder, providing scores for both 1969's *More* and 1972's *La Vallée*, aka *The Valley (Obscured by Clouds)*. In 1970, experimental German rock pioneers Can released an album entitled *Soundtracks*, consisting entirely of songs which had been featured in movies, including such sensational schlock as *Mädchen mit Gewalt* (1970), which translates literally as 'Maidens with Violence'. Released in America as *The Brutes* (it was also retitled *Cry Rape*) and boasting one of the most genuinely repugnant trailers I have ever seen, this is a movie which most people would rather gouge their eyes out than watch. But Can, eager for any celluloid association, provided tracks such as 'Soul Desert', presumably working on the assumption that *any* movie was good for business.

*

For many cineastes, the king of the cine-literate pop soundtrack is Martin Scorsese, who has earned a reputation as cinema's smartest musical magpie with films like *Mean Streets* (1973), *Goodfellas* (1990) and *Casino* (2006). In his preface to the BFI's *Celluloid Jukebox*, Scorsese declares that 'Popular music has the potential to give movies a forceful, dynamic edge', and goes on to cite the early example of William Wellman's 1931 gangster film *The Public Enemy*, which 'uses popular tunes in the background played out against the chilling violence on screen, creating a sense of bitter irony and authenticity'. For Scorsese, 'popular music formed the soundtrack of my life . . . and so it was only natural that it would become such an important part of my work as a director, beginning with my first student films.'

One of these was the student film *Bring on the Dancing Girls*, which was originally completed in 1965, but later expanded into the feature-length work *I Call First*, which screened at the Chicago International Festival in November 1967. The next year, distributor Joseph Brenner agreed to purchase the film on condition that Scorsese shoot and splice in a sex scene which could spice up the film's marketing. Reluctantly, Scorsese agreed, despite the fact that leading man Harvey Keitel now looked older than he did when shooting began in 1965.

Nevertheless, Scorsese concocted an artfully shot fantasy sequence in which Keitel's 'J.R.' romps naked on a bed with a series of beautiful women, a racy addition which he dutifully added to the newly retitled *Who's That Knocking at My Door* – a title taken from the 1959 Genies song which plays at the end of the movie. In order to raise the sex scene above the level of mere titillation, however, Scorsese slapped the 'killer awoke before dawn' segment from The Doors' 'The End' over the black-and-white scene, couching Keitel's erotic dreams within Jim Morrison's feverish narration about wanting to fuck his mother and kill his father. The scene, in which the camera circles restlessly around a spartan loft and lingers lovingly on close-ups of Keitel's eyes, face and body, is a perfect encapsulation of the blend of art, exploitation and pop music which would become the defining feature of Scorsese's oeuvre.

Years later, Francis Ford Coppola would follow Scorsese's lead by using 'The End' as the iconically ironic opening to *Apocalypse Now* (1979) – starting his film with a song that declares itself to be a finale. We see helicopters sweeping over lush vegetation, engulfing it in napalmed flames as Jim Morrison's droning voice tells us it's all over. As the camera pans slowly to the right, smoke fills the screen, and we cross-fade to the haggard face of Martin Sheen's Captain Willard, upside down, lost in dreams of the war-torn jungle, the blades of the helicopters transmuting into the blades of a hotel ceiling-fan.

The sounds of The Doors (about whom Oliver Stone would make a bloatedly indulgent biopic in the early nineties) had also turned up in Monte Hellman's 1971 cult classic *Two-Lane Blacktop*, one of several low-budget American pictures which used pop music to tap into the youth market in the wake of the runaway success of *Easy Rider*. Alongside The Doors' 'Moonlight Drive', other tracks used in Hellman's movie included Kris Kristofferson's 'Me and Bobby McGee' and Arlo Guthrie's 'Stealin'', while musician James Taylor starred as 'The Driver' and Beach Boy Dennis Wilson played 'The Mechanic'.

In each of these very different movies, pop songs (and pop stars) were being used by film-makers to lend an air of zeitgeisty 'now-ness' to their creations. All that was to change in 1973, with George Lucas's nostalgic elegy to a bygone age *American Graffiti* – arguably the first and certainly the finest 'jukebox movie'. Like *Blackboard Jungle*, eighteen years earlier, *American Graffiti* opened to the distinctive sounds of Bill Haley calling his audience to 'Rock Around the Clock'. But unlike the template established by Brooks, Lucas used the sounds of the Comets, Chuck Berry, Frankie Lymon et al. to take his audience out of the 'now' and back into the *past*. If pop music had previously served to give movies a contemporary edge, now it seemed that the genre was coming of age and starting to feel nostalgic for its own childhood.

Despite its pop-packed soundtrack, *American Graffiti* (for which the advertising slogan asked, 'Where Were You in '62?') is *not* a drive-in movie; rather, it is a remembrance of a drive-in movie, a poignant homage to the jukebox cinema culture that was already receding into the past. Set during the last summer night of 1962, the film follows a group of teenagers in Modesto, California, marauding together for one final time before adulthood beckons to tear them apart. Crucially, the film was specifically constructed by Lucas and sound designer Walter Murch to create a world in which the jukebox tracks that play throughout are part of the very fabric of the film – coming out of car radios, diners and transistor sets. Wherever you go in *American Graffiti*, the sounds of the songs (from 'Rock Around the Clock' to 'Johnny B. Goode' and 'Why Do Fools Fall in Love') are everywhere, jockeyed by legendary DJ Wolfman Jack, who becomes the film's unofficial narrator.

The origins of *American Graffiti* lie in a student film Lucas made with Murch while he was at the University of Southern California. Entitled *The Emperor* (1967), the film centred on the figure of Bob Hudson, a disc jockey who commanded the airwaves in Los Angeles in the mid-sixties. The pair would go on to collaborate on Lucas's ice-cold dystopian science fiction picture *THX 1138* (1971), in the wake of which fellow film-maker Francis Ford Coppola challenged Lucas to make a 'popular' film about young people. Inspired, Lucas screened Fellini's *I Vitellone* (1953), a European classic about Italian teenagers living at home, trying to figure out what to do with their lives. Drawing together themes from Fellini's film with personal recollections of his own youth and elements of *The Emperor*, Lucas sat down to write *American Graffiti*, with the radio broadcasts of Wolfman Jack at the centre of the drama.

Born Robert Weston Smith, 'Wolfman Jack' emerged as a gravelly-voiced radio DJ whose act took inspiration from a heritage of monster movies, and who broadcast to the US from Mexico, just across the Del Rio, Texas border, thus putting him out of the reach of the American authorities. His act was anarchic, irreverent and piratical, and he became a huge hit with kids who would call in to his show, creating a lively countercultural conversation that outraged the old and delighted the young.

With over forty songs on its soundtrack, *American Graffiti* featured wall-to-wall music, a bold move about which the studio was extremely nervous. There had been precedents, of sorts, such as Peter Bogdanovich's 1971 coming-of-age movie *The Last Picture Show* which leaned heavily on the diegetic retro sounds of songs from the early fifties by the likes of Hank Williams and other contemporaneous country and western stars. But *American Graffiti* was literally plastered with the kind of pop hits that would have been heard on radios and jukeboxes in 1962, leading to a total music-licensing cost of somewhere in the region of $80,000 – a huge sum for such a comparatively cheap movie, roughly a tenth of the total budget.

Universal begged Lucas to drop some of the songs, or to get cheaper soundalike bands to re-record the hits for a fraction of the cost. But having written his script with a 45 rpm record player by his side, putting the specific details of each disc into every scene, Lucas refused to compromise. As Murch told me: 'He would put on the record and go into a sort of dream-space and he would write the scene. And then at the head of the scene he would write out what the music was to go with this scene.'

The first assembly of *American Graffiti* was wrapped by editor Verna Fields (who would go on to work on Steven Spielberg's *Jaws*) in the autumn of 1972. Murch remembers that Fields took him aside and told him that the film was 'wonderful', but added: 'Please ask George not to use so much music. Because after fifteen minutes of this, people are just going to say "Turn off the music!"' To which Murch replied: 'Verna, I know where you're coming from, I know why you're saying that, but we have a plan . . '

The plan, which Murch had used on *THX 1138* and then on Coppola's *The Godfather*, was a process that he nicknamed 'worldizing'. It involved taking a piece of music or a sound effect, and then rather than running it through an electronic echo-chamber in order to create an artificial ambience, Murch would simply re-record it in the actual environment in which it appears in the film. 'So, if somebody turns on a radio and they're in a bathroom, take that piece of music and re-record it *in a bathroom*.' For *American Graffiti*, Lucas and Murch took the two-hour Wolfman Jack radio programme that Marcia Lucas had assembled to provide the backdrop to the film and went into the backyard of the house where they were editing. 'I had a Nagra tape recorder with a microphone, and George had a Nagra tape recorder with a speaker. And we stood about as far away from each other as we could in that backyard, turned on the tape recorders at the same time, and at oscillations of around five to ten seconds, George would move the speaker to the left and then 180 degrees to the right. And I would move my microphone counter to him.' Occasionally they would face each other for a direct recording, and at other times they would face away, picking up reverb within the quiet suburban location. This produced a 'worldized' track that could be mixed in with the film's dialogue, allowing the audience to 'focus on the dialogue when they need to focus on it, and then to enjoy the music at maximum impact when that's necessary. So that thing that Verna Fields was nervous about – the audience wanting us to turn the music *off* – never happened.'

The effect was uniquely immersive, creating the illusion of an 'entire town that was the pickle-jar full of the vinegar of this sound. No matter where you were in the town, you heard this music and the voice of Wolfman Jack'. Murch and Lucas had wanted the songs to be part of the sound design, rather than an after-the-fact addition. And they are! This was a key element often lacking from the inferior jukebox movies that followed in the wake of *American Graffiti*, as film companies got wise to the popularity of coming-of-age dramas such as the *Lemon Popsicle* series (1978–88), in which retro hits did all the period work.

Murch remembers that Universal 'didn't like the film, they didn't like the title, they didn't like the music', but that the audience's positive reaction to the first preview of *American Graffiti* affirmed they were onto something. Murch also recalls Francis Ford Coppola pulling out his chequebook and offering to buy the film from Universal executive Ned Tanen, who was convinced that it would flop. 'He was working on writing out a cheque for seven hundred and eighty thousand dollars – *Godfather* money – and Ned said, "Well, wait a minute, let's not be hasty . . ."' Coppola later told Murch that he should have just kept writing the cheque because *American Graffiti* became such a huge hit.

It's hard to understate the importance of *American Graffiti*'s legacy, and the effect that it had on the use of retro pop music in movies. Far more than the spate of throwback rock 'n' roll romances that followed in the seventies and eighties, *American*

Graffiti continues to be a template that is as relevant in the twenty-first century as it was back in 1973. Look, for example, at Reggie Yates's 2021 film *Pirates*, about three young Black British men spending a last night together on the cusp of the millennium – New Year's Eve 1999. Like *American Graffiti*, the film has a pirate radio backdrop that allows for a fairly constant barrage of garage and jungle tunes, from the likes of Sunship, Wookie, DJ Zinc, So Solid Crew, DJ Luck, MC Neat, Scott Garcia, Ms Dynamite and Hardrive, all of whom serve to establish the exact period milieu. While Yates cites Mathieu Kassovitz's *La Haine* (1995) as a primary influence for *Pirates*, he also acknowledges the shadow of *American Graffiti* that hangs over his movie, in which three kids cruise the streets of South London. To all intents and purposes, *Pirates* is a twenty-first-century British reworking of *American Graffiti*, tapping into the uncanny power of pop music to transport us back to a bygone place and time.

*

As British film producer Stephen Woolley once memorably told *Mojo* magazine: 'Pop music in movies is like a knife. You twist it, and nostalgia comes pouring out.' If George Lucas proved that point in *American Graffiti*, then director Philip Kaufman built upon Lucas's legacy in his initially underrated 1979 film *The Wanderers*. Based on a novel by Richard Price (author of *Clockers* and *Lush Life*), *The Wanderers* is set in the Bronx in 1963 and follows an Italian greaser gang's confrontation with imminent obsolescence. This is a time of massive social upheaval; Kennedy's assassination, which looms in the near future of *American Graffiti*, plays a key narrative role in Kaufman's film. Smartly using such period tracks as The Four Seasons' 'Walk Like a

Man', 'My Boyfriend's Back' by The Angels, Dion's 'Runaround Sue' and The Surfaris' 'Wipe Out', Kaufman marvellously blends aloof irony and loving admiration in his depiction of the gang's street-crawling escapades. Yet the Wanderers' greaseball life-style is under attack, and Kaufman dramatizes the generational threats to their existence through adroitly placed pop tunes. The arrival of proto hep-cat Nina – who unwittingly causes a rift in the gang – is signalled, for example, by the mellow refrain of 'Strangers on the Shore', which interrupts the pounding rock 'n' roll rhythms associated with the Wanderers. More bizarrely, appearances of the surreal, zombie-like Ducky Boys (a real-life Irish gang known as the 'Boogeymen of the Bronx') are accompanied throughout by discordant electronic wails and free-form drumming which, in one memorable fight scene, enter into an aural battle with Dion's 'The Wanderer'. At the end of the movie, anti-hero Richie – by now a man out of time – follows Nina to a darkened club where a silhouetted Bob Dylan plays 'The Times They Are A-Changin''. Richie, the old-school rock 'n' roller, cannot enter the club to follow the object of his desire. Instead, he is left alone, out on the street, literally locked out of the future.

Perhaps the most memorable scene from *The Wanderers* is the moment in which Richie and his estranged girlfriend stand outside a television shop on which the assassination of John F. Kennedy is playing out on the screens. The gathering crowd stand in stunned silence as Walter Cronkite confirms the tragedy, and the sounds of Ben E. King's 1962 recording 'Stand by Me' flood the film, bridging the transition from the historical assassination to the personal reconciliation of two key characters. Elsewhere, The Shirelles' 'Soldier Boy' accompanies a scene in which the Wanderers' sworn enemies the Baldies are drunkenly enlisted into the US Army – a mishap that sees them promptly dispatched, presumably to Vietnam, where the war was on the brink of massive escalation.

Unsurprisingly, the depiction of the Vietnam War, which became a staple subject of American movies in the late seventies and throughout the eighties, has leaned heavily on pop-music soundtracks, as directors sought to portray the slide from the comparative innocence of the early sixties into the catastrophe that followed. Whereas war movies were once played out to glorious orchestral themes (Eric Coates's stirring 'March' from *The Dam Busters*, 1955; Ron Goodwin's instantly recognizable title music for *633 Squadron*, 1964; Goodwin and William Walton's patriotic music for *The Battle of Britain*, 1969), pop songs began to be used to provide clashing discord to the onscreen action. Time and again, the Vietnam War has been depicted on screen as being fought to the strains of Jimi Hendrix and The Doors. Seven years after Coppola used 'The End' to open *Apocalypse Now*, Oliver Stone's 1986 war drama *Platoon* (which makes heavy use of Samuel Barber's Adagio for Strings – a piece that had been played on radio and TV when JFK's assassination was announced, and was performed at Roosevelt's funeral) was being trailered using images of bloody and explosive jungle combat overlaid upon the jarringly sweet and tender strains of Smokey Robinson's 'Tracks of My Tears'. Meanwhile, Barry Levinson's *Good Morning, Vietnam* (1987) labours the well-worn point that while American radio was blaring James Brown's 'I Got You (I Feel Good)' the country was gearing up for national trauma and international humiliation.

In 1991, Mark Rydell's *For the Boys* melodramatically charted the changing nature of war from the Second World War to Vietnam by following a pair of singers entertaining the troops through the years. After the joys of watching Bette Midler's Dixie Leonard perform such early forties foot-stompers as 'Stuff Like That There', the film's darkest scene finds Dixie crooning the melancholic Beatles tune 'In My Life' in the middle of a Vietnam battlefield, directly before watching her son get torn apart by a bomb. It may not be subtle, but it stands as yet further proof of the power of pop music to evoke the changing nature of the past.

*

None of this is to suggest that, in the wake of *American Graffiti*, the use of pop music in movies became entirely retrospective. On the contrary, the dual themes of 'now-ness' and 'then-ness' have continued to co-exist. The year before *American Graffiti* opened, Perry Henzell's *The Harder They Come* (1972) struck one of the most convincingly contemporary blows for urgently immediate pop cinema, becoming that rarest of things – a movie whose soundtrack actually kick-started a pop revolution.

A super-low-budget drama hailed as 'the first genuinely Jamaican feature film', *The Harder They Come* caused a press sensation when it premiered at the Venice Film Festival in 1972. Ska and reggae legend Jimmy Cliff stars as Ivan, a figure inspired by real-life Jamaican outlaw Vincent Ivanhoe Martin, widely regarded as the original rude boy. During the course of the movie, we watch this poor countryman arriving in Kingston, where he attempts to make a name for himself in the Jamaican music industry but gradually drifts into a life of crime.

Alongside Cliff, who wrote and performed the hit title song, *The Harder They Come* featured a host of cameos and support-ing roles: from ska legend Prince Buster to Beverley Anderson, who went on to marry Jamaican Prime Minister Michael

Manley, and Carl Bradshaw, who became a mainstay of the Jamaican film and TV industry after making his screen debut in Henzell's film. A huge hit in Jamaica, where audiences were amazed to see people on screen who spoke like they did, *The Harder They Come* was deemed to require subtitles for audiences in America, where it became a midnight movie hit. As for the soundtrack album, it made the US charts and has been listed as one of the greatest albums ever by publications as influential as *Time* magazine and *Rolling Stone*, bringing reggae music to a mass audience worldwide.

'Many films had been made *in* Jamaica, but never before had there been a film about Jamaican culture,' commented Barbara Blake-Hannah, a journalist who was enlisted by Henzell to work as publicist on *The Harder They Come*. Speaking to my Radio 4 *Screenshot* colleague Ellen E. Jones, Blake-Hannah recalled hearing 'the great soundtrack, which was the reggae music, which the world hadn't really heard yet. Bob Marley was not yet a star when that movie was made. Reggae was just coming forward, and this film gave us an entire soundtrack of some of the greatest reggae songs that have ever been recorded, and the spiritual content of reggae lyrics was explained for the first time *in context*. People could *see* what people were singing about – the life they were singing about.'

British DJ, musician and film-maker Don Letts, who co-directed the 1997 Jamaican independent feature *Dancehall Queen*, has similarly profound memories of seeing *The Harder They Come* as a teenager. 'It was a major cultural reference for a generation that was like a lost tribe, trying to work out where we fit in. It definitely set me off on this visual journey that made me want to become a film-maker. I was totally taken by the film's power to inspire, inform and entertain. What other movie can claim to have single-handedly broken a genre of music around the planet?'

In the wake of *The Harder They Come*, films like Theodoros Bafaloukos's *Rockers* (1978), Franco Rosso's *Babylon* (1980), Perry Henzell's *Countryman* (1982) and (some years later) Letts's *Dancehall Queen* continued to build upon the legacy of that collision of film and emergent reggae. Music supervisor Ed Bailie, who worked with British director Steve McQueen on his *Small Axe* TV series (2020), also acknowledges that there's an ongoing debt to *The Harder They Come*. 'The thing that really strikes me still about that film is that it is one of those pieces that documents a time almost unknowingly. These days you'd work really hard to look back and recreate that time. But that film was *creating* it, almost not knowing how much of a document it would be for the future.'

The most memorable scene in *Lovers Rock* (part of the *Small Axe* series, and named after a laid-back sub-genre of reggae) plays out at a party where revellers dance and sing along to Janet Kay's 'Silly Games'. McQueen had a very specific vision for the use and re-use of the song over a nearly ten-minute-long sequence, and Bailie recalls: 'It was fascinating to see the film-maker interacting with the music in such a way that the cast themselves were part of this real energy that was buzzing through him, because of his love of that track'. Bailie praises the 'repeat needle-drops' of 'You Can Get It if You Really Want' in *The Harder They Come*, describing it as 'a great choice narratively as a song, because it's telling the lead's story – if he really *wants* to become this musical star, to become famous, he *can* get it. But the song is used at different parts of the film where he's at completely different parts of that narrative arc. So it's not just a great movie for the time that it was made, but craft-wise it was very intelligent in how it curated its musical moments.'

We might compare the impact of *The Harder They Come* in 1972 with that of Spike Lee's *Do the Right Thing*, nearly two decades later, in 1989. Furthermore, I would argue that you can draw a direct line from the opening sequence of *Do the Right Thing*, in which Rosie Perez dances frenetically to the confrontational sounds of Public Enemy's 'Fight the Power', to the opening moments of *Blackboard Jungle* back in 1955, when 'Rock Around the Clock' first rang out through movie theatres. Like Richard Brooks's film, *Do the Right Thing* approaches complex questions of racism with an in-your-face attitude that was not to everyone's liking. Having banned László Benedek's *The Wild One* in January 1954 for providing 'a spectacle of unbridled hooliganism', the British censors had been equally suspicious of *Blackboard Jungle*, which they similarly rejected for being filled with scenes of 'revolting hooliganism'. They later reneged and agreed to grant the film an X rating (with cuts) while still remaining anxious about the effect it might have on impressionable audiences.

A similar anxiety greeted the arrival of *Do the Right Thing*, which (like *American Graffiti*) featured the voice of a DJ – in this case Samuel L. Jackson's Mister Señor Love Daddy – providing unofficial narration for the time-compressed action (he even howls like Wolfman Jack). Over the course of one blisteringly hot summer day, racial tensions simmer in the film's one-block setting, building to an inevitable explosion. And, as had been the case with such milestone films as *The Wild One* and *Blackboard Jungle*, *Do the Right Thing* arrived in cinemas amid a flurry of controversy suggesting that it would incite riots and violence wherever it played. Despite now being recognized as one of the most important films of the late twentieth century, *Do the Right Thing* was attacked on first release by some high-profile American critics, most notably two writers for *New York* magazine, Joe Klein and David Denby. In the magazine's 'City Politic' column, Klein called *Do the Right Thing* 'reckless', and hoped that the movie wouldn't be opening in too many theatres near his readers, since the spectre of 'large black audiences' reacting violently to the film could not be ruled out. Meanwhile, David Denby declared that *Do the Right Thing* could cause an 'uproar', and opined that 'if some audiences go wild, [Spike Lee is] partly responsible'.

Exactly why *Do the Right Thing* got under these writers' skin is a matter for debate. Yet it's clear from the film's declarative opening that Lee knew how to use popular music to hit a contemporary nerve, just as Richard Brooks had done three decades earlier. While the rise of rock 'n' roll was viewed as the fall of civilization by some conservative commentators back in the mid-fifties, so rap music in general (and Public Enemy in particular) seemed to embody everything that terrified the white American establishment at the end of the eighties. For its fans, that opening was an act of defiance; for its critics, it was an act of provocation.

Do the Right Thing was shot by Ernest Dickerson, the cinematographer who studied with Lee at New York University, forming a collaboration that would last from the student film *Joe's Bed-Stuy Barbershop: We Cut Heads* (1983) through *She's Gotta Have It* (1986), *School Daze* (1988), *Jungle Fever* (1991) and *Malcolm X* (1992). Dickerson well remembers shooting that fiery opening sequence but still believes that it could have been even *more* powerful. Apparently, the original plan was for Perez to be dancing in front of filmed footage of Brooklyn, but that wasn't within their budget. As Dickerson told me in a *Do the Right Thing* episode of *Screenshot* for Radio 4, 'I found a place that had some big high contrast transparencies of Brooklyn buildings and brownstone buildings. So I decided to just use that, with the coloured light behind. We shot that in the studio, and while we were shooting it, always in the back of my head I'm saying: "Damn, I wish I could have shot it the way we originally wanted to with the rear screen projection!"'

A decade after its incendiary opening, *Do the Right Thing* was selected for the National Film Registry by the Library of Congress. That same honour had been bestowed upon *American Graffiti* just four years earlier, in 1995, but it would take another seventeen years for *Blackboard Jungle* to enter the pantheon of movies deemed 'culturally, historically or aesthetically significant' in 2016.

*

In 2022, British writer/director Dionne Edwards' film *Pretty Red Dress* proved that the rebellious spirit of *Do the Right Thing* was still very much alive and kicking. A slyly subversive tale of cross-dressing and gender identity, *Pretty Red Dress* stars Natey Jones as Travis, a young man whom we meet at the end of a spell in prison. Waiting for him is partner Candice, played with understated flair by British *X Factor*-winner-turned-chart-topper and star of stage and screen Alexandra Burke. A huge fan of Tina Turner (who died just weeks before the film's UK opening), Candice is facing a dream role – an opportunity to audition for the lead in a West End show about her idol. While shopping with Travis for something eye-catching to wear for the audition, Candice comes upon the titular red dress – a tassled garment, as dazzling as it is expensive. Yet when she asks the storekeeper if he can hold the garment back for a month, Edwards focuses our attention on *Travis*'s face, across which a series of conflicting emotions dance. Is he anxious because they cannot afford such a pricey item? Does he want to buy the dress anyway, in order to prove his love for Candice? Or is there something else that Travis cannot admit, even to himself? It's a complex story, touching on a number of hot-topic issues (race, gender, sexuality), but doing so in a way that is proudly populist and accessible. And according to Edwards, it takes direct inspiration from her 'favourite film ever', *Do the Right Thing*.

'*Do the Right Thing* starts with a bang, ends with a bang, and is rhythmically genius,' she explained to me. 'It's like a piece of jazz in a way, from the cinematography to the colour palette to the sweat on people's faces. I feel like I'm going to melt myself when I'm watching it. Rosie Perez dancing, shadow-boxing, kicking, doing the most amazing performance in that title sequence . . . just really sets the tone of what's going to happen in the film.'

According to Edwards (who is of Jamaican and Nigerian heritage), it was this memorable opening that gave her the courage to begin her own film with an equally arresting tone-setting title sequence, putting a new twist on the Tina Turner hit 'You Should'a Treated Me Right'. 'It's this very energetic performance, full of colours and lights. It's pretty unexpected in a way for *Pretty Red Dress* to start like that if you go in understanding that it's a film about this interesting take on what gender is. *Do the Right Thing* was so influential, because it starts in a way that is trying to grab the audience and tell them: "OK, this is what we're watching".'

Just like *Blackboard Jungle*.

While the publicity for *American Graffiti* asked 'Where Were You in '62?' (answer: I wasn't born yet), so *Do the Right Thing* continues to inspire a new generation of film-makers too young to remember its divisive first release. Today, it is an acknowledged masterpiece, brilliantly showcasing the ongoing power of film and popular music.

I have a suspicion that, at some point in the not-too-distant future, Jordan Peele's *Us* (his 2019 follow-up to 2017's *Get Out*) will also be recognized as a genuine masterpiece, not least because of the way it intertwines pop music with an original orchestral score to tell its deliciously twisty story . . .

A *Twilight Zone*-style mash-up of Dostoevsky's *The Double* and Jack Finney's *The Body Snatchers*, *Us* is a modern fable that opens in 1986 with a young girl in a 'Thriller' T-shirt wandering away from her parents at a Santa Cruz beach fairground. Entering the Vision Quest hall of mirrors, the child sees something terrifying and traumatizing – or is it just her own reflection? Thirty-something years later, the adult Adelaide Wilson (Lupita Nyong'o) returns to that same beach with her family – a family who play Luniz's 1995 banger 'I Got 5 On It' ('that's a classic right there') on the car stereo. 'I don't feel like myself,' Adelaide insists, pleading to leave the summer home that is bringing back so many memories. But when a shadowy family of doppelgangers arrive on the Wilsons' doorstep, it soon becomes clear that they can run, but they can't hide from themselves.

Slipping nimbly between the registers of domestic sitcom and sociopolitical shocker, *Us* takes time to establish its down-to-earth domestic dynamics before throwing the Wilsons (and us, the audience) to the wolves. Amplifying the underlying themes of Peele's script is Michael Abels's exhilarating score, which blends brooding polytonal drones with stabby strings, interspersed with inventive use of the human voice. The quasi-gothic choral 'Anthem' evokes the chills of Jerry Goldsmith's

'Ave Satani' from *The Omen*, while jukebox tracks by Minnie Riperton, NWA and Luniz are used to powerful effect, skirting the borders between horror and satire. Most pointedly, a key confrontation between two mirrored souls plays out to a haunting theme in which Abels turns the main riff of 'I Got 5 On It' into a spine-tingling orchestral refrain.

'This is an example of the macro and the micro,' Abels enthuses. 'The macro is the lead character, Adelaide. Growing up she studied ballet, and we see her as a young girl and a young teen in a tutu at the barre. In dance there's a thing called a *pas de deux*, which is a dance of two people, and it's normally the principal ballerina and the principal male dancer. That's the whole intellectual back-story. *Us* is a film about duality and people being attacked by their doppelgangers. So of course, the final battle would come down to the lead character and her doppelganger in a *pas de deux* to the death.'

The original plan had been for Abels to soundtrack that scene with a darker version of the *pas de deux* from Tchaikovsky's ballet *The Nutcracker*, and for the Luniz track to feature near the beginning 'as a way to get to know the family. They're getting to know each other by listening to music. And what you get as an audience member, early on, is that they're a regular ordinary family, yet they're listening to a piece of music that specifically Black parents of a certain age would remember from when they were growing up. So Jordan set up this scene in a way that's culturally specific and universal at the same time. Then it became clear to Jordan that "How can we do Tchaikovsky when we have *this* great tune?" It was really clear that that was the direction we had to go in.'

That direction involved stripping down and remixing/ reorchestrating/reimagining the hooks of the Luniz song, turning

271

it into a brilliantly threatening piece – a playfully balletic work, spiced up with scary Herrmann-esque strings and low bass growls, yet still retaining the 'culturally specific' pop sensibility that enables Peele to tell the story of *Us* (for which read 'U.S.') through music as much as words.

Let's close this chapter with a glimpse into the possible future of the creative marriage between pop music and movies, in the form of Beyoncé's 2020 film *Black Is King*. One of a series of increasingly ambitious 'visual albums' that accompany her music releases, *Black Is King* is a full-length feature film, described by Beyoncé as a 'visual companion' to the 2019 album *The Lion King: The Gift* ('sonic cinema . . . a new experience of storytelling'), curated by the musician for Disney's photoreal-ist remake of their animated 1994 hit. A fantastical tale with a down-to-earth message, *Black Is King* was filmed across three continents by eight different directors (including Beyoncé) and draws on the Afro-futurist aesthetic that gave us Sun-Ra's 1974 screen extravaganza *Space Is the Place* and more recently inspired Marvel's *Black Panther* (2018). Released globally on Disney+, it is perhaps the quintessential example of the modern union of pop music and movies – lavish, immersive and eclectic.

But it also takes us right back to the roots of the genre – to Bessie Smith in 1929, starring in a dramatic musical short that helped to launch a cinematic art form that is still thriving today. On the surface, *St Louis Blues* and *Black Is King* may seem to be from different worlds. Yet look closer and you'll see two films made nearly a century apart, both showcasing extraordinary Black female artists, in a perfect union of film and popular music.

Soundtrack Selection:
Never Let Me Go (2010)

During the five years that Jenny and I made our weekly two-hour film music show for Scala Radio, few soundtracks featured more regularly than Rachel Portman's score for *Never Let Me Go* (2010). Adapted from a dystopian novel by Kazuo Ishiguro, the film follows a group of young people at an isolated boarding school who are encouraged (or perhaps *forced*) to be fit and healthy despite the fact that they all apparently face the prospect of dying young. Gradually it is revealed that these young people are clones, grown to provide spare transplantable organs for their counterparts out in the 'real' world – sourced-at-birth human-repair-kits destined to expire (or 'complete') once they have served their regenerative purpose.

In 2024, a stage adaptation of Ishiguro's novel by Suzanne Heathcote played in the UK to rave reviews, with Mark Lawson writing in *The Guardian* that: 'Unlike the operations in the novel, this transplant of Ishiguro's book is entirely justifiable and successful.' Responses to director Mark Romanek's screen adaptation of *Never Let Me Go*, however, were generally less positive. Despite boasting a starry cast that included Carey

Mulligan, Keira Knightley and Andrew Garfield, the film opened to mixed reviews and dispiritingly low box-office takings, racking up a net financial loss on its comparatively frugal $15 million budget. In an October 2010 article entitled 'Why didn't audiences spark to *Never Let Me Go*?', *Los Angeles Times* writer Steven Zeitchik reported that 'five weeks into its release, Mark Romanek's film has been an undeniable disappointment', adding that 'the movie widened to more than 200 theatres last week, but its per-screen average was so low that the movie will start to lose screens in the coming weeks'. A few weeks later, *Never Let Me Go* had indeed disappeared from US cinemas.

On the subject of composer Rachel Portman's contribution to the film, however, things were more harmonious. Having won the San Diego Film Critics Society Award for Best Score, Portman's music would go on to have a life of its own outside the movie. Today, it is one of my favourite film scores of all time – music to which I return on a regular basis, and which never fails to move me. Clearly the Scala listeners felt the same, voting it one of *their* favourite scores from the past decade in a 2019 poll conducted by the station. That's a remarkable feat considering the cool reception the film got in cinemas, suggesting that many (if not *most*) of the people who now love that score didn't see the movie – at least not on its initial release.

One of the difficulties of marketing *Never Let Me Go* was the problem of how to define it – was it a sci-fi film, a dark romance, or a tragic tale of doomed youth? Portman remembers that this sense of uncertainty dated right back to her earliest involvement in the project, and discussions about what sort of music the film required. 'They had been a *long* time thinking about *how* to score it,' she remembers. 'Because of the nature of the human experiments, it had always, I think, attracted slightly creepy music. Whereas I saw only the film's beating heart and its emotion. It felt to me that it was all about *love*.'

Despite Portman's own certainty about the film's central theme, that sense of questioning the movie's identity continued. Speaking to journalist Nev Pierce for *Empire* magazine, screenwriter Alex Garland noted that there had been a 'background debate' about whether *Never Let Me Go* was science fiction ('It seems perfectly obvious it is') but concluded that 'it's not a genre movie – it's a literary adaptation about mortality. And about hard things that people have to swallow'.

Portman saw *Never Let Me Go* as a profoundly human drama about connection, and she was certain that the music should reflect *those* qualities rather than leaning into any genre elements. 'The score needed just to be about *that*,' she tells me, 'and I don't think they had identified that until I came along. I actually did a demo, and I chose a scene with Carey Mulligan's character on this really depressing seventies bus, clothes on the washing line, and yet her words are the words of a young person who loved being with this boy. There's so much pain and heart in it that I was immediately attracted to write the theme.' Indeed, the title of the film (and book) helped to inspire this theme because 'It never really lets go of the upper register, giving this pulsing sense of not letting go of love.'

Using a forty-eight-piece orchestra, incorporating piano, strings and harp with mournful solos for violin and cello, Portman's score feels like a passion project – a work that is filled with pain and yearning, expertly capturing the conflicting emotions at the heart of the story. 'All of us who worked on the film were completely and utterly in the thrall of it,' remembers Portman. 'It seemed so incredibly important. It was a film that mattered so hugely and so deeply; I can hear it in the music that I wrote.'

Returning to the 'Is it science fiction?' debate, I ask whether there was ever any temptation to use more traditionally generic elements, such as futuristic electronica for the film. 'No,' replies Portman definitively, before going on to add: 'We *did* have a slightly creepy solo girl's voice. It was a young girl's voice, used in a slightly dissonant way over a couple of scenes. There *are* some sinister elements in there, but none of it is electronic.'

For Portman, it was always the down-to-earth elements of the story that were of paramount importance, with the futuristic cloning themes simply serving as a narrative device to explore a world that is familiar to us all. Tellingly, she found the all-important sense of inspirational excitement she was looking for in 'some of these beautiful external shots of grey, leafless landscapes. They were really evocative to me to write music to.'

The result is a score that encourages the audience to consider the universal themes of the story: 'How much time do *we* have, while we're here, to connect with people? It relates to deeper issues which I think Ishiguro's work seems to be about. Love, and time, and caring.'

CHAPTER 9

A Frightful Noise

What does terror sound like? For William Friedkin, director of perhaps the most famously frightening movie of all time, *The Exorcist* (1973), it sounds (and feels) like an icy chill at the top of the spine. A tale of demonic possession, based on the bestselling novel by screenwriter William Peter Blatty, *The Exorcist* offered a groundbreaking (and ultimately genre-defining) collision of ancient religion and urban modernity. With the exception of its enigmatic Iraq opening sequence (and a brief sojourn to New York), the drama plays out almost entirely within a few square miles of the Georgetown district of Washington DC. The setting is contemporary, focusing on a movie actor (Chris MacNeil, brilliantly played by Ellen Burstyn) who is making a film in that area, and whose young daughter becomes increasingly troubled by symptoms that doctors and psychiatrists are at a loss to explain. Eventually, when all else has failed, Chris turns to Father Karras, the priest/counsellor whom she asks to perform an exorcism on her daughter, and who responds by telling Chris that he'd have to get the young girl into a time machine and back to the sixteenth century because 'it just doesn't happen anymore . . .'

This tension between the past and the present, between the mundane and the uncanny, the down-to-earth and the out-of-this-world, lies at the very heart of *The Exorcist*'s dark spell. In both novel and film form, it conjures a portrait of a familiar world torn apart by *un*familiar forces. As Friedkin told me: 'This is a story about a normal girl, in a normal house, on a normal street, who just *happens* to be possessed by a demon.'

The challenges that Friedkin faced in bringing Blatty's novel to the screen were multitudinous, not least because Friedkin had declared that he wanted to bring the same air of documentary realism to the drama that had defined his Oscar Best Picture-winner *The French Connection* (1971). Cinematographer Owen Roizman, who had injected such a sense of gritty verisimilitude into *The French Connection*, was enlisted to repeat the trick with *The Exorcist* – a film whose in-camera special-effects sequences would include levitations, head-spins, bed-bounces and copious amounts of green vomit. All these were to be captured on film as if they were happening *right there in the room*, rather than added later through clever visual effects trickery. (For the most part, Friedkin and Roizman, aided by mechanical-effects whizz Marcel Vercoutere and make-up artist Dick Smith, managed to do just this, although the finished film *does* include a few blink-and-you'll-miss-them post-production opticals.)

When the tough work of getting *The Exorcist* in the can was completed, Friedkin and his editors began the equally challenging task of assembling the film in a manner that would draw the audience deep into its spell. Foremost among their challenges was constructing the film's most notorious sequence – a scene that involved a life-size mannequin of child star Linda Blair, whose head appears to rotate 180 degrees on her stationary torso while a cacophony of conflicting elements (crashing furniture, flying records, grotesque obscenity, head-spinning weirdness, thunderous sound effects) batter the audience into stunned submission.

Followed by echoing silence.

'I deliberately designed *The Exorcist* so that it would play like a battle between light and dark,' Friedkin told me. 'You have these extremely brightly lit sequences – almost *over*-lit – juxtaposed against these shadowy interiors and night-time exteriors. And the same was true of the soundtrack – these moments of very intense sound that cut very abruptly to absolute silence. There were moments that we'd actually cut leader-tape into the soundtrack so that the sound literally disappeared altogether.'

One critic astutely described *The Exorcist* as being a film filled with 'loud silences'.

Among the barrage of noises that assail audiences of *The Exorcist* are a number of natural sounds recorded by musician, sculptor and experimental recording artist Ron Nagle. Having been tasked by Friedkin to find and record 'sounds of absolute horror', Nagle took his tape recorder to an abattoir where pigs were being slaughtered. He also recorded the sound of angry bees trapped in a jar, the buzzing of which was then amplified and distorted by Nagle to generate a noise which created what he called 'the mohawk – you know, when the hair on the back of your head literally stands up in fear. That's when we knew we were on to something.'

As for the score, Friedkin knew only that he wanted music that would unsettle and distress the audience without dispelling the air of documentary realism. Yes, the film was full of dramatic moments, many of which were designed to be as terrifying as possible. But as far as Friedkin was concerned, any music that made *The Exorcist* feel like 'a drama' (or, worse still, a 'horror movie') would simply remind viewers that what they were watching was fiction, thereby eroding the carefully constructed illusion of rigid verisimilitude.

Friedkin's first instinct – which turned out to be the first of several dead ends – was to try to enlist the services of his musical hero, Bernard Herrmann . . .

*

Herrmann had scored two of Friedkin's favourite films: Orson Welles's *Citizen Kane* (1941) and Alfred Hitchcock's *Psycho* (1960). But by the early seventies Herrmann's output had (as previously noted) become significantly scaled back, as he found himself out of step with the contemporary movie business. Nevertheless his career experienced a late-in-the-day resurgence thanks in no small part to his reputation among a younger generation of film-makers working within the horror genre.

In 1972, rising talent Brian De Palma (who would go on to direct *Carrie*, 1976, and *Dressed to Kill*, 1980) turned to Herrmann when making *Sisters*, a psychological horror/thriller that was hailed in press quotes splashed across its poster as 'The most genuinely frightening film since Hitchcock's *Psycho*'. Herrmann would collaborate with De Palma again on his subsequent feature *Obsession* (1976), for which the composer earned a posthumous Oscar nomination. He also provided a memorable score for Larry Cohen's scary-baby shocker *It's Alive* (1974), which was marketed as a cross between *Rosemary's Baby* (1968) and *The Exorcist*. (Cohen really wanted Herrmann to score his 1976 sci-fi/horror thriller *God Told Me To*, but the composer reportedly said 'God told me *not* to'.) While Herrmann's final recorded score, for *Taxi Driver* (1976), may be considered his definitive late-period work, it was his reputation as the maestro of terror, with *Psycho* standing as the high water mark, that kept him employed throughout the seventies.

Herrmann's relationship with Hitchcock had always been a mix of productivity and conflict, their collaborations built to some degree upon a layer of creative tension that brought out the best in both of them. In the case of *Psycho*, the shower scene spawned an entire genre of imitators, as screeching violin strings became the default setting for composers attempting to convey the frenzied terror of yet another bloody assault. Yet Hitchcock had originally wanted this celebrated sequence to play out *without* any musical accompaniment, just the sounds of Janet Leigh's screams melding with the splash of water on the bathroom tiles, and the post-produced noise of a blade slicing through the air and striking bare flesh. (It's also possible that Hitchcock had the censors in mind when deciding to eschew music for this scene, since deleting images that have been precisely cut to music is more complex – and therefore more expensively time-consuming – than removing them from an unaccompanied sequence.)

Herrmann, however, had a different idea, and pressed ahead with his now-infamous 'Murder' cue despite Hitchcock's insistence that the scene would be unaccompanied. It was only late into the editing process that Hitchcock started to express his disappointment with the carefully montaged images that Saul Bass had so meticulously designed, and that cinematographer John L. Russell had shot virtually frame-for-frame to Bass's template. (As viewers of my 1991 Channel 4 documentary *Fear in the Dark* will know, it is possible to create an uncannily accurate reproduction of the shower scene using Bass's storyboards alone.) For Hitchcock, who had envisaged this sequence so clearly as a terrifying highlight of *Psycho*, the scene lacked . . . punch.

Herrmann took this as his cue to reveal that he had an 'idea' for the sequence which he then played for the director – a series of jarring violin strikes that take the audience within the mind of Marion Crane, as if we are hearing the sound of *her* shock and *her* terror as the assailant's blade slices through the air. Hitchcock was delighted and insisted that the music be added to the sequence. 'But you said no music,' Herrmann is reported to have teased, to which Hitchcock replied: 'Improper suggestion, my boy. Improper suggestion.'

The sound of Herrmann's shower-scene cue would become so iconic that it has effectively passed into common parlance, with the onomatopoeic phrase 'eek eek eek' becoming a modern shorthand for crazed behaviour of any kind. When making her 2017 film, *You Were Never Really Here*, Scottish director Lynne Ramsay found herself having to contact the rights-holders to Herrmann's most instantly recognizable composition after leading actor Joaquin Phoenix dropped an improvised vocal 'eek eek eek' into a scene between a troubled man and his mother, and everyone understood *exactly* what the throwaway sound meant, and where it came from.

Yet for all the ubiquity of the shower-scene-murder cue, it is arguable that *Psycho*'s most striking musical moment actually lies elsewhere. As fans of the movie will know, the opening credits include an equally iconic musical cue that perfectly sets the scene for what is to come. To match the black-and-white visuals of Hitchcock's film, Herrmann had said that he wanted to create a form of monochromatic music, using a limited palette of often-muted stringed instruments to conjure a stripped-back accompaniment unlike his previous, more expansive work with

Hitchcock. The decision to use only the string section may have been partly practical (*Psycho* was a comparatively low-budget production, shot with the same sparse ethos of Hitchcock's TV shows) but Herrmann clearly relished the enforced constraints, making a virtue out of a necessity.

The chord that opens *Psycho* (now popularized in common parlance as the 'Hitchcock chord') is a distinctive hammered minor/major seventh. The chord is repeated five times – two crotchets, three quavers – in a tight motif that brilliantly establishes the conflict between the light and dark elements that lie at the centre of Hitchcock's picture. As Herrmann himself observed, 'After the main titles, you *know* that something terrible must happen. The main title sequence tells you so, and that is its function: to set the drama.' When the hammered chord returns, with its unsettling inner tension, it 'again tells the audience, who don't know something terrible is going to happen to the girl, that it's *got* to.'

That dreadful sense that something monstrously abnormal is going to happen to this very 'normal' girl (and in the utterly mundane setting of a roadside motel) was clearly something that chimed with William Friedkin when he went searching for a composer for *The Exorcist*.

The story of Friedkin's negotiations with Herrmann about the project are conflicting. According to one account, widely attributed to Larry Cohen, Friedkin showed Herrmann a cut of *The Exorcist* and said: 'I want you to give me a better score than the one you did for *Citizen Kane*,' to which Herrmann (who, in this version of the story, *hated* the film) replied: 'Well, why didn't you make a better picture than *Citizen Kane*?' An alternative version of the story has Herrmann turning Friedkin down because the director insisted that he should receive co-credit as composer and musical director, with Herrmann submitting each day's work to Friedkin for his approval and/or alteration. Neither of these accounts seem particularly credible, although both are in widespread circulation.

A third retelling of these events has Herrmann (who, in this version of the story, *loved* the movie) saying to Friedkin that he'd be interested in doing the score, but insisting on recording it in London, using the organ at St Giles Church in Cripplegate, a building with unique acoustic qualities. Accounts of Friedkin's response to Herrmann's suggestion (including those given by Friedkin himself over the years) are once again at variance with one another. One has Friedkin considering Herrmann's idea about the St Giles organ to be creatively excellent but practically impossible, since Friedkin was cutting the film in New York and didn't want his composer to be on the other side of the Atlantic. More likely is the story Friedkin told me on several occasions: that he admired Herrmann, but felt that the use of a church organ would be out of keeping with the film's urban, gritty aesthetic – a gothic intrusion of the kind he was specifically trying to avoid.

Whatever the truth, Herrmann and Friedkin parted ways.

*

Friedkin's next port of call was composer Lalo Schifrin, best known at that point for his music for the TV series *Mission: Impossible*, and his score for *Bullitt* (1968), the car chase from which had set the bar high for Friedkin's own nail-biting work on *The French Connection*. Once again, a degree of uncertainty surrounds the breakdown in relationships between director and composer. According to Friedkin, he specifically instructed Schifrin to create a score that would conjure up the feeling of 'a

cold hand on the back of the neck', preferably something ambient and atonal that would blend with the film's already extremely
complex aural track. What Schifrin came up with (according to
Friedkin) was 'a big scary wall of sound', striking elements of
which were used in a proposed early trailer for *The Exorcist*
filled with flash-frames and quasi-subliminal demon-face cuts.
The trailer (which is now widely available on YouTube) proved
unpopular with audiences, with Schifrin alleging that it caused
people to faint and vomit. According to the composer, his music
(which the orchestra had apparently spontaneously applauded
during recording sessions) became the victim of the trailer's
unpopularity, with Friedkin firing him in order to reassure the
studio, who were freaked out by the initial audience responses.

It is certainly true that that early trailer has none of the
understated subtlety which would come to define the publicity through which *The Exorcist* was ultimately sold to cinema
audiences. And it is also the case that Schifrin's music is exactly
as Friedkin describes – a 'big scary wall of sound', filled with
swirling discordant strings, pitched somewhere between the
gripping tension of Herrmann's *Psycho* score and the disorientating atonality of Krzysztof Penderecki, of whom Friedkin was
a huge fan. Yet Friedkin reports that when he first heard Schifrin's cues he was appalled, and there are stories of him pulling
the master tape off the spools of the tape recorder and throwing
them out into the parking lot at the post-production company
Todd-AO, while shouting words to the effect of 'Get this shit out
of my movie!'

Whatever the truth, it is hard to imagine how Schifrin's
score would have fitted with Friedkin's film, although to the
composer's credit, he *did* create something genuinely alarming. (He would go on to work on such horror hits as 1979's *The*

Amityville Horror, and those with a keen ear can hear certain elements of his rejected work on *The Exorcist* being repurposed elsewhere.) Perhaps Friedkin himself was uncertain as to how much he should lean into the horror-genre elements of his film. He would often tell me that he 'never thought of *The Exorcist* as a horror film' but instead saw it as 'simply a damn good story'.

With Schifrin out of the picture, Friedkin (who had yet to encounter the electronic music of Tangerine Dream and was clearly starting to doubt that any film composer could give him what he wanted) turned instead to a selection of existing pieces by composers like Penderecki, George Crumb, Anton Webern and Hans Werner Henze, with some additional bridging work for which he enlisted the help of Jack Nitzsche. Fleeting fragments of pieces such as 'Polymorphia' and 'Night of the Electric Insects' are sprinkled throughout the film, their appearance often indistinguishable from the sound-effects track for which Chris Newman and Robert 'Buzz' Knudson would ultimately win an Oscar. Indeed, so embedded within the fabric of the film are these pieces that it is entirely possible to watch *The Exorcist* and come away with the impression that the film has no musical score whatsoever. Was that the sound of the springs creaking on Regan's bed, or a distantly heard fragment of experimental music adding to the cacophony of the richly textured sound design?

Over the course of *The Exorcist,* only two cues stand out as traditionally 'melodic'. The most dramatic of these is an excerpt from Hans Werner Henze's 'Fantasia for Strings', the strident sounds of which play out over the film's closing credits, with a series of descending staccato cello stabs abruptly breaking the comparatively tranquil air of the film's briefly reflective closing moments. Interestingly, this piece originated in the

1966 soundtrack of another film – German director Volker Schlöndorff's *Der Junge Törless/Young Törless*, an acclaimed adaptation of a 1906 novel by Robert Musil, which was seen as a key cinematic text in Germany's post-war examination and re-evaluation of its national psyche.

The other overtly melodic piece to feature in *The Exorcist* is Mike Oldfield's 'Tubular Bells Part 1', the introductory bars of which are used fleetingly in the film (and, more prominently, in the closing credits, cross-fading from 'Fantasia for Strings'), earning the popular title 'Theme from *The Exorcist*'. When Friedkin first encountered the 12-inch *Tubular Bells* LP (which would go on to become one of the biggest-selling albums of all time), he had no idea who Mike Oldfield was, or that his solo-performed album would turn into 'kind of like an introduction to the orchestra, with this narrator [Viv Stanshall] somewhat ironically introducing all the different instruments that this guy was playing.' Instead, Friedkin told me, he was simply browsing through white label recordings, either on the Warner lot or at the offices of Ahmet Ertegun's Atlantic Records, which had become a wholly owned subsidiary of Warner Bros in 1967. The debut album of Richard Branson's newly formed Virgin Records, *Tubular Bells* had been released to little fanfare in the UK in May 1973, and wouldn't be issued by Atlantic in the US until October. We know that Branson had been looking for a potential movie tie-in to boost flagging record sales, so it is entirely possible that the disc was simply doing the rounds of films currently in production. Friedkin told me that he dropped the needle on the opening bars of *Tubular Bells* and decided to use them in his movie. He never listened to anything else on the record.

What Friedkin heard was a deceptively complex yet strangely

simple-sounding melody, a repeated A-minor riff played on the upper notes of a Steinway grand piano, the sound of distance enhanced by the natural reverb of the room. This is then joined by a glockenspiel, a bell-like chime mirroring the repeated piano pattern, continuing in perfect sync with it for several bars. Gradually, other instruments are introduced, but it's this hypnotic opening stanza that Friedkin thought was '*exactly* what I needed'. Recorded at Branson's Manor Studio in 1972, it had 'an almost nursery-rhyme quality to it – kind of like a child's tune. I had been looking for something with that childlike quality, as a kind of theme for Regan, and this just seemed perfect – a gift from the movie gods.'

In terms of horror cinema, Friedkin's search for a childlike 'nursery rhyme' theme to lie at the centre of a film that would scare the life out of a generation of adults was not as unusual or unprecedented as it may have seemed. When visiting Abbey Road Studios for a Scala Radio special on the studio's ninetieth anniversary, head of audio products Mirek Stiles told me that one of the treasures almost accidentally unearthed in their vaults was a tape of Mia Farrow singing the lullaby from Roman Polanski's 1968 devil-child horror movie *Rosemary's Baby*. Adapted from a darkly satirical novel by Ira Levin, who also wrote *The Stepford Wives* and *The Boys from Brazil*, *Rosemary's Baby* is a modern-day tale of a young woman living in contemporary New York who finds herself the victim of a demonic cult. Impregnated by Satan himself, Rosemary becomes the mother of the Antichrist, all amid the somewhat chintzy settings of apartments within the German Renaissance-style Dakota Building on the Upper West Side.

With its central ancient/modern tension, and the use of a mother and child as the focus of its innocence/evil duality,

Rosemary's Baby laid the groundwork not only for *The Exorcist* but also for a string of devil-child seventies hits. The score for *Rosemary's Baby* was composed by Krzysztof Komeda, and the most memorable track is the 'Lullaby', on which Farrow's vocals are spine-tingling – a breathily performed 'la-la-la' pattern, ascending and descending in a circular manner that eerily prefigures the spiralling oscillations of the main theme from *Tubular Bells*. The melody is simple yet haunting, climbing note by note in single-step intervals, then falling back down through the same pattern. It's the kind of tune a child could sing, or (more precisely) the kind of tune that a mother would sing to her child, the melody progressing in baby-steps.

Alternatively titled 'Sleep Safe and Warm', the lullaby became a hit single on the American Billboard easy-listening charts in an arrangement by George Tipton. (There's a fascinating recording of Komeda composing the piece, playing the melody on the piano and apparently improvising the 'la-la-la' vocal line in real time.) Umpteen cover versions have been recorded since Komeda's score was nominated for a Golden Globe, with jazz musicians such as Chet Atkins and Tomasz Stańko finding their own distinctive way through the melody. But it's the simplicity of that ascension/descension that lies at the heart of the piece, lending it an air of magical innocence that ironically serves to amplify the horrors of the film for which it was composed.

*

Five years later, in 1973 (the year that *The Exorcist* was released) we find another childlike ascension/descension pattern at the core of yet another score for a celebrated horror film – Nic Roeg's *Don't Look Now*. Adapted from a story by Hitchcock-favourite Daphne du Maurier, *Don't Look Now* follows a couple in Venice who are haunted by the apparition of their deceased daughter Christine. In Du Maurier's source, Christine has died before the story begins, a victim of meningitis. But in Roeg's film, brilliantly scripted by Allan Scott and Chris Bryant, she drowns in the opening stanza, setting the scene for a water-logged tale of mystery in which the lost child appears to be eerily resurfacing through the canals of Venice.

With Donald Sutherland and Julie Christie in the lead roles as differently grieving parents John and Laura Baxter, *Don't Look Now* became one of the defining chillers of the decade, released in the UK by British Lion, who put it out with an abridged cut of *The Wicker Man* (1973) as the supporting feature! It is now considered to be one of the greatest British movies ever made, ranked at Number 8 in the BFI's turn-of-the-century poll of the 100 best 'culturally British' movies, ahead of such classic fare as *The Red Shoes* (1948), *Get Carter* (1971) and *Trainspotting* (1996).

The score for *Don't Look Now* was written and partly per-formed by Italian musician and composer Pino Donaggio, who had co-written the 1965 hit 'Io Che Non Vivo', which was recorded in English-language versions as 'You Don't Have to Say You Love Me' by such superstars as Dusty Springfield and Elvis Presley. By the early seventies, Donaggio's pop career had waned somewhat, but when *Don't Look Now*'s casting director Ugo Mariotti spied him on a vaporetto in Venice, he took it as a sign, and asked him if he'd like to score the film. Donag-gio, whom I interviewed on stage in Trieste in 2023 following a fiftieth anniversary screening of *Don't Look Now*, initially demurred, claiming that he had never scored a movie (although he had in fact been the credited composer on Alberto Caval-lone's 1959 film *La Sporca Guerra*). But Mariotti and Roeg, who prided themselves on being rule-breakers, were persuasive, and Donaggio began work on a score which would kick-start an entirely new career. In the wake of *Don't Look Now*'s success, he wrote music for a couple of Italian mystery chillers before taking over from Bernard Herrmann as Brian De Palma's regular composer of choice, providing eerily note-perfect scores for films such as *Carrie* (1976), *Home Movies* (1979), *Dressed to Kill* (1980), *Blow Out* (1981), *Body Double* (1984) and *Raising Cain* (1992), alongside collaborations with horror legends Dario Argento and George Romero, among many others. He is now regarded as the maestro of modern suspense movies, his work with De Palma in particular drawing comparisons with the classic collaborations of Hitchcock and Herrmann.

Listening to Donaggio's score for *Don't Look Now*, it's easy to see why he was so appealing to De Palma. A skilful violinist, Donaggio's compositions for Roeg's Venice-set mystery make superb use of strings to conjure a profoundly Herrmann-esque air of suspense, anxiety and (equally importantly) emotional clout. Listen, for example, to the cue 'Searching for Laura – Part 2', in which the strident bass strings suggest some darkly ominous fate awaiting John, while the urgent triplets of the violins' top-line evoke a cat-and-mouse chase through darkened streets and canals. Or how about the screeching stabs of 'Christine is Dead' which give way to groaning bass strings as the child is hoisted from the mire of the pond into which she has fallen – a perfect synthesis of dread and horror.

Yet alongside the atmosphere of fright and anxiety, there is much that is simply beautiful about Donaggio's *Don't Look Now* score. The recurrent 'Laura's Theme' plays out in several variations during the course of the movie, most majestically in the closing musical montage, in which the strangely triumphant sounds of a waterborne funeral segue into a romantic air, with soaring violin melodies, underpinned by a poignant piano motif.

This lays the groundwork for the rapturous 'Main Title' from *Carrie*, a deceptively enticing introduction to the movie in which swooning strings and a lilting flute lull us into a sense of dreamy reverie before the first drops of blood fall. Throughout Donaggio's genre film scores, that balance between the beautiful and the monstrous is a key ingredient, as if the composer instinctively feels that an audience can only be terrified if they are first emotionally involved.

Alongside *Don't Look Now*'s lush string arrangements, there's also the simpler piano strains of 'John's Theme', which recurs throughout the film, most poignantly in an early variation subtitled 'Children Play'. Just as Polanski and Komeda had built the score for *Rosemary's Baby* around a childlike lullaby, so Roeg wanted his tale of a lost child to have a central theme that evoked innocence rather than danger and threat – a quality that would heighten the movie's ability to chill its audience. Donaggio responded with a theme in which the top-line melody could be played on a piano as if by a child slowly learning the instrument, whose hands could barely reach the keys. Although later variations (such as the flute-filled 'Love Scene', the string-and guitar-led 'Laura Leaves Venice', and the final melancholy 'Flashbacks') add rather more complex musical curlicues to this theme, it is the 'Children Play' incarnation that is the most poignant.

When I interviewed Nic Roeg about *Don't Look Now* in 2008, he told me that he had wanted the right and left hands of the piano part to create the air of an early musical exercise, establishing a motif that would become more lyrical and flowing during the course of the piece, and of the movie. The top-line melody revolves around five notes that can be played with the right hand hardly moving, starting with the little finger on the perfect fifth top note, then moving down to the root note on the thumb, and back up – step by step, finger by finger – to the fifth, back to the little finger. Meanwhile, the bass clef/left-hand part recalls the kind of slow-stride walking exercise that would be familiar to anyone raised on *A Tune a Day* books, usually played to the accompaniment of a sotto-voce 'ONE two, THREE four' as the novice player struggled to coordinate both hands.

'We were in the recording studio,' Roeg told me of the session in which this particular track was cut, and in which he tried to get the musically accomplished Donaggio to play as if he had never seen a keyboard before. 'Pino sat down at the piano,' he laughed, 'and he just *couldn't* play it like a child. I kept saying: "It's too good, Pino! It's too good!"' During our conversation in Trieste, Donaggio confirmed Roeg's recollection, remembering how he had to work hard to *un*learn the instrument, while protesting that, as a violinist, the piano wasn't really his forte anyway.

*

Don't Look Now opened in the UK in October 1973, just two months before *The Exorcist*'s Boxing Day premiere in New York. It seems unlikely (although not impossible) that William Friedkin saw *Don't Look Now* before finalizing *The Exorcist* in the run-up to Christmas. He had, though, definitely seen Polanski's *Rosemary's Baby* and would have been well aware of its use of a lilting lullaby as a central part of the score. Friedkin had noted that the opening movement of 'Tubular Bells' had a childlike quality; a delightfully innocent motif. As with 'John's Theme' from *Don't Look Now*, the notational steps are comparatively straightforward, clusters of two side-by-side notes, moving in tight formation, up and down a very limited five-note group. Simplicity itself!

And yet . . . there is something far more complex going on – not in the notation, but in the time signature. For while Oldfield's composition does indeed have a nursery-rhyme ring to the notes, they are clustered in alternating bars of 7/8 and 8/8 couplets – or, more accurately, the piece is written in the deliberately disorientating time signature of 15/8. It's hard to describe the effect of such an unusual time signature, not least because it doesn't *sound* unusual unless you try to count it, or indeed to play it. Then it suddenly becomes clear that the well-ordered pattern of the tune has a recurrent skipped beat that seems to wrongfoot the piece, but so subtly that you almost don't notice it's happening. As Oldfield confirmed in a 2014 interview for *The Telegraph*: 'Most music is in 4/4 time, but that curious little figure at the beginning is in 15/8. It's like a puzzle with a little bit missing. That's why it sticks in the brain. And that's why it worked so well as the soundtrack to *The Exorcist* – with that little bit missing everything is not quite right . . .'

That sense of something being 'not quite right' is, indeed, central to the power of 'Tubular Bells' and its placement within Friedkin's film. We first hear the piece as Ellen Burstyn's character Chris walks home from the Georgetown University set of her film *Crash Course* to the house that she is renting on Prospect Street. As she walks, in apparently carefree fashion, the sounds of Oldfield's music start to tinkle in the autumnal breeze, the strange time signature suggesting an air of mystery and magic in these modern streets. A group of children rush by, dressed in

Halloween costumes, and the roar of a motorbike briefly over-powers the tune, which seems to chime with the ever-so-slightly distraught thoughts in Chris's head. Her smile turns to a frown, and soon she is overhearing young priest Damien Karras telling a troubled cleric that 'There's not a day of my life that I don't feel like a fraud . . '. Chris may be on her way home to her beloved daughter Regan, and the tune of 'Tubular Bells' may be in sync with that mother–daughter reunion, but there's an element of the world being slightly *out of* sync with itself – a suggestion that the natural order is on the brink of unbalance.

The next time we hear 'Tubular Bells', it plays briefly over a videotape of a restrained Regan, strapped to a medical bed, her face ravaged, raving at the doctors who have failed to diagnose her ever-more distressing condition. Here, the magical dysfunc-tion of that time signature rings clear as a bell, telling us that what we're witnessing is not something that can be explained by science, but by forces altogether more otherworldly. This is the point where medicine has run its course, leading into the scene in which Chris – when asked if she's ever heard of exorcism – incredulously replies: 'You're telling me that I should take my daughter to a witch doctor?'

The third appearance of what is now known as the 'Theme from *The Exorcist*' comes at the very end of the film when (at least in its original version) Father Dyer stands at the top of the precipitous steps leading from Prospect Street to M Street and remembers his friend Damien Karras who gave his life to save a young girl when falling down these steps. As the lonely priest is silhouetted against the Georgetown skyline, we briefly hear a few bars of 'Tubular Bells', the spiralling tune now suggesting that Regan has been returned to her youthful self, while the off-kilter time signature reminds us that this is a world in which demons (and therefore angels) are *real*, and the down-to-earth certainties of secular modern life have vanished into thin air.

*

If, as Oldfield suggests, the key to the uncanny nature of 'that curious little figure' is that the time signature makes it seem 'like a puzzle with a little bit missing', then we can hear a clear echo of that temporal disruption in John Carpenter's self-penned theme to his 1978 shocker *Halloween*, the film that effectively kicked off a new wave of saleable slashers such as the *Friday the 13th* franchise which followed hot on its heels in the eighties. Originally pitched under the working title *The Babysitter Murders*, *Halloween* was a low-budget affair (it cost around $300,000) which took inspiration from Hitchcock's *Psycho* (it stars Janet Leigh's daughter, Jamie Lee Curtis), and which in 2006 was selected for inclusion in the Library of Congress National Film Registry.

Having discussed the film with Carpenter on several occasions (most notably for the BBC Two documentary *The Night He Came Home*), his account of the creation of that score has remained remarkably consistent: that it was written and recorded in three days, with the 'Main Theme' reportedly being knocked off in little more than an hour. Yet that theme has gone on to become one of the most iconic riffs of modern horror cinema – instantly recognizable, endlessly parodied.

As Carpenter told me, he wanted the 'Main Theme' to be something that could be played with two fingers, again achieving that almost infantile simplicity that would also contain a powerful element of threat (the first time we meet Michael Myers, he is a knife-wielding six-year-old). The riff he came up with has a distinct similarity to 'Tubular Bells', albeit played with a more overtly urgent sense of staccato unrest. As with Oldfield's piece, the *Halloween* theme consists of a sustained lower note, with a higher top-line note, oscillating/alternating in tight repetitive clusters. While the root note remains constant, the top-line moves up and down in semitonal intervals, creating a tension between the two. The intervals are simple: a fifth followed by a flattened sixth, then back to the fifth. But what gives the piece its edge is the time signature, which can be read as either 5/4, or more accurately as 10/8. Effectively, each bar consists of three note clusters: two triplets, made up of a top note followed by two lower notes, and one quadruplet, in which the third beat moves the top note *up* one semitone before resolving back *down* in the next bar.

Again, as with the Oldfield piece, the added beat (5/4 rather than 4/4) creates a disruption that is not immediately obvious to the listener, but quietly generates a sense of repetitive anxiety and anticipation. And, unlike the *swung* 5/4 time signature of the jazz standard 'Take Five', Carpenter's use of rigidly regimented (and distinctly *un*-swung) staccato beats means that this disordering is wholly sinister, rather than casually laid-back. (It is, weirdly enough, *possible* to play the theme from *Halloween* with a swung back-beat. Try it – the tension dissipates entirely.)

*

As noted in Chapter 6, 'Switched-On Electronica', Carpenter's music for *Halloween* was part of a tradition of film electronica that included *Sorcerer*, Friedkin's tense follow-up to *The Exorcist*, for which synth pioneers Tangerine Dream provided a score whose central piece 'Betrayal' used a similar repetitive half-tone pulse that eerily pre-echoes Carpenter's timeless theme. It also located the movie alongside a tradition of European *giallo* chillers by directors like Dario Argento, whose work with prog-rock band Goblin on films such as *Profondo Rosso* (1975) and *Suspiria* (1977) dovetails neatly with Carpenter's own compositions. This was a period in which the sound of modern horror was shifting somewhat from the orchestral scores of yore into something with a more stripped-down home-made aesthetic, and so it's perhaps unsurprising that several horror scores produced in this period seem to mirror one another.

This was also the period that produced a series of otherwise disparate international horror films that would be randomly bracketed together in the UK in the early eighties under the catch-all banner 'Video Nasties' (a term beloved of the tabloids that should *always* appear in inverted commas). For UK horror fans, 'Video Nasties' offered a heady mix of freedom and repression. For decades, Britain had been sheltered from the more *outré* elements of international cinema by the British Board of Film Censors (as they were called before becoming the British Board of Film *Classification* – BBFC), which rated, cut or rejected outright films submitted for public exhibition. But when the new medium of home video surfaced in the early eighties, movies that were being released on VHS did not require a BBFC certificate – at least, not at first. Spotting a loophole in the law, a few industrious entrepreneurs took the opportunity to release on video movies that the BBFC had not passed for cinematic exhibition. Key examples included Abel Ferrara's *The Driller Killer* (1979), Sergio Garrone's *SS Experiment Camp* (1976), Meir Zarchi's *I Spit on Your Grave* (1978) and, most infamously, Ruggero Deodato's *Cannibal Holocaust* (1980), all of which suddenly became available uncut on tape.

The last of these is of particular interest for soundtrack fans, since it presents perhaps the definitive example of an extremely nasty movie being made all the more terrifying by the somewhat paradoxical beauty of its score. Among his many other film credits, Italian composer, conductor and orchestrator Riz Ortolani had previously co-written the music for the 1962 docsploitation classic *Mondo Cane*, a string of shocking vignettes from around the world that launched the 'mondo' movie genre, inspiring a rash of increasingly grisly offerings that reached its nadir in the *Faces of Death* series (1978–90) that also became part of the 'Video Nasties' scare.

Ortolani and co-composer Nino Oliviero's music for *Mondo Cane*, however, was contrapuntally romantic, with its signature instrumental theme tune being repurposed with English-language lyrics by Norman Newell as 'More', earning a nomination at the 36th Academy Awards for Best Original Song. Deodato was a huge fan of Ortolani's work on *Mondo Cane* and asked him to repeat the trick for *Cannibal Holocaust*, which owed a stylistic debt to the burgeoning 'mondo' genre in its use of scenes of apparently unsimulated atrocities. (The entire picture is constructed as a 'film within a film' in which lost 'documentary' footage made by a now-missing group of explorers is retrieved from the Amazon rainforest and then viewed in New York, creating the illusion of verisimilitude.) Using a combination of acoustic orchestration and electronica, Ortolani came up trumps, composing a sublimely melancholy 'Main Theme', which recently resurfaced as the end-credits music for Season 2 of the American teen drama *Euphoria* (2022). Other cues with such distressingly violent titles as 'Crucified Woman' have a similarly lyrical feel, with the tenser and more agitating moments of Ortolani's score constantly interrupted by themes of great beauty and transcendence. While *Cannibal Holocaust* may be almost unwatchably grim viewing, the music strives to keep the audience onside, appealing to their emotional core even as the screen is filled with images of vile degradation and actual cruelty.

Like so many UK horror fans, I first saw *Cannibal Holocaust* when it was released on unrated video, swiftly becoming one of the most notorious 'Nasties'. Even then, I was struck by the counterpoint between the grotesquerie on screen and the beauty of the score, and I remain convinced that this is one of the key elements of the film's longevity. Gore alone cannot account for the movie's enduringly infamous reputation. There has to be something else getting under the audience's skin – and I think that something is the music. But almost as soon as *Cannibal Holocaust* became available in the UK, it began to disappear from video stores amid a spate of Obscene Publications Act prosecutions, with the Director of Public Prosecutions (DPP) drawing up a famously ad hoc list of impoundable titles which were potentially in violation of UK law. In their 1983 manifesto, the Conservative Party made the spectre of 'Video Nasties' an election issue, promising to 'introduce specific legislation to deal with . . . the dangerous spread of violent and obscene video cassettes'. Following a landslide victory, they did just that, rushing through the 1984 Video Recordings Act, which empowered the BBFC to classify or cut video releases with 'special regard to the likelihood of video works . . . being viewed in the home'. This deceptively mild phrase was to have far-reaching consequences, establishing in law the principle that home-viewing was inherently dangerous in a way that cinematic exhibition was not. In effect, it called for videos to be treated more punitively by the censors than cinema releases – and that meant that alongside the video banning of films like *Cannibal Holocaust*, William Friedkin's 1973 masterpiece *The Exorcist* was also removed from UK video shelves, not to return until 1999.

*

Fast-forward to 2021, when the 'Video Nasties' panic provided the backdrop for one of the most exciting horror movies of the twenty-first century – Prano Bailey-Bond's *Censor*. A serpentine tale of trauma, repression and liberation mediated through the deliciously tactile medium of illicit videotapes, Bailey-Bond's feature debut stars Niamh Algar as Enid, a film censor who spends her days watching, cutting and classifying scenes of violence in mid-eighties Britain. To evoke the time period, Bailey-Bond and her team (which included executive producer/adviser Kim Newman) conjured a series of fictional titles like *Asunder* and *Don't Go in the Church* that resembled movies on the DPP's list of impoundable titles. The key was evoking the aesthetic of films that had been feverishly viewed on VHS and Betamax in the eighties without descending into parody or mimicry – a complicated balancing act that involved a mixture of homage and update.

To cinematographer Annika Summerson, Bailey-Bond gave a collection of Lucio Fulci films, while cast and crew were asked to study everything from Tobe Hooper's *The Texas Chain Saw Massacre* (1974), Romano Scavolini's *Nightmares in a Damaged Brain* (1981) and Joe D'Amato's *Absurd* (1981), to Hélène Cattet and Bruno Forzani's *giallo*-inspired 2009 Belgian oddity *Amer*. Bailey-Bond also suggested that her team watch John Hancock's cult seventies offering *Let's Scare Jessica to Death* (1971) and Michael Haneke's sadomasochistic romance *The Piano Teacher* (2001). 'I also used scenes from *Cannibal Holocaust* that I showed to the actors playing the censors during rehearsals,' Bailey-Bond told me in 2021. 'I wanted them to engage with the idea that they weren't just watching sausages-for-intestines type stuff and fake exploding heads. I did want to keep them in that headspace that it's not just something to look back and laugh at. I wanted to make it *real* for them.'

A throbbing electronics-led soundscape score by Emilie Levienaise-Farrouch (who had worked intimate wonders on the romantic 2018 Brit-pic *Only You*) adds immeasurably to the period feel, with Blanck Mass's spiralling track 'Chernobyl' (which, as noted in Chapter 6, was previously heard in Ben Wheatley's trippy folk horror *A Field in England*) upping the ante in the film's climactic sequence. When I ask Levienaise-Farrouch to describe the process of composing the music for *Censor*, she begins by explaining that, for her, the music needed to 'mirror the intensity of the actors' performances'.

'Something like *Censor*,' she tells me, 'in which everything is very intense, is going to be very different to approaching a film like, for example, *Living* [the 2022 English-language remake of Kurosawa's 1952 Japanese classic *Ikiru*]. I had read the script of *Censor* in advance, and the starting point for the score was writing a suite of musical ideas which included the title sequence cue. It also needed the kind of sounds that you have in the dream sequence, and I remember that I didn't write it to picture, I just relied on what I knew from the script and from my conversations with Prano.'

Levienaise-Farrouch cites Goblin's music for Argento's *Suspiria* as a specific influence. 'They started putting my music into *Censor* very early in the edit, and I remember being asked to write in a "giallo" style. I had a lot of fun integrating loads of sounds from those early soundtracks.' She recalls listening to the *Suspiria* CD on repeat when she used to work in a record shop. 'What I love about that score, and about all my favourite horror scores, is the tension between something that is beautiful and disgusting. That's certainly true of *Suspiria* – there's great beauty beneath the scares.'

For Levienaise-Farrouch, the key challenge was 'to avoid creating anything that sounded like pastiche'. Despite the period setting, she didn't want to approach it as a period film. 'It was more the idea of scoring Enid's trauma, giving musical form to her inner life,' she says. 'And because we're scoring her inner life, and you have the auto-fiction that she's starting to build in the second half of the film [in which Enid's reality starts to blur with the fictional worlds of the "Video Nasties"], we started to integrate period sound – *not* because we were doing a period movie, but because those are the sounds that would have been permeating *her* reality.'

During the editing and composing process, Levienaise-Farrouch found it particularly helpful to be able to sit with Bailey-Bond in front of a computer screen in which all the different elements of her score were clearly displayed so that the director could see the shape of the cue and, more crucially, the specific timings. 'Because Prano was sitting right next to me, we could just move or alter the audio files to suit her needs. I could just change the effects in front of her, and she was able to visualize and *verbalize* exactly what she wanted. So she might say: "I want something that sounds more like it's coming from the ground." And then we'd just try different things until we got it together.'

Levienaise-Farrouch worked on the *Censor* score during the Covid-19 lockdown, meaning that she had to rely in the first instance on what was immediately available to her in her home studio. 'We couldn't go anywhere, and I was very interested in using my own voice for this score – and I ended up using it *a lot*. I used a simple dynamic microphone, but I also used contact microphones which I would put on my throat and cheeks to record the female voice in a more internal way. To me that made sense because so much of the film was talking about repressed trauma.' She then experimented with the recordings using vintage equipment such as a sixties WEM Copicat programmable echo unit, and would feed the resulting sounds into the computer to form the groundwork of the score.

Looking back on the project, Levienaise-Farrouch remembers how the isolation of working from home during lockdown strangely worked to the benefit of her *Censor* score. 'It was interesting to be processing the kind of sadness, frustration and trauma of that period by just making a score about it, in a sense.'

For her, the process was both creative and cathartic – and also (as is so often the case with horror) strangely beautiful.

Soundtrack Selection: *Twin Peaks: Fire Walk with Me* (1992)

'Everything about David Lynch's "Twin Peaks: Fire Walk With Me" is a deception,' wrote influential critic Vincent Canby in his scathing *New York Times* review of the 1992 feature film prequel to Lynch's cult TV series that ran between 1990 and 1991. 'It's not the worst movie ever made', Canby continued, 'it just seems to be'. Canby's snarky dismissal of the film was very much in keeping with the general consensus. Having been reportedly booed at its Cannes premiere (a regular enough occurrence, admittedly, although Lynch's co-writer Robert Engels insists it didn't happen), the film was enthusiastically trashed by critics vying to outdo each other in knocking the once-revered American surrealist director off his perch.

Long before Canby's review appeared, his *New York Times* colleague Janet Maslin had labelled *Fire Walk with Me* 'disastrous' and wondered 'whether the film played worse to "Twin Peaks" fans, who already knew more than enough about the death of Laura Palmer, or to anyone happening onto this impenetrable material for the first time.' She concluded that 'Mr. Lynch's taste for brain-dead grotesque has lost its novelty, and it now appears more pathologically unpleasant than cinematically bold.' Meanwhile the trade bible *Variety* declared that 'there is no suspense involved in this story' (because we already *know* that Sheryl Lee's troubled high-schooler will die), and haughtily huffed that 'Laura Palmer, after all the talk, is not a very interesting or compelling character and long before the climax has become a tiresome teenager.'

Primed for a stinker by the damning reviews, audiences stayed away from *Fire Walk with Me* in droves. In America, it took less than $4.5 million, against a $10 million budget, and within weeks it was gone. 'After that, *Fire Walk With Me* was ignored for years', wrote Martyn Conterio in a 2017 *Guardian* retrospective, 'until a revival of its fortunes earlier this decade thanks to critics such as Mark Kermode who described the film as "maligned but frankly marvellous".'

Conterio was right – I absolutely loved *Fire Walk with Me* and had raved about it from the outset. I had not been entirely alone – a handful of other critics had embraced Lynch's misunderstood masterpiece, such as Alan Jones, Nigel Floyd and Kim Newman, the last of whom astutely noted that 'the film's many moments of horror [. . .] demonstrate just how tidy, conventional and domesticated the generic horror movie of the 1980s and 1990s has become'. For those of us who 'got' the film, *Fire Walk with Me* was first and foremost a great horror movie – something its detractors (who were presumably expecting a kooky, quirky TV spin-off) seemingly failed to notice, or appreciate. For me, it also boasted the finest soundtrack of the year – one of the great film scores of the decade, composed by Lynch's long-time collaborator, Angelo Badalamenti.

From the woozily jazzy 'Theme from Twin Peaks – Fire Walk with Me' that plays over an opening image of a TV screen waiting to be smashed, through the heartbreaking melancholia of Julee Cruise breathily singing 'Questions in a World of Blue' (for which Lynch provided the lyrics), to the ethereal transcendence of the angelic finale 'The Voice of Love', Badalamenti's music drags us deep into the world of Laura Palmer, the homecoming queen whose apparently idyllic life hides untold sadness and fear. If only the critics who derided *Fire Walk with Me* had *listened* to the movie (rather than just watched it) and concentrated more on the music and sound effects than just the dialogue, then perhaps they may have understood it better. Perfectly complementing Sheryl Lee's brilliant, near-operatic central performance, Badalamenti's music tells the *story* of the film – of a young girl's descent into hell after years of abuse that no one (not even Laura) is willing or able to acknowledge.

Badalamenti's collaborations with Lynch began on *Blue Velvet* (1986), for which he not only composed a lavish orchestral score, reminiscent of the finest works of Bernard Herrmann, but also played a cameo as a nightclub pianist accompanying Isabella Rossellini's sultry chanteuse, Dorothy Vallens. He pops up again on screen as the sinisterly coffee-spitting Luigi Castigliane in *Mulholland Dr.* (2001), a feature film that began life as a rejected TV pilot (first envisaged as another *Twin Peaks* spin-off) and then went on to be voted film of the decade by everyone from *Cahiers du Cinema* to the Los Angeles Film Critics Association.

The master of the suspended chord, Badalamenti's work with Lynch ranged from the violent Palme d'Or-winner *Wild at Heart* (1990) to the sentimental oddity *The Straight Story* (1999) via the psychogenic fugue of *Lost Highway* (1997). When I interviewed Lynch in Paris about the last of these, he told me that 'Lately I feel films are more and more like music. Music deals with abstractions and, like film, it involves time. Imagine the length of a type-written report that could honestly translate the feelings of a symphony into words. It would be pretty strange. It would really be like poetry.'

No wonder Lynch worked so well with Badalamenti, with their collaboration reaching its peak in the *Twin Peaks* TV series, and in *Fire Walk with Me*. In both of these, the main theme is built upon suspended chords – with two notes suggesting the existence of a *third* note that cannot be heard, only inferred. As Lynch told me, 'When you have a note, and another detuned note buzzes against it, there's something *in between* those two notes that's the magical area. I think since we live in a world of dualities – hot and cold, high and low, the whole thing – that any balancing point is very special.'

That sense of balance and duality made Badalamenti the perfect composer for the world of *Twin Peaks*. According to Angelo, whom I first interviewed on stage at the Edinburgh Film Festival, Lynch would stand behind him as he sat at a keyboard, and slowly describe the unfolding moods he wanted his composer to evoke. 'He'd have his hand on my shoulder, and he'd say "Oooo, we're in the woods, and there's *something* in the woods, it's very dark and mysterious, but then . . . what's that? . . . It's an *angel*! An angel of light! We're bathed in this light of love. And now . . . It's dark again."' As Lynch spoke, Badalamenti would experiment with the suspensions that were his trademark, the sound of notes 'buzzing against each other' perfectly mirroring the ongoing battle between light and dark, humour and horror. The result was magic.

That magic finds its purest, most distilled essence in Badalamenti's score for *Fire Walk with Me*, with the composer perfectly negotiating the shifts between the worldly and *other*worldly elements of the narrative. While Lynch's visuals juxtapose scenes of almost parodically homely Americana with images of terrifying demonic infestation, Badalamenti's subtly provocative music provides the emotional backbone, helping the audience to negotiate the potentially jarring moods of the movie rather than be baffled or alienated by them. I remember driving around America with a cassette tape of the *Fire Walk with Me* soundtrack playing on the car stereo a few months after the film's disastrous first opening, experiencing an almost transcendent sense of elation at the beauty of Badalamenti's score, and a great sense of sadness that the film's failure to find an audience might mean that the music too would disappear.

But it didn't. Over the years, a critical reassessment of *Fire Walk with Me* began to gather momentum, led by an enthusiasm for the score which gained cult status among fans. When that score was reissued by Death Waltz Records on collector's edition vinyl in 2017, I was thrilled to be asked by Lynch and Badalamenti to provide the liner notes. As I wrote in those notes: 'The simple truth is that, for years, too few people had heard the score because the film had been so widely, wrongheadedly dismissed. Today, *Fire Walk with Me* is recognized as a lost classic, and Badalamenti's music is right at the heart of its reassessment. Having loved it from the outset, I remain utterly devoted to this superb soundtrack album, and to the shimmering visions which it still conjures up after more than two decades of delirious, devoted listening.'

END TITLES

A Well-kept Secret

It's a wet Tuesday afternoon in November 2024, and I'm stomping around the square mile of London's Soho district that has been the backdrop to so much of my life as a film critic.

When I first came back down to London from Manchester in the late eighties, Wardour Street was home to the offices of the Warner and Rank film companies, while Soho Square had 20th Century Fox. All of these offices had plush screening rooms where critics would watch the new releases. There were also the independent screening venues, from Mr Young's on D'Arblay Street (now known as the Soho Screening Rooms) to the Bijou and the Coronet, which nestled between editing rooms across Dean Street and Frith Street.

Today, Warner have moved out to Theobalds Road, up by Holborn Station, and Fox have shut up shop after being devoured by Disney. But the screening rooms are still there, often in the basements of establishments like the Soho Hotel and the Dean Street Townhouse, or in the offices of Dolby on Soho Square, just next to the BBFC. What *isn't* there – as I ruefully notice every time I walk past – is 58 Dean Street Records, once London's best (and *only*) specialist film soundtrack emporium, the place where I first realized just how little I knew about film soundtracks.

I call Philip Masheter, who speaks to me from his home in the Czech Republic, where he now lives with his family. I ask him what happened to the shop that was once such a big part of the soundtrack collectors' market.

'I think it was round about 1996 when we moved on,' he remembers, as rent hikes in Soho priced them out of the area. The shop moved to Bloomsbury Street for the best part of a decade, but 'it was never as good as it was in Soho, because even though the new location was near the British Museum, it was slightly off the beaten track for the film industry.' Technological advances such as CD copiers affected the market, but the main problem was that 'the big stores like Virgin and HMV and Tower started to look at our market, and then quite aggressively tried to *catch* that market. They were able to get much better deals on supply.'

In effect, movie soundtracks went mainstream, emerging from what had once been a specialist niche into something altogether more all-encompassing. Today, soundtracks can be found and streamed at will, providing instant access to the music from movies you've just seen, or rediscovered. It's an Aladdin's cave of delights, available at the click of a button. And it's a world away from the once-vital service that shops like 58 Dean Street provided all those decades ago.

Masheter recalls the heyday of the eighties and early nineties, when the format of choice was the LP, and the 12-inch record sleeve formed a significant part of the collectability of a sound-track. Back then, rare records were precisely that, 'something you wouldn't see more than once or twice in ten years. Like *The Lady in the Car with Glasses and a Gun* [1970], or some of the really early soundtracks, which you'd rarely get in good condition. There was a big pride of ownership in a collection then – if you had something like that, you weren't going to sell it. Because there was absolutely no way to have it *except* to have the physical copy of it. That was probably the time when people were most hooked on the thrill of it as a *collectable* thing.'

So what does the film music market look like nowadays?

'Well, I think the main difference is that it doesn't have that stigma of *nerdiness* any more!' Masheter laughs. 'I always used to say that "When Jerry Goldsmith dies, this hobby will die with him." Because in the past, the market was really made up of hardcore devotees – people who were total fanatics for certain composers. But that has changed, and the market has widened.'

Just as the stigma of 'nerdiness' has started to vanish from the film soundtrack market, so the homogeneity of the *composing* field has also dissipated, as the world of movie-scoring has expanded and become more inclusive. Michael Abels, who co-founded the Composers Diversity Collective, says the organization was formed because 'there was a real need and desire for people who *didn't* feel like they fit in to have a space'. He recalls hearing companies expressing a desire to be more inclusive yet claiming they didn't have contacts for more diverse composers: 'Now, people don't say that any more – they say: "We want to be more inclusive and we know some people but they're all working!" Which counts as progress!'

But Abels is mindful that nurturing a more diverse and equal industry takes work. 'Inclusion pays off big time in many ways, but you have to understand it doesn't happen just by accident. The Composers Diversity Collective is there to represent and make us visible.'

As for what most attracts today's soundtrack collectors, Philip

Masheter believes that classic soundtracks are still the main draw, not least the limited-edition remastered or extended scores of which La-La Land Records are the industry leaders. 'That's great stuff, and the kind of quality you can get now people could only dream of in the eighties.'

Mike Matessino, who has worked extensively with La-La Land, confirms that while the world of the film soundtracks market may have changed beyond recognition, those enthusiasts – the hardcore *collectors* – are still there, and they're still as demanding as ever. 'They want to know that they really have the score,' Matessino says. 'It lives in their collections, in their libraries, on their personal listening devices. It's there to recapture the emotional impact that the music brought to the movie . . . You can do things like look at a book of costume designs, or you could watch a visual-effects reel, or behind-the-scenes photos. But as a finished piece of artistic presentation, the music is the *only* component of a movie that can be separated out and presented as its own thing. So even if you have terrible movies, of which there have been many over the years, some of them have *fantastic* scores. And sometimes they can create, in the imagination, a movie that might go with a great score that was originally done for a movie that was *not* so great.'

All of which takes me back to my earliest days as a soundtrack collector – listening to movie music while gazing at the images on a 12-inch LP sleeve, conjuring moving pictures that may or may not have actually featured in the original film. I think about Neil Brand recalling the earliest days of so-called 'silent' cinema, and how music was *always* a key part of the moviegoing experience. And I think of the strange chain of events that has led us to a place where movie music can be grabbed out of the ether onto our phones, but in which people have simultaneously discovered a growing love for live film score performance.

'In the silent era, live music to a film was the norm,' says Clint Mansell when I ask him about his wonderful score for Duncan Jones's *Moon* (2009) being performed at the Barbican by the London Contemporary Orchestra in 2019 – a performance that has passed into modern cineaste mythology as one of the best live film score performances of the century. 'It's quite a time-honoured tradition. As film composers, we don't usually get to interact with our work once it's been released with the film. It's not like a band that releases an LP, then goes on tour promoting it to an audience where you feed off the music and the audience response.'

So Mansell – like so many contemporary composers – looked back to the earliest days of cinema and found something of real inspirational value in the combination of live music and moving images. 'Most live scores tend to be of pretty big films, or iconic films,' he observes. 'My general repertoire doesn't quite fit into those categories so it becomes a task to perform a movie with perhaps more of a cult-like status.' Luckily, not only did July 2019 mark the tenth anniversary of *Moon*'s UK release, it also coincided with the fiftieth anniversary of man landing on the moon, and of the release of David Bowie's 'Space Oddity'. 'Seeing as Bowie was Duncan's father, it was just a great opportunity to bring these milestones together. So that sealed the deal.' The result was a truly memorable event. For Mansell, it was 'humbling, yet amazing – to experience my music being performed live and to feel the audience almost breathless at times, and exhilarated at others.'

It also demonstrated once again that the market for live movie scores is not limited to such grand-scale productions as

Christopher Nolan's *Interstellar*, with its soaring Hans Zimmer score, or the *Lord of the Rings* movies, to which Howard Shore lent such grandeur. On the contrary, a smaller-scale film like *Moon*, which is now considered something of a modern classic, can generate a live music event that 'feels more intimate, more personal, like a well-kept secret', says Mansell. 'Live concerts, theatre, opera, ballet, even football matches are so exciting – seeing and hearing something happening right in front of your eyes takes the experience to a whole new level. Hearing musicians bringing the notes to life (alongside a great performance by Sam Rockwell!) was a thing of beauty.'

It's a beauty that not only persists, but grows. Just as the market for soundtracks has expanded from specialist collectors and devotees to more widespread general music fans, so the growing demand for live film scores shows no signs of abating. In 2022, I had the pleasure of introducing the Grimethorpe Colliery Band accompanying Mark Herman's 1996 gem *Brassed Off* live at a packed Royal Albert Hall. The atmosphere was electric. And at the end of the evening, everyone said, 'We *must* do this again!'

Which we shall.

And so, in the end, we return to where we began – to images flickering on a screen while musicians of all stripes play along, joining the audience in the creation of that strange alchemical magic that happens when music meets the movies, in perfect harmony.

ACKNOWLEDGEMENTS

First of all, you'll notice that in 'Just the Music' we've credited all the composers and film music experts who took the time to speak to us for this book. However, it's worth thanking them again for providing so much insight about the art and intricacies of scoring for the screen.

Your help was indispensable.

Huge thanks, too, to the dedicated team at Picador, who have been both generous and meticulous in helping us to get this book over the finishing line. Take a bow Andrea Henry, Mary Mount, Nicholas Blake, Connor Hutchinson, Siobhan Slattery, Elle Gibbons, Nick Griffiths, Laila Kazzuz and jacket designer Stuart Wilson.

We'd also like to extend our gratitude to the great Jon Burlingame for offering his expertise; to indexer extraordinaire Tim Clifford; to ace conductor Robert Ziegler; to Chandler Poling and the team at White Bear PR; to everyone at La-La Land Records; and to Mark Robertson at Abbey Road.

And particular thanks to everyone at the wonderful BFI Reuben Library.

If you listened to the Scala Radio show and emailed in to suggest film scores for us to play, or to get involved in our numerous long-running features (Great Music Shame About the Film; Cinzano Time; Soundtrack Solace; Whistling Tunes – the list goes on), THANK YOU. Your kind words and encouragement meant, and *still* mean, a lot to both of us.

On a personal note, Jenny would like to thank:

My friends, who didn't laugh at me when I told them I was going to co-author a book during maternity leave, I appreciate your restraint. To my sister Sarah and my parents Tricia and Greg, I am so grateful for your support – and all the babysitting! Which leads me to Ezra, my little legend. Thank you for making my world shine brighter. And finally, thank you to Mark for putting your faith in me and asking me to join you on this project. I still can't quite believe it.

Mark would like to thank:

Linda, for your steadfast love, devotion and support, which is – and always will be – my guiding light; Hedda, for your wise professional counsel, friendship, and endless patience in the *ten years* it took your useless client to finish this book; Georgia and Gabriel, for being a constant source of joy and inspiration to me; and to Jenny, for digging me out of a hole by agreeing to co-write this book, and then for making it what it is – a truly collaborative effort. It would never have happened without you.

NOTES AND SOURCES

As noted in 'Just the Music', unless otherwise stated all the quotations used in this book come from primary interviews conducted by Mark Kermode and Jenny Nelson. Other sources are noted below.

INTRODUCTION: JUST THE MUSIC

6 **Of all the awards**   Yardena Arar, 'The Grammy Awards: A Night of Records', *The Free Lance-Star*, Virginia, 29 February 1984, p. 34.

6 **You should probably listen**   Edgar Wright, outtake interview with Mark Kermode for *The Soundtrack of My Life*, BBC Radio 2, 2015.

9 **my BFI Modern Classics volume**   Mark Kermode, *Silent Running* (London: Palgrave/BFI Modern Classics, 2014).

11 **William Harrison's source short story**   William Harrison, *Roller Ball Murder* (London: Robson Books, 1975).

CHAPTER 1: NEVER SILENT

34 **its style and canine subject matter**   'Rescued by Rover (1905)', screenonline.org.uk.

34 **able to hold its own**   'Rescued by Rover (1905)', screenonline. org.uk.

37 **the unusual structure explores**   Bryony Dixon, 'Silent Cinema: Body and Soul', BFI Southbank programme notes, October 2021.

37 **letting loose their feelings**   'Neil Brand on Oscar Micheaux: An Audience for Body and Soul', silentlondon.co.uk, 22 October 2021.

41 **In his excellent book**   Gerry Turvey, *The Phoenix Cinema: A Century of Film in East Finchley* (London: Phoenix Cinema Trust, 2010).Insert note

41 **[T]he two cinemas vied**   Turvey, p. 72.

SOUNDTRACK SELECTION: *IT'S A WONDERFUL LIFE*

47 **The weakness of the picture**   Bosley Crowther, 'It's a Wonderful Life', review, *The New York Times*, 23 December 1946.

52 **had left it to me**   Sleeve notes to the seventy-fifth anniversary edition of the *It's a Wonderful Life* soundtrack by Frank K. DeWald (La-La Land Records), p. 11.

52 **In general, I say "yes"**   Fred Karlin, *Listening to Movies: The Film Lover's Guide to Film Music* (New York: Schirmer Books, 1994), p. 12.

52 **The film has a life of its own**   Michael Pappas, 'It's a Wonderful Life: From festive flop to Christmas classic', bbc.co.uk, 17 December 2019.

CHAPTER 2: HOW DID WE GET HERE? – PART 1

53 **A Channel 4 documentary**   *Hell on Earth: The Desecration and Resurrection of 'The Devils'*, Channel 4, 2002. Director: Paul Joyce.

56 **Reinhardt needed a composer**   Mark Pullinger, 'Korngold: Defining the Hollywood filmscore', bachtrack.com, 9 November 2014 [2024].

58 **Music is music**   Jessica Duchen, 'Erich Wolfgang Korngold: A Prodigy Rediscovered', Longborough Festival Opera, 21 April 2022 (lfo.org.uk).

59 **When asked why**   Mark Chivers, 'Doreen Carwithen in Haddenham: The world's first full-time female film composer', carwithenmusicfestival.co.uk.

62 **There is an international language**   Mark Kermode, 'Indian Blockbusters', *Screenshot*, BBC Radio 4, 23 September 2022.

62 **Rahman was profiled**   Monya De, 'Keeping Score', *Los Angeles Times*, 3 December 2008.

62 **giant in the Bollywood world**   Greg Kot and Jim DeRogatis, *Sound Opinions*, show 169, 'Frightened Rabbit and Opinions on A. R. Rahman and Morrissey', PRX, 20 February 2009.

63 **abounded in montages**   Fred Karlin, *Listening to Movies: The Film Lover's Guide to Film Music* (New York: Schirmer Books, 1994), p. 5.

65 **You know, the reason I don't like this tune**   Mark Richards, 'Comparing Bernard Herrmann's Psycho Score and Sinfonietta (1936)', *Film Music Notes*, 18 January 2013.

66 **Do you want it good**   Rose Abdalla, Tess Fetherston, Conrad Clark, Jane Ridley and Robert Saxton, 'Composer Elisabeth Lutyens, Daughter of Edwin', lutyenstrust.org.uk.

67 **Norma Herrmann recalled**   Günther Kögebehn, 'Running with the Kids: A conversation with Norma Herrmann' (bernardherrmann.org/Bernard Herrmann Society), published 2006, from an interview in 2004.

68 **Herrmann had payback**   Ibid.

68 **the Vienna Opera House**   Karlin, *Listening to Movies*, p. 19.

69 **In the 2024 documentary**   Laurent Bouzereau, *Music by John Williams*, 2024.

72 **It was only after Williams played**   Steven Spielberg interviewed by Laurent Bouzereau, *Jaws 25th Anniversary Collector's Edition*, soundtrack sleeve notes (Decca, 2000).

72 **Thank you very much**   'M. M. Keeravani Calls John Williams "Inspiration" in His Acceptance Speech at LAFCA', ndtv.com.

73 **it didn't take much pushing**   Laurent Bouzereau, *Music by John Williams*, 2024.

73 **produce a beautifully set**   Karlin, *Listening to Movies*, p. 19.

75 **The director suggested** Laurent Bouzereau, *E.T. the Extra-Terrestrial 20th Anniversary Edition*, soundtrack sleeve notes (MCA, 2002).

75 **The oft-told story** Jamie Gangel, 'The Man Behind the Music of *Star Wars*', today.com, 5 May 2005.

75 **I owe a tremendous debt** Ian Bonhôte and Peter Ettedgui, *Super/Man: The Christopher Reeve Story*, DC/HBO, 19 January 2024.

76 **impossibly lucky** Bouzereau, *Music by John Williams*.

SOUNDTRACK SELECTION: *EYES WIDE SHUT*

78 **Kubrick had phoned him** Jeffrey Wells, quoting Jebediah Reed, *Radar Online*, at hollywood-elsewhere.com, 4 October 2006.

79 **first proper feature film** Jeff Bond, 'Ears Wide Open', *Film Score Monthly*, 4:8 (1999), p. 24.

80 **It's really the one** Rudy Koppl, 'Ears Wide Open: Jocelyn Pook Scoring Kubrick's Eyes Wide Shut', *Soundtrack! The Collector's Quarterly*, 18:71 (1999), p. 5.

80 **would describe the atmosphere** Bond, 'Ears Wide Open', p. 25.

80 **an encouraging collaborator** Koppl, 'Ears Wide Open: Jocelyn Pook scoring Kubrick's Eyes Wide Shut', p. 6.

80 **He might play a couple** Ibid.

81 **I have to know the whole** 'Scoring for Film and TV', panel hosted by Jenny Nelson, Abbey Road Equalise Festival, March 2023.

81 **the film company considering sending a man** Ibid.

81 **The director discussed the placement** Koppl, 'Ears Wide Open: Jocelyn Pook scoring Kubrick's Eyes Wide Shut', p. 7.

82 **jumping off a cliff** 'Scoring for Film and TV', Abbey Road Equalise Festival, March 2023.

82 **I was aware** Bond, 'Ears Wide Open', p. 24.

CHAPTER 3: THE DIRECTOR'S VISION

88 **Speaking in 1999**   Michael Schelle, *The Score: Interviews with Film Composers* (Los Angeles: Silman-James Press, 1999), p. 72.

91 **It's really challenging**   Interview with Mark Kermode on a panel for 'Scala Radio x Abbey Road Presents: Music for Film at Abbey Road', Amplify Festival 2022.

94 **I did something "Hildur-ish"**   'Scoring for Film and TV', Abbey Road Equalise Festival, March 2023, panel hosted by Jenny Nelson.

95 **You go on a call**   Ibid.

97 **simply showed him**   Autumn Wright, 'Joe Hisaishi Interview: Studio Ghibli's Legendary Composer on *The Boy and the Heron*', *Paste Magazine*, December 2023.

98 **often kept the scenes longer**   'Q&A – Ennio Morricone', *The Observer* Music Monthly, 18 March 2007.

98 **According to Shire**   Fred Karlin, *On the Track: A Guide to Contemporary Film Scoring* (New York: Schirmer Books, 1990), p. 162.

98 **This broader experimentation**   Ibid., p. 163.

98 **Zimmer has recalled**   Jennifer Nelson, *Saturday Night at the Movies* (London: Elliott & Thompson, 2018), p. 232.

104 **I tried to compose elegant and romantic**   Charles Chaplin, *My Autobiography* (London: Penguin Modern Classics, 2003).

105 **her original intention**   'Immortal longing: Sally Potter on Orlando', *Sight and Sound*, March 1993.

107 **rescue the characters**   Mark Kermode, 'Out of Blue – Carol Morley's Visionary Thriller', *The Observer* New Review, 31 March 2019.

SOUNDTRACK SELECTION: *UNDER THE SKIN*

113 **With *Under the Skin* I was relating it**   'Sound On with Daniel Lopatin and Mica Levi', *A24* podcast, 3 December 2018.

CHAPTER 4: HOW DID WE GET HERE? PART 2

116 **freshness** Joshua Rich, 'A High Scorer', *Entertainment Weekly*, 6 August 2004.

117 **Find out who that guy is** Jon Burlingame, 'Jerry Goldsmith: An appreciation', filmmusicsociety.org, 2 August 2004.

118 **I don't think he ever forgave me** Charlie Brigden, 'The Great Unknown: The story behind Jerry Goldsmith's score for "Alien"', rogerebert.com, 17 May 2017.

119 **I don't know if I've worked with any geniuses** Burlingame, 'Jerry Goldsmith: An Appreciation'.

119 **saved the picture** Ibid.

123 **godfather of braaams** Seth Abramovich, '"Braaams" for Beginners: How a horn sound ate Hollywood', hollywoodreporter. com, 5 May 2015.

124 **I always write from a personal point** Jennifer Nelson, *Saturday Night at the Movies* (London: Elliott & Thompson, 2018), p. 220.

124 **I have an idea** Interview with Mark Kermode, Scala Radio, July 2019.

126 **There are sounds that are not of humanity** Ryan Britt, 'How Hans Zimmer Brought the Dune Soundtrack to Life', denofgeek. com, 2 November 2021.

126 **truly one of the most incredible** Jon Burlingame, 'Shirley Walker: An appreciation', filmmusicsociety.org, 7 December 2006.

126 **major-star composer** Michael Schelle, *The Score: Interviews with Film Composers* (Los Angeles: Silman-James Press, 1999), p. 365.

126 **It was great to have Shirley boss me** Burlingame, 'Shirley Walker: An appreciation'.

127 **and to support the illusion or delusion** Schelle, *The Score: Interviews with Film Composers*, p. 364.

128 **I had had too much** Ibid., p. 365.

128 **a little, terribly frightening** Ibid., p. 364.

128 **those whose achievements** Shirley Walker Award, ascap.com.

131 **very disciplined in his work**   Interview with Mark Kermode, Scala Radio, July 2019.

134 **in recognition of his magnificent**   'The 79th Academy Awards Memorable Moments', oscars.org, 2007.

134 **Only a composer like Ennio Morricone**   A. R. Rahman, Twitter/X, 6 July 2020.

138 **Music is music**   Jessica Duchen, 'Erich Wolfgang Korngold: A Prodigy Rediscovered', Longborough Festival Opera, 21 April 2022 (lfo.org.uk).

SOUNDTRACK SELECTION: *DRIVE MY CAR*

141 **feels almost like the scenery**   A. D. Amorosi, ' "Drive My Car" Director and Soundtrack Composer on Crafting Film's Emotional Score: "Our Film Language Was Very Similar" ', *Variety*, 11 March 2022.

CHAPTER 5: THE LONG AND WINDING ROAD

145 **I'm prepared to do whatever**   Michael Schelle, *The Score: Interviews with Film Composers* (Los Angeles: Silman-James Press, 1999), p. 59.

150 **Lean's initial choice**   Jessica Duchen, 'Homage to a Misfit', *The Independent*, 24 August 2004.

152 **He had six weeks**   John Riley, 'Maurice Jarre: Composer who Won Three Oscars for His Work with David Lean', *The Independent*, 30 March 2019.

152 **I did it by getting exactly fifteen hours**   Fred Karlin, *Listening to Movies: The Film Lover's Guide to Film Music* (New York: Schirmer Books, 1994), p. 192.

152 **You haven't made it**   Amie Cranswick, 'The Top 10 Rejected Film Scores', flickeringmyth.com, 2 September 2021.

153 **It happens to everyone**   'Scoring for Film and TV', Abbey Road Equalise Festival, March 2023, panel hosted by Jenny Nelson.

194 **All of us were listening**   Danny Scott, 'Tangerine Dream's Peter Baumann: "There was no preparation. We just switched on the synths, smoked a joint and made some noise!"', musicradar.com, 1 April 2020.

196 **autonomous composition**   Chris Nelson, liner notes for *Clockwork Orange: Wendy Carlos's Complete Original Score* (excerpt at wendycarlos.com).

197 **My music is simply**   Robert Moog, *The Soundtrack of Tron*, Keyboard magazine, November 1982, pp. 53–7.

197 **Some of [the] music**   Wendy Carlos, 'Rediscovering Lost Scores, Volume One', wendycarlos.com.

SOUNDTRACK SELECTION: *BLADE RUNNER*

204 **He will sit and watch**   *On the Edge of Blade Runner*, Noblesgate Productions for Channel 4, 2000. Director: Andrew Abbott. Writer/Presenter: Mark Kermode.

204 **I remember when**   Ibid.

205 **What interested me the most**   Ian Freer, 'Synth Job', *Empire*, 218 (August 2007), pp. 112–13.

206 **When I compose**   Howard Maxford, 'Blade Runner Sound and Vision', *Starburst*, 271 (March 2001), pp. 63–8.

209 **I was just feeling**   Freer, 'Synth Job'.

209 **I have never felt**   Ibid.

CHAPTER 7: PLAY THROUGH THE ACTION

211 **I would hate to be stuck**   Fred Karlin, *Listening to Movies: The Film Lover's Guide to Film Music* (New York: Schirmer Books, 1994), p. 199.

213 **the function of music**   Ibid., p. 82.

215 **He even admitted**   Ibid., p. 79.

215 **Mickey Mousing for Steiner**   Paul Cote, 'Fathering Film Music: A Max Steiner retrospective', filmmusiccritics.org.

216 **the most influential music score**   Chris Willman, 'Max Steiner Biographer Breaks Down How the "King Kong" Composer "Established the Grammar of Film Music"', *Variety*, 4 June 2020.

216 **Steiner grew fearful**   Willman, 'Max Steiner Biographer'.

216 **this awful Wagnerian illustration**   Cote, 'Fathering Film Music: A Max Steiner retrospective'.

217 **Nothing is as loud**   Karlin, *Listening to Movies*, p. 11.

219 **the seed of all modern action**   Peter Debruge, William Earl, Todd Gilchrist and Owen Gleiberman, 'The 50 Best Action Movies of All Time', *Variety*, 14 July 2023.

219 **Ian Fleming was so impressed**   Ian Fleming, telegraph to Eric Ambler, September 1959, lettersofnote.com, 2 May 2012.

222 **And I think that's the key**   Adam Chitwood, ' "Mission: Impossible – Fallout" Composer Lorne Balfe on crafting an epic score', collider.com, 30 July 2018.

223 **if they were scoring**   Wes Phillips, 'Jerry Goldsmith, 1929–2004', soundandvision.com, 27 July 2004.

224 **hugely effective**   Janet Maslin, 'Back on the Trail of a One-Armed Man', *The New York Times*, 6 August 1993.

225 **out of a need**   'About the AFC', theawfc.com.

228 **he described his role**   Scott Mendelson, 'Interview: Richard King of "Dunkirk" talks the art of sound editing', forbes.com, 8 August 2017.

228 **this illusion of a continuing rise**   Jennifer Nelson, *Saturday Night at the Movies* (London: Elliott & Thompson, 2018), p. 223.

229 **In the editing**   Ibid., p. 236.

SOUNDTRACK SELECTION: *CRASH*

234 **the jury's attempt**   Ryan Lattanzio, 'Cronenberg Says Coppola Didn't Want Him to Win a Cannes Jury Prize for "Crash" in 1996', recordedpicture.com, 16 March 2021.

234 **I've run into**   Ibid.

235 **psychopathic hymn**   Faxed letter from J. G. Ballard to Robert Louit, British Library, Add. MS 88938/4/2, 16 November 2004.

235 **a 'cautionary' tale**   J. G. Ballard, introduction to the French edition of *Crash* (Paris: Calmann-Lévy, 1974).

235 **a new sexuality**   J. G. Ballard, *Crash* (London: Random House, 1973).

CHAPTER 8: POP GOES THE MOVIES

241 **Watching *Blackboard Jungle***   Marshall Crenshaw (ed.), *Hollywood Rock: A Guide to Rock'n'Roll in the Movies* (London: Plexus, 1994), p. 41.

241 **"St. Louis Blues"**   ' "St. Louis Blues" to be New Picture', *The Afro American*, 29 June 1929, p, 8.

245 **It seems that with the coming of film**   Mike Hammond, interview with Mark Kermode, 2024.

245 **The old groove**   'Sound Makes Possible More Novelty in Shorts', *The Film Daily*, 15 September 1929.

247 **a 'beautiful' work**   'Cryin' for the Carolines', *Photoplay*, July–December 1930 (PFA Library and Film Study Center, UC Berkeley Art Museum and Pacific Film Archive, Chicago).

251 **coined by Jiles Perry**   'First Music Videos', guinnessworldrecords.com.

252 **It is more than just a case**   Mike Curb, president of MGM Records, sleeve notes for MGM Super *Zabriskie Point*, 1971.

253 **Popular music has the potential**   Jonathan Romney, Adrian Wootton (eds), *Celluloid Jukebox: Popular Music and the Movies Since the 50s* (London: BFI Publishing, 1995), p. 1.

257 **He would put on the record**   Ellen E. Jones and Mark Kermode, 'The Jukebox Soundtrack', *Screenshot*, BBC Radio 4, 11 August 2023.

260 **While Yates cites**   Ellen E. Jones and Mark Kermode 'The New Year's Eve Movie', *Screenshot*, BBC Radio 4, 31 December 2021.

260 **Pop music in movies**   'Twisting the Knife', *Mojo*, June 1994, p. 54.

264 **Many films had been made**   Ellen E. Jones and Mark Kermode, 'The Harder They Come at 50', *Screenshot*, BBC Radio 4, 5 August 2022.

264 **It was a major cultural reference**   Ibid.

265 **The thing that really strikes me**   Ibid.

267 **reckless**   Joe Klein, 'The City Politic: Spiked . . . Dinkins and *Do the Right Thing*', *New York* magazine, 26 June 1989, p. 14.

267 **uproar**   David Denby, 'He's Gotta Have It', *New York* magazine, 26 June 1989, p. 53.

268 **I found a place**   Ellen E. Jones and Mark Kermode, 'Do the Right Thing', *Screenshot*, BBC Radio 4, 23 July 2024.

269 **It's like a piece of jazz**   Ibid.

SOUNDTRACK SELECTION: *NEVER LET ME GO*

273 **Unlike the operations**   Mark Lawson, 'Never Let Me Go Review – Fresh Life Found in Kazuo Ishiguro's School Dystopia', *The Guardian*, 28 September 2024.

274 **five weeks into its release**   Steven Zeitchik, 'Why Didn't Audiences Spark to "Never Let Me Go"?', *Los Angeles Times*, 21 October 2010.

275 **Alex Garland noted**   Nev Pierce, 'Alternative Reality', *Empire*, 258 (December 2010), pp. 106–9.

CHAPTER 9: A FRIGHTFUL NOISE

279 **the mohawk**   Interview with Mark Kermode, *The Fear of God: 25 Years of The Exorcist*, BBC Productions, 1998.

282 **Hitchcock was delighted**   Robert Siegal, 'Bernard Herrmann's Score to "Psycho"', npr.org, 30 October 2000.

283 **After the main titles**   Dr Tim Summers, 'Bernard Herrmann's Film Music: Psycho and Others', royalholloway.ac.uk.

294 **Most music is in 4/4**   Helen Brown, 'Mike Oldfield Interview: "I Am a Man of Extremes"', *The Telegraph*, 7 March 2014.

296　**Most notably for the BBC Two**　*The Night He Came Home: John Carpenter's Halloween*, BBC Productions, 1999.

SOUNDTRACK SELECTION: TWIN PEAKS – FIRE WALK WITH ME

305　**Everything about David Lynch's**　Vincent Canby, 'Review/Film: One Long Last Gasp for Laura Palmer', *The New York Times*, 29 August 1992.

305　**whether the film played worse**　Janet Maslin, 'Critic's Notebook; Lament at Cannes: Rarities Are Rare', *The New York Times*, 19 May 1992.

306　**there is no suspense**　Todd McCarthy, 'Film Review: Twin Peaks: Fire Walk with Me', *Variety*, 18 May 1992.

306　**After that, *Fire Walk with Me***　Martyn Conterio, 'Fire Walk with Me: How David Lynch's Film Went from Laughing Stock to the key to Twin Peaks', *The Guardian*, 2 September 2017.

306　**the film's many moments**　Kim Newman, 'Review: Twin Peaks: Fire Walk with Me' *Sight and Sound*, November 1992.

307　**Lately I feel films**　Mark Kermode, 'Weirdo', *Q magazine*, September 1997.

308　**He'd have his hand on my shoulder**　Angelo Badalamenti in conversation with Mark Kermode, Edinburgh International Film Festival, 2001.

INDEX

ABOUT THE AUTHORS

Mark Kermode is a film critic, writer, broadcaster and musician. He is the co-presenter of the Sony podcast *Kermode and Mayo's Take* and the BBC Radio 4 programme *Screenshot*. He is the author of several books on film and music including *Hatchet Job* and *How Does it Feel?*. He is co-founder and double-bassist of the skiffle & blues band The Dodge Brothers, who (with pianist Neil Brand) provide live accompaniment to silent movies.

Jenny Nelson is an award-winning audio producer and writer. She produced Mark Kermode's film music show at Scala Radio from 2019 to 2024, and in her previous role as Executive Producer at Classic FM she wrote a book about creative collaborations between film directors and composers. Jenny has hosted panels about screen music at London's Southbank Centre and Abbey Road, and is a former trustee at the Cambridge Film Festival.

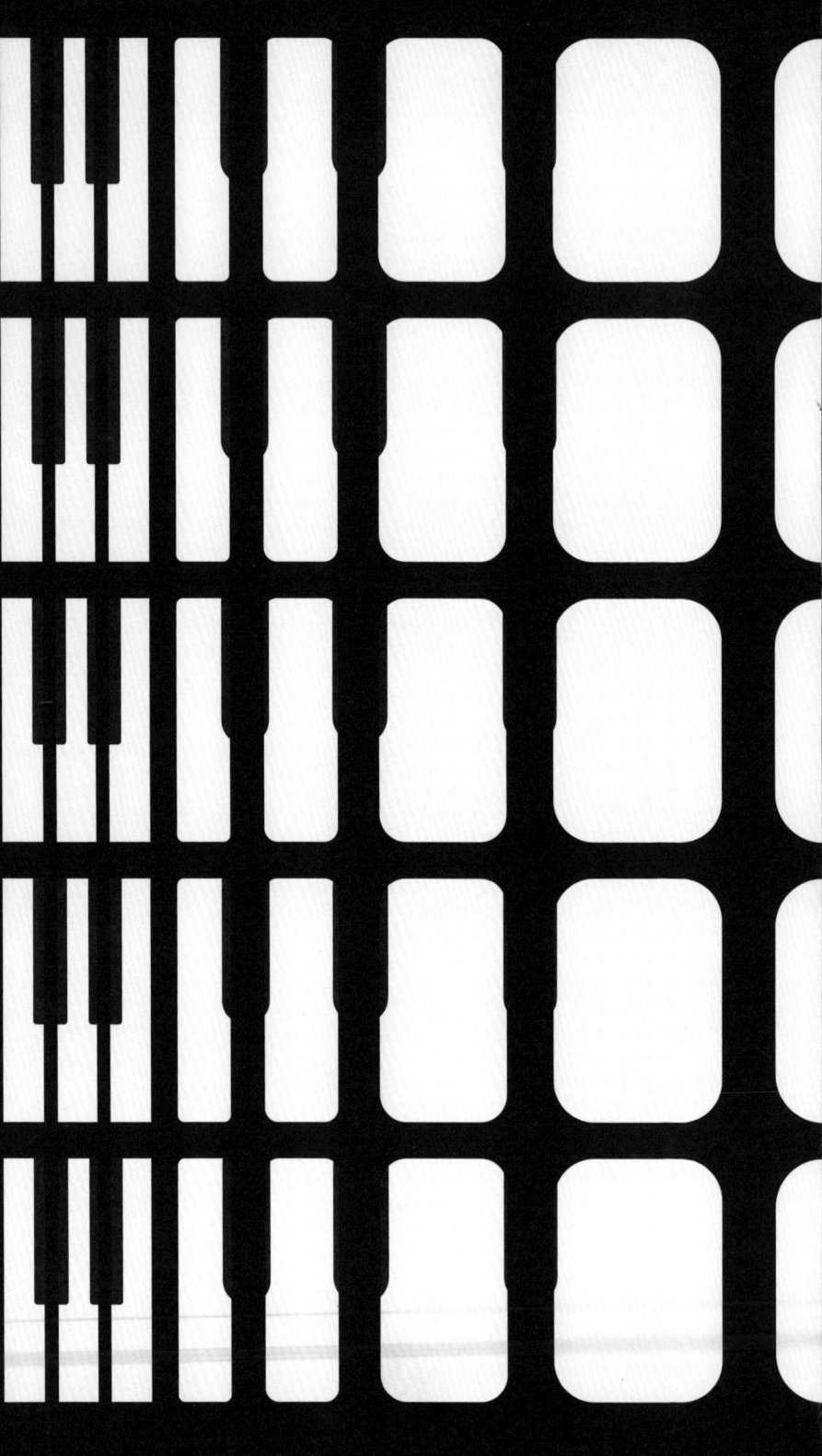